Teaching
Cooperative
Learning

SUNY SERIES, TEACHER PREPARATION AND DEVELOPMENT
Alan R. Tom, editor

The University of New Mexico
At Gallup

Zollinger Library

TEACHING
COOPERATIVE
LEARNING

The Challenge for
Teacher Education

EDITED BY
Elizabeth G. Cohen
Celeste M. Brody
Mara Sapon-Shevin

STATE UNIVERSITY OF NEW YORK PRESS

Published by
State University of New York Press, Albany

© 2004 State University of New York

For information, address State University of New York Press,
90 State Street, Suite 700, Albany, NY 12207

Production by Diane Ganeles
Marketing by Jennifer Giovani

Library of Congress Cataloging in Publication Data

Teaching cooperative learning : the challenge for teacher education / edited by
    Elizabeth G. Cohen, Celeste M. Brody, Mara Sapon-Shevin.
        p. cm. — (SUNY series, teacher preparation and development)
    Includes bibliographical references and index.
    ISBN 0-7914-5969-1 (alk. paper) — ISBN 0-7914-5970-5 (pbk. : alk. paper)
        1. Group work in education—Cross-cultural studies. 2. Teachers—Training
of—Cross-cultural studies. I. Cohen, Elizabeth G., 1931– II. Brody, Celeste M.
III. Sapon-Shevin, Mara. IV. SUNY series in teacher preparation and development.

LB1032.T42 2004
371.39'5—dc21   2003045654

10 9 8 7 6 5 4 3 2 1

CONTENTS

ILLUSTRATIONS

FOREWORD

A Teacher Educator's Perspective

YAEL SHARAN

Teacher educators who value and practice cooperative learning will welcome the rich and varied menu of programs this book offers. The program descriptions deal with the daily realities and complexities of running courses, programs, and teacher education models that have cooperative learning at their core. Each chapter summarizes what the authors learned from their program and the implications they see for the continued development of teacher education programs.

There are many clear guidelines to be gleaned from the authors' collective experience. Two main questions helped me focus on the implications of the programs described in this book: "What are their salient features?" and "What should teacher educators consider when designing a cooperative learning program?"

One way to learn from the richness of this book is to organize the programs as a series of four concentric circles of their salient features. At the core of the circles is *experiential learning*. All programs described here construct a setting that includes the traditional components of the experiential learning cycle: experience, reflection, conceptualization, and planning. The programs offer a first round of the cycle in the university or college classroom, where candidates encounter the many personal and some of the professional implications of cooperative learning. This is based on a broader conception of the ideal teacher, described by Rolheiser and Anderson (chapter 1), as "a more complex image of teachers as interdependent professionals working collaboratively with one another and with other partners in education."

The second circle extends the experiential feature of learning how to teach cooperative learning methods by stressing the need for *mastery of specific skills and strategies*. Not all chapters specify the required skills but all assume the need for clarity in this area. They also assume that teacher educators teaching cooperative learning are familiar with the full range of cooperative learning methods and strategies.

The third circle of salient features extends to the faculty. In varying degrees of detail, all chapters describe how *faculty collaborate in planning and designing a program's goals and methods*. Faculty who value and practice cooperative learning use it among themselves to learn, to plan their teaching, to design the teacher training program, and to reflect upon its effectiveness. By working within their own cooperative culture they model cooperative learning values and strategies in their own work, and enhance the cooperative element of the students' learning experience. The modeling of faculty collaboration adds a necessary element to the training program, by reinforcing the experiential and mastery features of the first two circles.

An underlying assumption in teaching how to use cooperative learning is that the program is built on a strong philosophical perspective congruent with the values implicit in cooperative learning (Schniedewind, chapter 3). Yet teacher educators cannot rely on professing their belief in cooperative learning and modeling it to ensure effective practice. Modeling, in and of itself, with the hope that teacher interns will absorb the elements of cooperative learning by osmosis, or from one or two courses, is insufficient. A strong message transmitted by the accumulation of experience presented in this book is that the three circles are interdependent. A cooperative culture among faculty in a program where cooperative learning is well integrated, preferably across the curriculum, where candidates learn about cooperative learning as well as the "what," "how," and "why," seems to be one of the essential requisites for sustained change.

The final circle of the main features of teacher education programs takes us outside the training institution for *coordination between what the interns see and do at the university and what they see and do in actual classrooms*. Interns are quick to notice discrepancies between their cooperative learning experiences at the university and college level and their observations in actual classrooms. Mentor teachers and classrooms must be chosen as carefully as possible so that student teachers can observe proficient practice of cooperative learning strategies and practice them in the classroom.

The close collaboration between faculty and field-placement schools brings the salient features of teacher education for and by cooperative learning full circle, deepening the metaphor. Classroom practice allows student teachers to apply directly the methods and strategies they learned, experienced, and observed at the university. Yet this is the thorniest of all the essential features of a teacher education program, because it is the one over which faculty have the least control. Authors point out the various pitfalls in this collaboration and note that faculty expectations are not always met. An optimistic view comes from those programs where the nature of the collaboration was negotiated over time, or evolved, resulting in a permanent partnership in the framework of a learning consortium or professional development center.

This book could provide a helpful resource for teacher educators in their efforts to design and carry out their own programs. The cooperative premises underlying the programs in this book suggest a possible strategy for doing this: A team of teacher educators responsible for a particular program, ideally with teachers from cooperating schools, could form an investigating team to generate a list of all the strengths and problems in their particular programs. Armed with this analysis, they could then conduct a deliberate search through the descriptions of the various programs and commentaries in this volume, trying to find "answers" or at least "responses" to their questions. This volume could serve as a reference tool for teacher educators hoping to evaluate and redesign their own programs.

Planning and implementing a teacher education program is very hard work. It is a complex effort based on the coordination of a great number of organizational details, personal preferences, practical and conceptual issues. All the programs take this complexity seriously as is evident by the rigorous way they are conducted and analyzed. Judging by the tenacity that characterizes the authors' involvement, the effort is worth their while. This is probably due not only to the generally satisfactory results, but also to the authors' need for creative problem solving and flexibility, and for intellectual challenges. After all, teacher educators enjoy doing just that—educating and nurturing future teachers. With this volume as a model, things are looking good for meeting these challenges.

ACKNOWLEDGMENTS

The editors of this volume gratefully acknowledge the financial and moral support of the International Association for the Study of Cooperation in Education (IASCE). This organization was a pioneer in the introduction of cooperative learning to classrooms. The Board of IASCE has encouraged the publication of books, articles, and a magazine that aid the classroom teacher who wants to use strategies of cooperative learning and the staff developers who have made it possible for so many teachers to introduce groupwork to their classrooms. Members of IASCE include outstanding researchers who have documented the positive effects of cooperative learning and many features of its context and its implementation. The organization is now truly a worldwide network of researchers, staff developers, teacher educators, and classroom teachers.

Celeste Brody is currently serving as copresident and Mara Sapon-Shevin is a past president of this organization; Elizabeth Cohen served on its Board for many years. As cooperative learning began to gain wide acceptance in education, we saw the need to document the programs of teacher educators with long-term experience in teaching cooperative learning. By so doing, teacher educators who are attempting to integrate this strategy into their programs could gain the benefit of the accumulated knowledge of their colleagues. From the inception of this project, the Board has encouraged our work. Copresident Lynda Baloche is a contributing author along with a number of other past and present Board members, including Neil Davidson, Yael Sharan, and Mark Brubacher.

INTRODUCTION

MARA SAPON-SHEVIN

As schools have become increasingly diverse, the demands on teachers have changed accordingly. Many schools of education that prepare teachers now recognize that all teachers must have the skills, abilities, and attitudes necessary to teach heterogeneous groups of learners within their individual classrooms and schools. It is undisputed that teachers today are expected to be culturally sensitive and have the knowledge, skills, disposition, and commitment for teaching a wide range of children (Ladson-Billings, 1995; Holmes Group, 1990; Sleeter & Grant, 1999; Zeichner, 1993 & 1997). Both the popular press and professional literature are full of references to the increasing heterogeneity of schools and the need for teachers to teach to that diversity.

Although many social changes, legislative decisions, and educational innovations now make the heterogeneity of classrooms more apparent, the truth is that there never was such a thing as a "homogeneous" classroom; we must acknowledge all the forms of diversity that have always been present in schools as well as the differences among students that have only recently been recognized or attended to (Sapon-Shevin, 1999).

INCREASING DIVERSITY IN SCHOOLS

The growing diversity in America's schools is undeniable. Classrooms include more students of color, students whose primary language is not English, and recent immigrants. According to the Federal Interagency Forum on Child and Family Statistics (1998), one of every three students enrolled in elementary and secondary schools today is of racial/ethnic minority background. Demographers

1

predict that students of color will make up about 46 percent of this country's school-age population by the year 2020 (Banks & Banks, 2001). By the year 2035, this group is expected to constitute a numerical majority of the K-12 student population. Children of immigrants make up approximately 20 percent of the children in the United States, bringing a host of cultural and language differences to many classrooms (Dugger, 1998).

One in five children under eighteen years of age currently lives in poverty, making children the fastest growing poverty group in the United States. In American cities, 30 percent of all students live in poverty (U.S. Department of Education, 1995), and there is a growing population of homeless children, many of whom attend school sporadically or not at all.

The number of school-age children who speak a language other than English at home and have difficulty speaking English was 2.4 million in 1995, or 5 percent of all school-age children in the U.S. (Federal Interagency Forum on Child and Family Statistics, 1998). Growing numbers of migrant families whose children attend school intermittently also present challenges to schools.

At the same time, efforts towards mainstreaming and then inclusion mandated by federal legislation and evolving educational practice have brought hundreds of thousands of new students identified as having mild, moderate, and significant disabilities back to general education classrooms, further increasing the heterogeneity found in typical schools. It is estimated that approximately 11 percent of school-age children, or approximately 5.3 million students are classified as disabled (U.S. Department of Education, 1995). Many of these students were previously served in special programs, sometimes in separate schools or completely unserved; their return to their neighborhood or community schools represents another major shift in the school population.

WHY COOPERATIVE LEARNING?

As schools move closer to the goal of providing education for all children within inclusive classrooms and schools, increasing amounts of attention and energy are being devoted to developing pedagogical approaches that are appropriate in heterogeneous classrooms. Teachers must structure the educational and social environment so that students develop the knowledge, skills, and attitudes required to interact across both perceived and actual differences and disabilities. Many teachers who are working in diverse or inclusive classrooms are particularly eager to develop modes of instruction that do not isolate and stigmatize learners with different needs: "Everyone write your book reports, and Michael, come over here and draw a picture" is an approach that not only separates children unnecessarily, but also denies all children the opportunity to learn and interact with others in ways that will enhance their academic and social growth. The realization that complete individualization is not a practical or even desirable solution to meeting the diverse needs of children within a single classroom has led many inclusion advocates to promote cooperative learning as the pedagogy of choice.

Over the last ten years, cooperative learning has become accepted as one of the "best practices" in education. School districts hiring new teachers expect that the teachers they hire will be at least comfortable, if not skilled, in implementing cooperative learning strategies in the classroom. Consequently, many teacher education programs have increased the number of courses and opportunities for novice and experienced teachers to learn how to design and implement cooperative/collaborative learning.

Cooperative learning has been used extensively within "regular education" classrooms (McTighe & Lyman, 1988; Jones & Steinbrink, 1991; Almasi, 1995; Gambrell, 1996) and "special education" classrooms (Hoover & Patton, 1995). Cooperative learning is of value for all students including those who have been identified as "at risk," "bilingual," "gifted," and "normal." Cooperative learning encourages mutual respect and learning among students with varying talents and abilities, languages, racial, and ethnic backgrounds (Marr, 1997). Sudzina (1993) reports that cooperative learning is effective in reducing prejudice among students and in meeting the academic and social needs of students at risk for educational failure. All students need to learn and work in environments where their individual strengths are recognized and individual needs are addressed. Many educators today strive to ensure that multiple intelligence theory and differentiated instruction are incorporated into their curricula (Gardner, 1993; Armstrong, 1994, Tomlinson, 1999). Emotional intelligence is also an important facet of classroom community (Goleman, 1995) that requires teacher attention. All students need to learn within a supportive community in order to feel safe enough to take risks (Sapon-Shevin, 1999). Cooperative learning arrangements have been found to be useful for increasing achievement, encouraging student involvement, and enhancing motivation for learning (Polloway, Patton, & Serna, 2001.)

One of the goals of cooperative learning is to disrupt typical hierarchies of who is "smart" and who is not; Cohen (1994) has extensively documented the ways in which issues of societal status are often reproduced within cooperative learning activities unless specific steps are taken to alter that relationship. Cooperative learning can allow all students to work together, each student experiencing the role of teacher and of learner, and each student modeling recognition of and respect for many different skills and learning styles. If teachers or students are uncomfortable with cooperative learning, it is often because they have adopted a particular technique without a firm understanding of the underlying principles and do not have sufficient support to implement creative, multilevel cooperative learning activities that allow students to participate at different levels, with differentiated goals and varying levels of support.

CHANGING HOW WE PREPARE TEACHERS

Teachers are confronted on a regular basis with educational innovations that must be incorporated into their teaching: whole language, critical thinking, authentic assessment, and so forth. Some teachers (and administrators) hope they can ignore what they would categorize as "fads" in education, waiting for them to pass and be replaced by "the next thing," thus saving themselves the time and energy needed to learn about and implement new practices. Not only is there a compelling research base in support of cooperative learning, but it is also fully compatible with other currently prominent "best practices" such as differentiated instruction, hands-on learning, and authentic assessment (Gambrell, 1996).

How do institutions of teacher education teach cooperative learning? Is it simply a course students take or does a focus on cooperative learning permeate the central design and mission of the program? What, precisely, do teacher educators think beginning (and experienced) teachers need to know about cooperative learning? How are those skills best acquired and evaluated? Are there sufficient opportunities for students to practice their beginning cooperative learning skills during their field experiences and practica?

This volume explores practices in teacher education programs that teach cooperative learning strategies to their students. The project grew out of an investigation by the International Association for the Study of Cooperation in Education (IASCE); teacher educators from across the United States and across the world were asked to identify programs that might offer others an understanding of best practices in preparing teachers in cooperative learning.

Most teacher educators were reluctant to claim that their institutions had "figured it out" and could claim the best cooperative learning preparation possible. Indeed, one of our findings was the paucity of research in this area. Many teacher education programs acknowledged that they had limited follow-up data on the long-term effects of their preparation programs. All of those surveyed admitted that changing teacher education programs is slow, hard work, fraught with institutional pitfalls and constraints.

We selected teacher education programs from ten institutions with long-term experience in teaching cooperative learning. These were all programs implemented with thoughtful self-criticism and considerable experimentation with new and better ways to teach and embody cooperation. The authors were all able to talk about how they have confronted the dilemmas and challenges involved in using cooperative and collaborative learning approaches within their programs. The description of each program or process was illustrative of one or more of the issues and concerns that become manifest when teacher education programs attempt to change the ways in which teachers are prepared. An examination of these programs can help us to understand the complexities of contemporary teacher education and help us to analyze and critique our own practices in preparing teachers.

THE ORGANIZATION OF THIS BOOK

The teacher education programs described in this volume vary along many dimensions. Represented here are large, public universities (both urban and rural); small, private colleges; elite private universities; campuses that are part of a larger statewide university system, a Canadian university and a German university. Part 1 includes cases that represent a range of models of teacher education: those that offer education as an undergraduate major; credential programs restricted to graduate students; final certification for previously credentialed teachers; programs that certify elementary teachers; and those that prepare middle- and secondary-level teachers as well. Some of the programs presented here are small and cohesive, in which a number of faculty work closely together, utilizing a shared approach and ideology. Others represent one of several specializations within larger programs that offer a variety of approaches. In some of the programs, cooperative learning is a primary strategy taught to students, and the emphasis on cooperative learning is coupled with a focus on teaching for social justice. In other programs, cooperative learning is seen as a critical strategy for teaching diverse students in urban settings. Still others align cooperative learning closely with a particular subject matter such as literacy or science.

In chapter 1, Rolheiser and Anderson present a Canadian perspective in their description of practices in a fifth-year master's program featuring cooperative learning at the Ontario Institute for Studies in Education at the University of Toronto. They include seven strategies for teaching about cooperative learning that are part of the program, as well as a discussion of the ways in which the existence of various program options within the same teacher education design is both advantageous and problematic.

In chapter 2, Brody and Nagel from Lewis & Clark College in Portland, Oregon, give us a glimpse of a program in which an extensive internship experience for their preservice Master's program focuses on the role of teacher as decision maker. The authors explore the importance of the internship experience in shaping new teachers as well as the challenges to faculty as they attempt to maintain program ideology and consistency in the face of changing state licensure structures and other outside constraints.

Schniedewind, in chapter 3, describes a perspective, known as Socially Conscious Cooperation Learning, in which cooperative learning is both a pedagogical strategy and a philosophical worldview. She analyzes data from program graduates to determine the influence on teachers' practice of instruction that integrates cooperative learning pedagogy and philosophy.

Hanley and Harris of Anderson College, in South Carolina, consider their undergraduate teacher education program in chapter 4, in which cooperative learning strategies are sequenced in a way that the designers find logically defensible and pedagogically sound. The chapter also explores the challenges of encouraging beginning teachers to use cooperative learning consistently once they have left the program.

Lyman and Davidson describe the teacher education program at the University of Maryland in chapter 5. They illustrate the ways in which the program works with teacher education centers that are evolving into professional development schools. The authors conclude that cooperative learning must be modeled, experienced in the learner's role, practiced repeatedly in the field, seen as part of a constellation of allied strategies and techniques, and understood in relationship to social and academic outcomes in order for implementation to be successful.

Although most of the programs described are those that prepare elementary level teachers, Foote and associates in chapter 6, present a teacher education program for secondary education teachers at Niagara University, in New York. The challenge of reforming secondary teacher education lies in merging a focus on the powerful pedagogy of cooperative learning with subject matter that is more often taught through lectures.

In chapter 7, Finkbeiner, from Kassel University in Germany, shares the ways in which she uses collaborative learning in the context of foreign language teacher training. She explores the attitudes and beliefs that are important prerequisites for enhancing novice teachers' ability to implement and integrate a cooperative and collaborative teaching approach into their own teaching repertoires.

Slostad, Baloche and Darigan in chapter 8 further explore issues of program coherence. They describe their elementary certification program at West Chester University in Pennsylvania in which multiple program options exist, only one of which uses cooperative learning as a central organizing value. The advantage of a program in which all faculty are strongly cohesive is discussed, as are the challenges of instituting broader level reform.

The chapter by Cohen and associates (chapter 9) presents lessons learned from systematic data collection and experience with teaching Complex Instruction (CI) to preservice teachers. Drawing from a collaborative project between Stanford University and five campuses of the California State University, the study explores the relationship between preservice teachers' coursework on cooperative learning and their expectations and skills implementing cooperative learning in their first year of teaching. The authors speak to the need for preservice coursework to be linked concretely to other experiences that encourage new teachers to implement cooperative learning.

The ways in which teachers' understanding of the classroom as a social system impinge on successful cooperative learning are explored by Lotan in chapter 10 on teaching beginning teachers at Stanford University. With an emphasis on the concept of delegation of authority, Lotan shares simulations designed to engage beginning teachers in the struggles of empowering students while remaining professionally responsible.

Part 2 provides commentaries on the cases by the three editors and a classroom teacher. In chapter 11 Brody considers what teacher education programs can learn from these cases about designing their curriculum and instruction for preservice teachers and considers the points of agreement on what novice teachers should understand and be able to put into practice during student teaching or by the end of program. Cohen, in chapter 12, notes the organizational constraints and challenges found in the cases, and suggests the need for teacher education programs to move to structural arrangements that will support and enable teacher educators to meet those demands. In chapter 13, Sapon-Shevin reminds us that there are issues and concerns about the ways in which broader societal concerns about justice, fairness, equality, voice, and power are linked to the teaching of cooperative learning. She addresses the question, "How does the cooperative learning modeled in these chapters link this promising pedagogy to broader societal and cultural conditions and concerns?" In chapter 14, Brubacher affirms how critical classroom teachers are in connecting coursework and practice. He draws out some promising practices in providing opportunities for preservice teachers to work with a classroom teacher who is a model and who provides guided experience in cooperative learning. Finally, in the conclusion, Sapon-Shevin and Cohen summarize the challenges for the reform of teacher education from the lens of cooperative learning and discuss the need and direction for further research.

ABOUT READING THIS VOLUME

The ten program descriptions and the commentaries that follow raise many questions. These can be used to frame the reading of this volume. Readers might want to ask these questions of their own programs and settings and think about their own challenges in the ways that we asked our contributors to think about theirs.

- How is cooperative learning presented to students, and how does that conceptualization affect students' willingness and ability to implement the approach? If cooperative learning is presented as a teaching strategy that is effective for certain kinds of instruction or specific populations of students, does this increase the likelihood that students will move towards comfortable adoption and implementation? Or, should cooperative learning be embedded within a more coherent orientation to teaching and education—part of an approach that values student engagement and constructivist theories of learning as well as teacher empowerment?

- When teaching students a new instructional strategy, what sequence of steps or sequence of complexity is the most effective? Is there a clear continuum of cooperative learning strategies that allows us to start with the "easier" strategies and then move to more complex ones as students gain mastery? Or does teaching students less cognitively taxing or less fully developed forms of cooperative learning contribute to increasing the chances that they view (and use) cooperative learning as a quick fix rather than as a complex instructional technique embedded in a demanding philosophical framework?

- What is the relationship between the coursework beginning teachers take and their work in the field? What kinds of practica and field work experiences are necessary to support teachers' learning in general and their acquisition of cooperative learning skills in particular? What kinds of relationships are necessary between the university and the field sites in order to ensure quality programs?

- Do all teacher education departments or program faculty members have to believe in the value of cooperative learning in order for students to learn the approach successfully? Do students learn more when there is total program cohesion? How do those faculty who are not members of a cohesive group maintain their support and focus?

- What do beginning teachers need to understand about resistance to cooperative learning? When teacher educators, teachers or administrators are reluctant to teach or implement cooperative learning, what are the possible sources of that resistance and how might they be overcome? Is it possible to *mandate* best practice, or are more empowering forms of school change necessary?

Each of the programs presented here allows us to understand a different dimension of teacher education. The range of programs forces us to think about our own understandings of what it means to learn to teach or to be a teacher. The programs represented encourage us to challenge the ways in which teacher education programs prepare future teachers to implement sophisticated instructional strategies such as cooperative learning. Successful teaching in diverse settings demands that teachers be treated as professionals who can and need to understand underlying educational theory and its link to practice rather than being forced to implement scripted teaching programs or teacher-proof curricula that assume limited aptitude on the part of teachers or students.

REFERENCES

Almasi, J. (1995). The nature of fourth-graders' sociocognitive conflicts in peer-led and teacher-led discussions of literature. *Reading Research Quarterly, 30*, 314–51.

Armstrong, T. (1994). Multiple intelligences in the classroom. Alexandria, VA: Association for Supervision and Curriculum Development.

Banks, J. A. & Banks, C. A. M. (2001). *Multicultural education: Issues and perspectives*, 4th edition. New York: John Wiley and Sons.

Cohen, E. G. (1994). *Designing groupwork: Strategies for the heterogeneous classroom*, 2nd edition. New York: Teachers College Press.

Dugger, C. W. (1998, March 21). Among young of immigrants, outlook rises. *The New York Times*, A1, A11.

Federal Interagency Forum on Child and Family Statistics (1998). *America's children: Key national indicators of well-being*. Washington, DC: U.S. Government Printing Office.

Gambrell, L. B. (1996). Creating classroom cultures that foster reading motivation. *The Reading Teacher 50* (1): 14–25.

Gardner, H. (1993). *Multiple intelligences: The theory in practice*. New York: Basic Books.

Goleman, D. (1995). *Emotional intelligence*. New York: Bantam Books.

Holmes Group (1990). *Tomorrow's schools: Principles for the design of professional development schools*. East Lansing, MI: Holmes Group.

Hoover, J. J. & Patton, J. R. (1995). *Teaching students with learning problems to use study skills: A teacher's guide*. Austin, TX: Pro-Ed.

Jones, R. M., & Steinbrink, J. E. (1991). Home teams: Cooperative learning in elementary science. *School Science and Mathematics, 91*, 139–143.

Ladson-Billings, G. (1995). Multicultural teacher education: Research, practice and policy. In J. A. Banks & C. A. McGee Banks (Eds.). *Handbook of research on multicultural education*. New York: Macmillan Publishing, 747–759.

Marr, M. B. (1997). Cooperative learning: A brief review. *Reading and Writing Quarterly: Overcoming Learning Difficulties, 13* (1), 7–20.

McTighe, J., & Lyman, F. G., Jr. (1988). Cueing thinking in the classroom: The promise of theory-embedded tools. *Educational Leadership, 47* (7), 18–24.

Polloway, E. A., Patton, J. R., & Serna, S. (2001). Strategies for teaching learners with special needs. 7th Edition. Englewood Cliffs, NJ: Merrill Prentice Hall.

Sapon-Shevin, M. (1999). *Because we can change the world: A practical guide to building cooperative, inclusive classrooms communities*. Boston: Allyn and Bacon.

Sleeter, C. E. & Grant, C. A. (1999). *Making choices for multicultural education: Five approaches to race, class, and gender*, 3rd Edition. New York: John Wiley & Sons.

Sudzina, M. (1993, February). *Dealing with diversity in the classroom: A case study approach*. A paper presented at the annual meeting of the Association of Teacher Educators, Los Angeles. (ERIC Document Reproduction Service No. ED 354 233).

Tomlinson, C. (1999).*The differentiated classrooms: Responding to the needs of all learners*. Alexandria, VA: Association for Supervision and Curriculum Development.

U.S. Department of Education (1995). *17th Annual Report to Congress on the Implementation of IDEA*. (Washington, DC: U.S. Dept. of Ed.).

Zeichner, K. M. (1993). *Educating teachers for diversity*. East Lansing, MI: National Center for Research on Teacher Learning.

———. (1997). Educating teachers for cultural diversity. In K. Zeichner, S. Melnick, and M.L. Gomez (Eds.). *Currents of reform in preservice teacher education*. New York: Teachers College Press.

PART I

THE CASES

CHAPTER 1

Practices in Teacher Education and Cooperative Learning at the University of Toronto

CAROL ROLHEISER AND STEPHEN ANDERSON

Preparing new teachers for today's classrooms, schools, and communities demands different approaches to teacher education. For many faculties of education this means creating cultures that are not only responsive to externally changing contexts, but are also proactive and explicit about working on the continuing development of their own institutional cultures. At the University of Toronto, teacher education faculty and school district staff began serious reform efforts about a decade ago. We changed our program to reflect and to contribute to evolving knowledge about effective teaching practices and principles (e.g., cooperative learning, constructivist approaches to student learning), and alternative forms of student evaluation (e.g., portfolios, peer/self-evaluation). We began to incorporate knowledge from the growing field of teacher development, both initial and continuing, into our programmatic changes to teacher education (e.g., emphasizing teacher-teacher collaboration for continuous learning, as well as teacher inquiry and reflective practice). We broadened our conceptions of the ideal teacher, and our corresponding goals for initial teacher education, from a limited focus on developing individual expertise in the classroom, to a more complex image of teachers as interdependent professionals working collaboratively with one another and with other partners in education. Our collective goals were aimed at achieving excellence in the classroom, and helping candidates become active agents of educational improvement and societal change. Finally, we challenged ourselves to apply similar understandings about teaching and learning, teacher development, and organizational effectiveness to our own roles as teacher educators and to the institutional culture in which our teacher education program was embedded. We begin this chapter by highlighting key institutional elements that have influenced the integration of cooperative learning into the preparation of preservice teacher candidates in one Ontario Institute for Studies in Education/University of Toronto (OISE/UT) elementary program option serving a cohort of sixty students. We then describe our framework for teacher development and how it interacts with the teaching of cooperative learning. We draw on our research and on our formative assessments of teacher candidate progress to support our perceptions of their development in the use of cooperative learning during the program.

THE INSTITUTIONAL CONTEXT

Most preservice teacher education programs in the province of Ontario, Canada are organized as consecutive undergraduate programs. Teacher candidates admitted to the programs have already earned at least a Bachelor's degree in some field of specialization other than education. Upon successful completion of the academic and practicum requirements of an eight- to ten-month teacher education program, a university awards candidates a Bachelor of Education degree and recommends them for an Ontario Teaching Certificate to be conferred by the Ontario College of Teachers.

Leadership and Faculty Renewal

This chapter draws mainly on our work since 1988. The appointment of a new dean of the faculty of education in 1988 was accompanied by the initiation of a process of faculty renewal. Although many of the older generation of faculty were deeply involved and provided leadership in the changes undertaken in this time period, there is no doubt that the openness to innovation was enhanced by the presence of new faculty, many of whom added considerable research expertise, as well as the traditional emphasis on classroom teaching expertise, to the faculty profile.

The process of faculty renewal involved vigorous administrative and collegial support for faculty development. Interested faculty, for example, began to meet as a study group to enhance each other's learning and efforts to integrate cooperative learning into their own instructional repertoires. This study group spawned other faculty learning groups focused on the use of varied instructional innovations such as portfolio assessment, case-based teaching, and action research. In sum, the institutional context was highly supportive of faculty innovation in teaching, including the use of cooperative learning. The pressure, support, vision, and leadership for program experimentation and change from the dean and his leadership team were, and continue to be, a key factor for innovation in our teacher education program.

Shift to Program Cohort Structure

Until 1988 teacher candidates took discrete courses in curriculum and instruction, educational psychology, the social foundations of education, and topics such as educational law and special education, which were taught by instructors who had little contact with one another. Practicum experiences were independently organized in four two-week blocks by a practice teaching unit with few direct links to their coursework experiences. One of the major changes was a shift to a "program" approach organized around cohorts of faculty and teacher candidates grouped into a variety of program options. A typical elementary program option involves about sixty teacher candidates and a group of five or six instructors. The faculty instructors plan and deliver the candidates' program as a team. The teacher candidates take all their in-faculty coursework as a cohort. Each program option collaborates with specific sets of elementary schools for the practicum components of their program. The shift to a program cohort structure created a context that is more conducive to coordination and coherence of all of the teacher candidates' professional learning experiences.

Development of Field-Based Programs and Partnerships

Closer links with the field were established in the planning and delivery of the program. The traditional block practicum experiences expanded to include weekly nonevaluated in-school days, and fewer but longer practice teaching blocks. The faculty negotiated partnerships with school districts and clusters of schools within those districts to participate as host schools for specific program options. These closer links to schools and teachers made it is easier to develop coherence in school and classroom support for specific foci of beginning teacher development, such as cooperative learning.

The Learning Consortium originated in 1988 as a teacher development and school improvement partnership between the faculty of education and four Toronto area school districts to collaboratively plan and deliver teacher education ventures extending from preservice, to beginning teacher induction, through the continuing in-service development of practicing teachers (Erskine-Cullen, 1995; Fullan, Erskine-Cullen & Watson, 1995). When the Learning Consortium began, the partners chose cooperative learning as an initial focus for teacher learning. This involved a series of summer institutes and follow-up support in cooperative learning for practicing teachers and interested university faculty. The partnership created a high profile for implementation of cooperative learning in these districts' schools, many of which served as practicum sites in the preservice program.

Change and Consensus on Program Goals

Along with the organizational changes, the faculty formalized six broad goals for teacher development that served as guidelines for programming and as outcomes for assessment of teacher candidate growth throughout the program. These goals oriented the program towards a multidimensional image of teacher learning focusing on student diversity and equity in the classroom, teachers' pedagogical knowledge (i.e., curriculum, instruction, classroom management, human development), school law and professional ethics, teacher commitment to ongoing professional growth, collaboration with colleagues and other stakeholders in education, and personal philosophies of teaching. Faculty consensus on these goals provided a programmatic foundation that related cooperative learning to a broader institutional image for initial teacher education.

In sum, three key conditions of the institutional context positively affected our efforts to incorporate cooperative learning and norms of professional collaboration into our elementary preservice program. One was the administrative and collegial support for experimentation with new strategies for teacher education, grounded in both research and in our own ongoing professional learning. Second were the programmatic and structural changes (e.g., program cohort structure, field-based programs, teacher education partnerships) that created an impetus for greater teamwork in the design and delivery of the program between preservice faculty and practicing teachers. These changes made it possible for faculty to coordinate plans and to infuse focuses of teacher candidate development, like cooperative learning, across the program. And third, consensus around a set of images or outcomes for teacher development legitimated the emphasis on cooperative learning, and positioned those focuses of teacher candidate learning within a holistic framework for teachers' initial and continuing professional growth.

A STRATEGIC FRAMEWORK FOR TEACHER LEARNING

Our approach to cooperative learning within the preservice program has been guided by three interrelated conceptions of teacher development. The first is the teacher-centered framework for classroom and school improvement designed by Fullan, Bennett, & Rolheiser (1990). One component of the framework identifies four possible areas of teacher development in the classroom, including content (e.g., knowledge of curriculum, human development, and learning), class-room management (e.g., addressing misbehavior, creating an inclusive class-room), instructional skills (e.g., questioning practices), and instructional strategies (e.g., cooperative learning, concept attainment). A second component of the framework targets four potential foci for school improvement, including developing shared goals, teacher collegiality, efforts towards continuous improvement, and the organizational arrangements (e.g., time, space, resources) necessary to enable other areas of classroom and school improvement. At the center of the framework is the teacher-as-learner, a professional striving to improve mastery of a technical repertoire of instructional practices, to develop the skills and attitudes to collaborate effectively with others, to become compe-tent researchers of their own practices and matters of school improvement, and to enhance their capacity as reflective practitioners. In theory, the more compo-nents of this framework for improvement and teacher development that are addressed and the closer the linkages among them, the greater the likelihood that positive results will occur. This model provided us with a powerful organizer for positioning our preservice work on cooperative learning and teacher collab-oration within a research-grounded framework for teacher growth.

The six broad program images or outcomes for effective teaching provided the second major conceptualization of teacher development shaping our work with cooperative learning and teacher collaboration in the preservice program. One outcome, for example, targeted the development of curriculum and instruc-tional expertise, including but not limited to cooperative learning strategies. Another outcome honed in on the vision of teachers as interactive professionals in the classroom and beyond with other teachers, parents, and the community. These program outcomes legitimized cooperative learning and collaboration as institutional goals for initial teacher development and propelled us to extend, deepen, and integrate teacher candidates' learning in ways that we might other-wise not have done.

The third concept of teacher development that has shaped our work on cooperative learning and teacher collaboration is the notion of alternative *forms* of teacher learning. The classroom and school improvement framework and the six program images guided our thinking about the content and outcomes of beginning teacher preparation, but they did not address the question of *how* teachers learn, and how knowledge about forms of teacher learning might be built into a preservice program. Table 1.1 highlights eight forms of teacher learn-ing that we have incrementally integrated into our program (cf. National Staff Development Council, 1999).

These three conceptual frameworks for teacher development allowed us to relate our preservice work with cooperative learning and teacher collaboration to a holistic, multidimensional, research-linked vision of teacher development.

Table 1.1. *Eight Forms of Teacher Learning Integrated into OISE/UT Teacher Education*

Forms of learning	Focus of learning
Technical training model (theory, demonstration, practice, feedback, coaching)	Introduce and support mastery of specific instructional strategies and skills (e.g., Jigsaw, mind-mapping)
Clinical supervision and mentoring	Practicum observation and feedback by faculty advisors and host teachers
Reflective practice	Teacher candidates create self-directed portfolios of growth targeted to the Six Key Images
Action research	Practicum-based inquiry on professional practice
Teacher study groups	Practicum-based literacy study groups of teacher candidates and key teachers
Peer support (critical friends)	Peer responses to portfolio entries; peer evaluations in some assignments
Professional reading	Required in major assignments (e.g., portfolios, action research, investigations of current education issues)
Technology-mediated learning	Computer conferencing about education issues; computer forums about subject matter pedagogy (e.g., math); internet use for research and locating resources

TEACHING ABOUT COOPERATIVE LEARNING WITHIN OISE/UT

Cooperative learning figures prominently in an overall approach to creating and modeling the development of a collaborative learning community within our program option of sixty teacher candidates and a dozen host schools. Here we describe and illustrate seven interrelated strategies for developing teacher candidate understanding of and skill in cooperative learning in our preservice program.

1. Setting expectations for collaboration
2. Community and team building

3. Modeling of cooperative learning strategies
4. Cooperative learning institute and follow-up
5. Expectation and support for trial use in practicum placements
6. Integration of cooperative learning with other program components
7. Cooperative assignments and accountability

We are confident about the positive effects of our approach on beginning teacher learning, but we are realistic about the limitations of a ten-month preservice program. This confidence and pragmatism arise from our research on cooperative learning among preservice and experienced teachers (Cullen, Rolheiser, & Bailey, 1993; Anderson, Rolheiser, & Bennett, 1995), as well as from data on teacher candidate learning collected and shared by our program team through assignments, supervision, and feedback.

Setting Expectations for Collaboration

In our first meeting with our teacher candidates during summer orientation we share the six institutional outcomes for teacher development. We communicate that our operation as a community is grounded in the tenets of cooperative learning. We discuss how candidates' previous experiences in university programs were likely structured individualistically or competitively, and highlight the key factors that may make for a different experience in their teacher preparation program at OISE/UT. To have them begin to value open sharing of ideas, expertise, and resources with colleagues means having experience with the benefits of cooperation (Rolheiser, 1996). Teacher candidates open a Time Capsule from previous graduates who communicate powerfully the rewards of collaboration through the cohort experience. In response to the prompt "One of the strengths I'm bringing to my career as a result of my experiences in the program . . . ," Time Capsule contributors make statements like the following: "Realizing the value and effectiveness of cooperative learning, as well as using it abundantly in the classroom"; "Collaboration. Share your ideas, experiences, issues, and learn with your teachers and peers. I've learned so much from teamwork." Setting expectations for collaboration is also communicated through teacher candidate involvement in community-building activities in the beginning period of their program.

Community and Team Building

The expectation of collaboration is accompanied by early community-building activities. The development of community, however, is dependent on constant and deliberate nurturing. To this end, we are conscious of building a learning community in a range of ways throughout the year using the model and many of the ideas described by Gibbs (2000). For example, every break (holidays, practicum, etc.) is followed by reconnecting in ways that include all group members. After the December break, students might engage in a Community Circle and share a cultural tradition they participated in over the holiday period. After each practicum we utilize cooperative methods to help our teacher candidates appreciate the variety of learning experienced. We might use a Four Corners activity (see Bennett & Rolheiser, 2001, for additional information on procedures for implementing the cooperative learning activities referred to in this chapter) where they move to the corner of the room with the movie title that best metaphorically represents their practicum experience (e.g., *The Titanic, As Good as it Gets, Mr. Bean's Escapades, The Full Monty*).

Team building operates in tandem with community building. Our teacher candidates experience a variety of different small group teams throughout the year. These teams range from short-term random groupings for class exercises or activities to strategically constructed heterogeneous groups for long-term projects or tasks. Whenever a new small group is created, or periodically with a long-term group, we use cooperative team building activities to help teacher candidates connect personally and create the conditions that enhance their work in joint learning tasks. We might use the process of a Three-Step Interview where groups of three or four take turns interviewing, responding, and recording to a question that invokes the sharing of opinions, experiences, emotions, etc. In preparation for an exploration of classroom management, for example, the interview questions might be: "Describe your first memory of a teacher that really made a difference to you as a student. What do you remember about that teacher?"

Base support groups (BSG) are the cornerstone of our cooperative learning approach. We establish BSG of four students within the first month of each year. BSG provide an opportunity for teacher candidates to experience working with a team that remains together over the course of an entire program and requires having a greater investment in working through conflict and developing trust and commitment. BSG are formed in conjunction with an activity we call "All About Me." In the first week of university classes we create an entire day of learning focused on children's literature; specifically, the use of picture books. Candidates examine, read, experience activities and analyze the various approaches used by authors and illustrators. They are then given the task to create a picture book targeted to the grade level they will teach in their first practicum. The book has to communicate something about themselves as people. Two weeks later they read this to three classmates and display it for other classmates. On the day of the "All About Me" book sharing they are put in heterogeneous BSG of four. We consider a mix of factors in forming the groups: gender, school, grade-level placements, and interpersonal traits. They participate in a peer sharing, oral response, and written peer-response process. Over time, these BSG become the foundation for starting and ending each class, and for general communication and support.

We have studied the effects of BSG on teacher candidate learning and collegial relationships over time (Rolheiser & Hundey, 1995). We found that the BSG were instrumental during the preservice year in (1) facilitating understanding in preservice course work, (2) enhancing teacher candidates' understanding of the learning process for their own students, and (3) focusing preservice teachers' intentions on working with peers in future professional communities. The study also revealed that norms of collegiality and collaboration continued into the beginning year of teaching.

Modeling of Cooperative Learning Strategies

We believe one of the most powerful means of learning is through what we model ourselves as instructors. In the first month of our program, and subsequently throughout the remainder of the year, the teacher candidates develop awareness of cooperative learning through experiential demonstrations. A variety of cooperative learning strategies and tactics are used (Bennett, Rolheiser, & Stevahn, 1991; Bennett & Rolheiser, 2001), including the Learning Together approach (Johnson, Johnson, & Holubec, 1994), Kagan's (1994) structures and tactics (e.g., Four Corners, Three-step Interview, Think-Pair-Share, Line-ups, etc.), Aronson's (Aronson & Patnoe, 1997) Jigsaw, and so forth. Instructors take time to ensure that the students debrief the experience, consider applications, and raise questions. These experiences, especially early in the year, provide a base for the explicit teaching of cooperative learning in an institute format. The modeling is valued and practiced throughout the year by all faculty on our team across all courses in the program.

Cooperative Learning Institute and Follow-up

We hold our first two-day institute on cooperative learning within the first two months of the academic year. It brings together teacher candidates with their host teachers from our partner schools. We found in prior research that the combination of preservice and inservice teacher colearning makes for a powerful learning environment, and creates the conditions that support experimentation and follow-up after the institute (Cullen, Rolheiser, & Bailey, 1993). Institute instructors use the skill training model (i.e., theory, demonstration, practice, feedback, coaching) to introduce and support the mastery of cooperative learning. Instructors also model the critical thinking skills they want to enhance for participants (Rolheiser & Stevahn, 1998). Participants use theoretical perspectives and research findings to facilitate the understanding of cooperative learning concepts (e.g., positive interdependence, individual accountability). They experience a range of cooperative strategies and structures (e.g., Learning Together, Teams-Games-Tournaments, Jigsaw, Inside-Outside Circles, Community Circle, Paired Reading, Placemat, Think-Pair-Share, etc.), and have the opportunity to design and coteach a cooperative lesson to peers during the institute. This lesson is followed by self and peer assessment that generates feedback and goals for future lessons. After the institute participants (candidates and host teachers) codevelop and teach cooperative lessons in our partner schools. Later, participants return to experience a three-day module focused on student evaluation in a cooperative classroom.

The most critical aspect of the institute design is that new and experienced teachers come together on equal ground as co-learners. The new teachers have the support of their host teachers to provide some coaching. The experienced teachers are accountable in that the new teachers are depending on them to jointly experiment. As one host teacher commented in a survey about the institute, "It gave me actual starting points to begin a newly structured program next week and working with the teacher candidates." In schools associated with the program for several years, the opportunity to study cooperative learning has extended to most teachers, thereby increasing the chances that candidates will be supported in their use of cooperative learning during their practicum.

At the conclusion of the cooperative learning institute we routinely collect feedback from the participants regarding the process and learning outcomes of the experience. Participants are asked to rate on a scale of 1 (low) to 5 (high) their knowledge of, and comfort with cooperative learning prior to the institute. Although they have already experienced cooperative learning in a variety of ways in the first two months of the program, the candidates tend to rate both their knowledge ($X = 1.75, N = 41$) and comfort levels ($X = 1.48, N = 41$) quite low (typical scores from one of the institutes). These findings suggest that modeling is not enough and that once participants begin to explore the conceptual and research dimensions of cooperative learning, along with its applications, they become more realistic about what they know in relation to what there is to know. The candidates give a high rating to the usefulness of the institute as a professional development opportunity that will impact their teaching practice ($X = 4.37, N = 41$). Analysis of.participant responses to open-ended questions about learning at the institute cluster into five domains: understanding the principles of cooperative learning, understanding the purposes and outcomes of cooperative learning, acquisition of practical methods and applications of cooperative learning, discriminating when to use cooperative learning, appreciation of the theory and research base for cooperative learning; and, ways of integrating cooperative learning into lesson planning (Rolheiser & Anderson, 2001).

Expectations and Support for Trial Use in Practicum Placements

We have developed mechanisms to encourage candidates to use cooperative learning in their school placements consistent with knowledge about the importance of job-embedded professional development (Wood & Killian, 1998) to the transfer and development of new skills. The cooperative learning institute coincides with the onset of the teacher candidates' first practicum. The evaluation of the candidates' practicum performance includes their ability to use a range of instructional approaches, including cooperative learning. Host teachers and university instructors observe the candidates teach and provide on-the-spot feedback to help refine their skills and knowledge related to cooperative learning. The frequency of experimentation with cooperative learning by teacher candidates during their practicum is evident in our personal records of classroom observations. Over a two-year period, for example, one of the authors conducted forty-two practicum observations involving twenty-nine students. Faculty feedback about the use of small group learning was evident in records of thirty observation episodes involving all but five of the students. These data confirm not only the teacher candidates' beginning efforts to transfer cooperative learning principles and methods into the classroom, but also the coaching process utilized to support that transfer (Rolheiser & Anderson, 2001). Common difficulties observed in early use include: (1) recognizing when cooperative group activities could be used to effectively enhance student learning; (2) shifting from the rote use of procedures (e.g., assigning roles to small group members) to the application of principles that can be enacted in multiple ways (e.g., positive interdependence to ensure cooperation); (3) structuring small group activities to make collaboration essential to the learning process and to include individual as well as group accountability; (4) incorporating both academic and social goals and skill development; (5) finding effective ways to monitor small group activity across the class; and, (6) anticipating and preparing students for the complexity of small-group learning tasks. The practicum following the cooperative learning institute is a time when new questions emerge that stimulate inquiry in the teacher candidates' portfolio entries (see next section) and in action research projects later in the year.

Further evidence of use of cooperative learning emerges during candidates' second-term practicum when they undertake instructionally focused action research projects. Teacher candidates formulate questions with their host teachers. Analysis of 166 action research questions covering a three-year period revealed that about 13 percent of our teacher candidates each year independently choose to study their use of cooperative group learning methods. Sample questions are as follows: "What effect does teaching students conflict-resolution skills have on their functioning in cooperative group tasks?"; "Will using the Think-Pair-Share technique help improve listening and communication skills in a junior/senior kindergarten?"; "Will students with low, average, and high mathematics achievement increase their performance on mathematical word problems as a result of cooperative problem solving in heterogeneous achievement groups?"

Integration of Cooperative Learning with Other Program Components

We connect cooperative learning to other areas that new teachers are exploring. We purposely focus on classroom management before cooperative learning. This decision is based on research related to the needs of new teachers (Veenman, 1984). The study of classroom management, however, allows us to highlight the importance of community building and team building as a basis for inclusion. Instructors emphasize the power of cooperative learning in proactive classroom management, including the teaching of social skills. Teacher candidates examine a variety of management approaches and the tenets underlying these approaches, for example, "How does a classroom management system where the teacher assumes responsibility for rules and behavior align to the values one might strive for in a cooperative classroom?"

When teacher candidates study lesson design they first master a basic planning model, and then plan for cooperative learning based on that model. They use the Johnsons's five basic elements (e.g., positive interdependence, individual accountability, face-to-face interaction, social skills, processing) as a lens for planning (Johnson, Johnson, & Holubec, 1994). We also encourage them to attend to both academic and social outcomes in their assessment and evaluation of students.

In the study of assessment and evaluation, candidates complete a three-day module focused specifically on these processes in cooperative classrooms. This module comes later in the program; our research suggests that it is only after some initial experimentation with cooperative learning that implementers are at a stage where they are focused on student outcomes (Anderson, Rolheiser, & Bennett, 1995; Ross, Rolheiser, & Hogaboam-Gray, 1998). The first day of this module participants examine assessment and evaluation issues in a cooperative classroom (e.g., needs and concerns of various stakeholders, options for grading cooperative activities, traditional versus alternative assessment practices). The second day they learn a model for helping students with self- and peer evaluation (Rolheiser, 1996). The third day they apply a decision-making model for portfolio assessment in a collaborative classroom (Rolheiser, Bower, & Stevahn, 2000). This combination helps teacher candidates probe the complexities of student learning through cooperative learning, and sets the stage for experimentation with alternative assessment methods in their second practicum.

Cooperative Assignments and Accountability

Our teacher candidates complete a number of major assignments that engage them in cooperative groupwork and in peer-supported individual learning. The assignments involve them in longer-term cooperative experiences. The assignments provide a context for modeling and deliberating issues and practices of student assessment and evaluation in cooperative groupwork. Assignments include one formally structured group investigation (Sharan & Hertz-Lazarowitz, 1980), and several individual but peer supported assignments (e.g., professional learning portfolio, action research project). The focus of the group investigations has varied from teacher experiences with educational change (Anderson, Rolheiser, & Gordon, 1998), to school-wide approaches to curriculum (literacy, math, etc.), and to exploration of the policies, practices, and theories associated with contemporary education issues (e.g., school violence, antiracism, parent involvement, bullying, special education, computers in schools). We require students to reflect on their experience as learners in a group investigation and to discuss applications of group investigation in elementary classrooms.

The Professional Portfolio

The professional learning portfolios are the most significant and integrative assignment for the teacher candidates. The candidates are expected to document their learning and growth across the six institutional outcomes for teacher development. The entries are self-directed. The candidates choose what learning experiences are most meaningful to their development and performance over the course of the year, and worthy of inclusion in their portfolios. The intent of the portfolio is to promote habits of reflective practice and to help the teacher candidates take ownership for their professional growth.

The portfolio development process has both individual and cooperative elements (Rolheiser, Bower, & Stevahn, 2000). Teacher candidates share an artifact or learning sample accompanied by a reflection, with a peer, members of the faculty team, or with educators in their practicum schools. They also request a written peer response to their entry. The intent of the peer response is to encourage candidates to experience the value of learning from and contributing to each other's learning experiences.

While the teacher candidates are not required to include cooperative learning-related entries, this is common given the emphasis on cooperative learning that pervades the program. Each member of our faculty team reads and comments on the portfolios of ten to twelve teacher candidates annually. We examined the portfolio feedback records maintained by one of the authors over a four-year period. For 35 students (about 15 percent of the students participating in our program over that period), 27 (77 percent) included one or more entries and reflections about their experiences with cooperative group learning.

Through the portfolio reflection process, candidates deepen their understanding and skill in the use of cooperative learning methods, as they deconstruct their classroom experiences in light of their theoretical knowledge of cooperative learning, compare their cooperative learning experiences over the course of the year, and anticipate future modifications in their use of cooperative learning. Assessment of the portfolio entries by the faculty team provide another opportunity for coaching linked to significant moments in the candidates' growth in cooperative learning, as illustrated in figure 1. Many include cooperative learning and collaboration as key elements of their philosophy of teaching, which they articulate in their portfolio submission at the end of their program (Figure 2).

CONCLUSIONS AND IMPLICATIONS

What have we learned from our experiences and research about the challenges of implementing cooperative learning in teacher education? We have identified four major ongoing programmatic challenges of our work at OISE/UT:

Need for Expert Coaching

Although most host teachers are comfortable with cooperative learning, they may not necessarily have the expertise or necessary skills to provide expert coaching to teacher candidates on a daily basis. Clearly, coaching facilitates implementation. Finding ways to provide such expert coaching on a sustained basis is a continuing challenge.

Varying Levels of Teacher Candidate Understanding and Expertise

We still see a range of cooperative learning expertise from those teacher candidates who see cooperative learning simply as "assigning roles" to those who are able to skillfully structure group tasks based on cooperative principles. Attention to these varying levels demands constant monitoring and adjusting of teacher candidate learning experiences and individual feedback.

Changing Staff and Curricula

Yearly staff and curricular changes in the school system demand that we constantly rethink and review our approaches in order to sustain the emphasis on cooperative learning and collaboration in the program and schools. In the province of Ontario, for example, the government has in the past five years introduced explicit subject-based learning expectations by grade level in the elementary panel, a standardized report card keyed to those expectations, and annual standardized testing and reporting of school results in literacy and mathematics for Grades 3 and 6. Adapting to these changes within the preservice program is critical to an evolving process.

Student A

"Cooperative Learning (title of entry). With this knowledge in heart and mind I hope to see more entries in the future that reflect upon and explore the development of your expertise in the use of various cooperative group structures and strategies in practice. Has it been that easy? Has everything worked according to 'theory'? Have you discovered things about the way that cooperative learning works that you hadn't anticipated? What cooperative learning structures have you actually tried, and with what results? Here you state a commitment to try. I don't think you'll really own cooperative learning as one component of your teaching philosophy except through experience and results that you feel validate the worth of those experiences."

Student B

"Pioneer Sisters/Cooperative Learning (title of entry). Good to see you experimenting with teaching strategies such as cooperative group learning. I saw you doing this as well with a science experiment. I was impressed with the level of responsibility for learning that you and [name of peer] gave to your students. Many teachers wouldn't even dream of organizing sixty primary kids into cooperative groups for a science experiment! You learned that socializing kids into the norms and processes of cooperative group work does not happen overnight. So it's useful, particularly when working with children who haven't had much experience with it, to ease in over the year . . . take a long-term planning perspective . . . beginning with community building activities, forming base support groups and engaging in some team building, working on some basic social skills perhaps in nonacademic work first, and then moving into academic work, practicing simple structures like Think/Pair/Share before getting into more complex group work, etc. I'd like to challenge you to reflect upon and deconstruct your cooperative group lessons in terms of all five basic elements. Here you are talking about assigning roles as an essential component of cooperative group learning. In fact, assigning roles is simply one of the nine ways identified in "Where Heart Meets Mind" of creating positive interdependence. There are other ways, and you still need to think about the other elements—face to face interaction, individual accountability, academic and social goals, and group processing! You probably shouldn't overdo the role assignment technique. Kids will tire of it. Refer back to your cooperative learning resources for more ideas. Soon you'll be having ideas of your own!"

Student C

"Cooperative Learning Centers (title of entry) You are obviously developing considerable experience and expertise in the use of a variety of cooperative group learning methods, Here you draw both from your own learning about cooperative group learning and integrate it with the knowledge your associate teacher brought to the task. You demonstrate considerable creativity in this unit in the use of multiple cooperative group activities. Important learning occurred in your response and observations of the two students who tried to opt out. Remember back to your second entry where you had to rely on your ability to convince a student to contribute. Here you let individual accountability and positive interdependence work their own magic, and you left the decision to join to the kids, so that when they did join in they did so of their own volition. This is clear evidence of growth in your cooperative learning expertise. I wondered what you learned about what makes team planning work/not work from this experience with your associate teacher? Perhaps that's another reflection."

Figure 1. *Instructor Feedback on Portfolio Entries to Support Different Stages of Understanding Regarding Cooperative Learning.*

"[Two of my portfolio entries] 'Successful Lesson (paleontologist)' and 'Read Your Students,' are examples of the knowledge and appreciation I have for cooperative learning. I have made this teaching strategy part of who I am. I have changed classroom environments to facilitate this type of learning. I recognize the instructional possibilities it provides, particularly the potential for integrating both academic and social skills. In addition, it facilitates creating an antiracist environment and it helps build collaboration, partnerships, and support systems. It allows each individual to contribute their uniqueness to better the whole class. The degree of required interaction promotes an appreciation and respect for each other. The multicultural society we live in needs children that know how to make connections with others who may be different from themselves."

Figure 2. *Teacher Candidate Final Portfolio Reflection on Cooperative Learning.*

Small-Scale versus Large-Scale Implementation

The case we described in this chapter is not representative across all program options within our institution. The challenge is how innovative approaches in teacher education are shared with colleagues and diffused over time within a large preservice program such as ours (over 1100 teacher candidates yearly). Such knowledge sharing is pivotal to quality programming across our institution.

CONCLUSION

In this case study we have highlighted our strategies for teaching about cooperative learning in our teacher education program, as well as the conceptual foundations and institutional context underlying and supporting those strategies. We believe that the positive results we have been able to achieve in the teacher candidates' development as cooperative learning educators are strongly linked to the conceptual coherence and research-based support for the pedagogical approach described in the case. At the same time, we recognize that the implementation of any educational change is not just a technically and theoretically driven process; it is influenced by the institutional context and culture within which it is enacted. At OISE/UT our efforts to incorporate cooperative learning and collaborative norms into the initial preparation of teachers at the University of Toronto have been enhanced by key elements of our institutional context: administrative leadership and support, faculty renewal and development, consensus on program images or outcomes, teacher education partnerships with schools and school districts, and the shift to a cohort-based design for planning and delivering the preservice program. The case illustrates our sense that teacher candidate development occurs through the deliberate combination and interaction of various elements over a period of time. A strong introduction to cooperative learning for new teachers does not happen by "accident, good will, or isolated projects, no matter how worthy" (Fullan, Erskine-Cullen, & Watson, 1995, p. 189). Rather, it requires the conscious development of new structures and new values, and a rethinking of traditional approaches and experiences, supported by multiple and complementary forms of teacher learning that actually engage teacher candidates in the practice of cooperative learning. It also requires appropriate catalysts that bring the key elements together in an interactive and dynamic process. The conceptual frameworks for teacher development underlying our programmatic approach to cooperative learning and collaboration have served as catalysts for combining and fusing diverse components of the preservice program. Several of the teacher candidates' major learning experiences, such as the creation of professional learning portfolios, have had a similar effect in their development over the course of the program. Achieving a synthesis in the teacher candidates' development requires the right mix of ingredients. The seven strategies for teaching about cooperative learning we described reflect our current sense of an effective mix of pedagogical strategies to support initial development as cooperative learning educators. Our goal is to continue coming together and creating connections in our quest to prepare teachers who value collaboration and cooperative learning not only at the start of their careers, but also throughout their careers as professional educators.

REFERENCES

Anderson, S. E., Rolheiser, C. & Bennett, B. (1995). Confronting the challenge of implementing cooperative learning. *Journal of Staff Development*, 16(1), 32–39.

Anderson, S. E., Rolheiser, C. & Gordon, K. (1998). Preparing teachers to be leaders. *Educational Leadership*, 55(5), 59–61.

Aronson, E., & Patnoe, S. (1997). *The jigsaw classroom*. New York: Addison-Wesley Longman.

Bennett, B. & Rolheiser, C. (2001). *Beyond Monet –The artful science of instructional integration*. Toronto: Bookation.

Bennett, B., Rolheiser, C. & Stevahn, L. (1991). *Cooperative learning: Where heart meets mind*. Toronto: Educational Connections.

Cullen, E., Rolheiser, C., & Bailey, B. (1993). *Learning together: The impact of joint professional development experiences for pre-service and in-service teachers*. Paper presented at the Canadian Society for Studies in Education Annual Conference, Ottawa, ON.

Erskine-Cullen, E. (Ed.). (1995). The Learning Consortium. *School Effectiveness and School Improvement*, 6(3), 187–282.

Fullan, M., Bennett, B. & Rolheiser, C. (1990). Linking classroom and school improvement. *Educational Leadership*, 47(8), 13–19.

Fullan, M., Erskine-Cullen, E., & Watson, N. (1995). The Learning Consortium: A school-university partnership program. *School Effectiveness and School Improvement, 6*(3), 187–191.

Gibbs, J. (2000). *Tribes.* Sausalito, CA: Center Source Systems.

Johnson, D. W., Johnson, R. T., & Holubec, E. J. (1994). *The nuts and bolts of cooperative learning.* Edina, MN: Interaction Book Company.

Kagan, S. (1994). *Cooperative learning.* San Juan Capistrano: Kagan Cooperative Learning.

National Staff Development Council (1999). Powerful designs. *Journal of Staff Development, 20*(3).

Rolheiser, C. (1996). Partnership and program renewal: Moving forward. In D. Booth and S. Stiegelbauer (Eds.), *Teaching Teachers.* Hamilton, ON: Caliburn Enterprises.

Rolheiser, C. (Ed.). (1996). *Self-evaluation: Helping students get better at it!* Ajax, ON: Visutronx.

Rolheiser, C. & Anderson, S.E. (2001). *Cooperative learning and preservice teacher education: Creating fusion in the mix.* Paper presented at the Annual Meeting of the American Educational Research Association, Seattle, WA.

Rolheiser, C., Bower, B. & Stevahn, L. (2000). *The Portfolio Organizer.* Alexandria, VA: Association for Supervision and Curriculum Development.

Rolheiser, C., & Hundey, I. (1995). Building norms for professional growth in beginning teachers: A Learning Consortium initiative. *School Effectiveness and School Improvement, 6*(3), 205–222.

Rolheiser, C., & Stevahn, L. (1998). The role of the staff developers in promoting effective teacher decision-making. In C. Brody and N. Davidson (Eds.). *Professional development for cooperative learning: Issues and approaches.* Albany: State University of New York Press, 63–78.

Ross, J. A., Rolheiser, C., & Hogaboam-Gray. (1998). Student evaluation in cooperative learning: Teacher cognitions. *Teachers and Teaching: Theory and Practice, 4*(2), 299–316.

Sharan, S. & Hertz-Lazarowitz, R. (1980). A group-investigation method of cooperative learning in the classroom. In S. Sharan, P, Hare, C. Webb, R. Hertz-Lazarowitz (Eds.). *Cooperation in education.* Provo, UT: Brigham Young University Press, 14–46.

Veenman, S. (1984). Perceived problems of beginning teachers. *Review of Educational Research, 54*(2), 143–178.

Wood, F. & Killian, J. (1998). Job-embedded learning makes the difference in school improvement. *Journal of Staff Development, 19*(1), 52–54.

CHAPTER 2

TEACHER DECISION MAKING FOR COOPERATIVE LEARNING IN A PRESERVICE MASTER'S PROGRAM

CELESTE M. BRODY AND NANCY G. NAGEL

Lewis & Clark College is a small, liberal arts college in the Pacific Northwest. Influenced by the Holmes Group (1986) regarding the desirability of graduate-level teacher preparation, in 1986 the teacher education faculty redesigned its preservice program to become a fifth-year master's program (fifteen months) to prepare elementary, middle, and secondary teachers. Students are in cohorts of approximately twenty students each; they opt for the early childhood/elementary levels (age 3 to grade 8), or the middle/secondary levels (grades 5 to 12).

Several of the faculty who designed the program were strong adherents of whole-language philosophy as the basis for literacy development, of constructivist theories of learning as derived from John Dewey and Lev Vygotsky; others were feminists and critical theorists committed to social justice. The faculty agreed on the value of collaborative learning for organizing the college learning experiences. We wanted to encourage students to confront and deal with ethical and social issues and other dilemmas of practice, multiple viewpoints, and issues about social, political, and ethnic diversity. We also expected them to learn how to create collaborative learning environments in their classrooms. Our unique circumstances—a small faculty (10 to 12 regular, full-time teachers in addition to a number of part-time adjunct faculty), who work closely together and share a similar philosophy of education, a rigorous selection process, and a graduate level program—have enabled our teacher education faculty to grapple with how to prepare teachers who are likely to become future curriculum and instructional leaders.

In this chapter we consider the components of our preservice master's program that support the novice teacher's capacity to step into complex, socially and economically diverse learning environments with the ability to use cooperative learning beyond simple, routine use. We explain why and how the framework of collaborative learning helps us organize both in-class and fieldwork experiences to cultivate the idea of the "teacher as decision maker." We also discuss some of the difficult choices we have made and continue to make in response to internal factors, challenges created by changing state licensure structures, and changes within schools due to mandated testing. We conclude with an assessment of our faculty's ability to sustain substantial student preparation in cooperative learning while continuing the program within the collaborative learning tradition.

COLLABORATIVE LEARNING AND DEVELOPING TEACHERS AS DECISION MAKERS

Our teacher preparation emanates from the premise that good instruction should be guided by the more general orientation of collaborative learning—and the goal to develop teachers who are capable and creative decision makers. This means that learning contexts should be intentionally structured as learner-centered rather than teacher-centered and should foster multiple ways for peer learning to occur, preferably through rich, intrinsically motivating tasks that drive purposeful talk and cooperative work among students (Brubacher, 1991). We want our students to learn to discern and understand a range of peer learning experiences that support different purposes, for example, peer tutoring, simple and complex forms of cooperative learning, peer response groups in writing, literature circles, and real-world problem-solving investigations in science and mathematics. In our view collaborative learning subsumes approaches to cooperative learning (e.g., approaches developed by Johnson, Johnson & Holubec, 1987; Kagan, 1993; and Cohen, 1994). The larger organizer, collaborative learning, grounds the program's emphasis on collaboration in the learning process vis-à-vis the theories of Dewey, Piaget and Vygotsky: the construction of shared meanings for continual conversations, conceptual learning and integrative experiences. Instructors also teach *about* cooperative learning as a particular subset of approaches that are important to a teacher learning to manage a classroom, develop a task and reflect on group work processes in terms of group cohesion, interdependence and individual accountability. We continue to make choices about what is specifically taught and emphasized given the limited time with our students, and the reality that they may not have systematic support for instructional improvement once they begin teaching.

EVALUATION OF OUR PROGRAM AND GRADUATES

For the past thirteen years the faculty have relied on close working relationships with one another to adjust the program quickly in response to state licensure changes, our own experiences and data about the program. We evaluate our program four ways on a regular basis:

1. Students complete an evaluation of different facets at the conclusion of their program—their cooperating (mentor) teachers, the quality of their field placement and supervision, and the coursework. We periodically conduct interviews of graduates about their teaching and the factors in the program that enhance or limit their job performance.
2. Annual surveys are completed by administrators regarding the performance of their first-year teachers who are our graduates.
3. End-of-the-program evaluations are completed by mentor teachers.
4. Notes are reviewed from meetings with supervising faculty and mentor teachers.

Instructors also visit classrooms to observe teacher graduates and to interview prospective cooperating (i.e., mentor) teachers—some of whom are graduates of our program. We analyze supervision reports by college supervisors to understand the effects of variations in classroom environments on our students.

In addition to the four sources of data on students and the program, for this chapter we also interviewed eight faculty who teach key courses and/or coordinate the preservice programs. We asked them to elaborate on questions ranging from their own definitions of cooperative learning and collaborative learning to the expectations they hold for the application of cooperative learning. The interviews helped the authors understand how the preservice programs evolved over the last five years in regard to the way in which strategies for cooperative learning are and are not taught. We draw on these data in describing why we designed the program the way we have; but we specifically refer to the faculty interviews in our analysis of issues that emerged in this process.

LEARNING THROUGH COLLABORATIVE LEARNING

There are a number of ways in which students experience *learning through collaborative learning* in the program. In this chapter we discuss two features in depth: the cohort approach and the year-long internship. *Learning about* cooperative learning occurs in all methods courses but in different ways in the elementary and middle/secondary programs; we will discuss one of the common experiences, the year-long classroom management course where cooperative learning is supported.

A Cohort Approach

Students. Despite ongoing, aggressive efforts to recruit minorities, the majority of our students are white and middle-class. There are more females than males at the elementary levels but at the middle to secondary levels there are about the same number of males as females. Our students tend to be liberal, progressive, and favor educational change. They range in age from twenty-two to forty-five and bring a variety of life and professional experiences. During the admissions process we weigh favorably several factors: living or working with diverse populations here or abroad, speaking a second language, and teaching or work experience with children. We look for evidence of reflective habits, creativity, a strong content and disciplinary knowledge in order to develop curriculum, an openness to learn through an internship-type experience, and flexibility toward handling competing work demands. We organize the candidate selection process to emphasize the importance of learning from one another in this program. We now conduct interviews in a group setting with issues for small groups to discuss and resolve as part of the screening process. (Candidates from afar are interviewed by phone.)

Students' experiences in small groupwork before or during college are often limited. The strategies they experienced often emphasized using groups for individual motivation, or fulfilling social aspects of peer relationships. Initially students might say, "I am grouped out. I usually did all the work." If they have had positive experiences or believe that cooperative learning correlates with better understanding of concepts, they are usually at a loss to explain what worked, for what purposes and why. Few understand the relationship of peer learning to cognition.

Cohort structure. A teacher's ability to work effectively as a team member is a skill critical in school settings. To develop this skill, we organize the entire fifteen-month experience around a learning group, called a cohort. Interns quickly realize that their learning is deeply affected by the level of student commitment to work together within the cohort. Interns take the majority of their coursework with their cohort, with the exception of subject electives and master's degree requirements. During the first summer, the curriculum is sequenced to provide community building experiences—issues regarding norms of participation, tensions regarding individual needs versus the good of the whole, and assessment of individual and group products—are regular grist for discussion.

Two of the courses in the middle to secondary program for example, writing and writing processes, and mathematical thinking, provide structured group-building experiences within the context of content.

The first summer's coursework for all students includes (but is not limited to): (1) child or adolescent psychology, combined with educational psychology and with learning to help students with special needs be successful in school, and (2) the social and historical foundations of education. In these courses there are a number of exercises assigned to introduce interns to methods of observing, interviewing, and understanding children or adolescents in school, community, or natural settings. They are also expected to explore the larger socioeconomic and political factors that affect schooling and society in terms of justice, equality, and equal access. To accomplish their tasks, compare experiences, and learn from one another, the cohorts are broken into small working groups of three to five interns. Instructors employ a number of cooperative processes, ranging from pair-sharing, discussion groups, jigsaws, and group investigations depending on course goals and their own instructional repertoires. Interns work on projects such as synthesizing field data, generating explanations for their observations, and applying child developmental theory to curriculum activities. Assignments involve individual accountability along with group products, depending on the goal. Systematic reflection is required at several points to assist the intern to understand the pedagogical processes that help or hinder them in their learning.

Although the cohort is a living laboratory for many forms of peer learning, we should not leave the impression that life in a cohort is always easy or constructive. Accepting differences among members of the cohort as to strengths and weaknesses on any number of characteristics, competencies, and proficiencies communicates the idea that professional growth and learning is more than technique; it involves a full range of individual and group considerations. Individual actions and accomplishments must be balanced against the ability to work as a member of a team. On the other hand, persistent, negative attitudes by a few individuals, resistance among the students about shifting from being passive, traditional learners to professional learners, and status issues within the group have made some cohorts less than satisfactory learning contexts. Conflicts and challenges are part of group life but when they persist beyond a level that is healthy for learning, they tax faculty and students, requiring numerous meetings and endless strategizing.

The Internship

We designed a year-long practicum experience in a school and classroom as an essential feature of the teacher preparation program. Evaluation data indicated that the year-long teaching experience was a critical variable in the ability of the intern to master complex teaching processes. The full year's "internship" in a school setting continues to provide a strong context for teacher preparation because it allows the intern to tackle progressively more challenging teaching tasks throughout the school year and to observe children's development over time. We use the term "interns" to call attention to a qualitatively different kind of learning for both the student and the cooperating teacher, one where both parties are more likely to benefit from the relationship because there is more time for both to learn from one another.

Interns are matched with mentors in a careful process involving initial visits, interviews, and discussion. Cohort leaders consider the temperament, strengths, interests, and anticipated challenges of the intern, as well as the school setting, the skills and background of the mentor teacher. Beginning with the first meetings for the start of the school year, interns are in schools learning to understand the full range of teachers' roles in the classroom, school, and community. During the fall term, interns are in their classrooms and schools for a prescribed number of hours each week. In the winter this time increases continually until early March when they are in the schools full-time.

We value coteaching processes and consider learning to be a team member and communicating with another teacher as a peer to be one of the benefits of the internship. Interns are required to systematically observe students, and to attend to the way in which mentors establish norms and set up classroom routines in their early fall experiences. They are expected to find ways to be a resource to the mentor and the students—tutoring, supporting small groupwork, handling routines, and implementing parts of lessons. Eventually, planning becomes a joint process, with the intern taking increasing responsibility for teaching and learning. This does not always happen, but when it does it appears to be the key in the intern's ability to go beyond simply managing routines in a classroom, to organizing teaching, including cooperative learning and other peer-learning processes.

We expect mentors to allow students to experiment with different forms of peer learning depending on the academic discipline and the situation in the class. Sometimes we have to require that these opportunities to experiment occur, using cooperative learning and college supervisors' observations to be sure that this occurs. Many of our mentors have had training with cooperative learning approaches and assist interns in implementing practices similar to those we teach on campus. Other mentors may not use cooperative learning, leaving the intern to develop an approach without observing the practice—in this case the intern visits other teachers, or may even be moved to another mentor if there is strong resistance to allowing the intern to develop cooperative learning strategies. We require mentors to attend seminars each semester, which provides a critical context for discussing expectations. We make it a point of approaching their concerns: (e.g., can you (the mentor) allow the intern to teach a lesson using cooperative learning even when you don't think it will work?).

Interns who are able to construct complex tasks resulting in observable learning through peers for social and academic purposes usually have the benefit of mentors who modeled these aspects, and the interns were astute enough to discern the elements that they must master. Skilled mentors who understand the theory behind their classroom management and the reasons for using cooperative and collaborative learning, and communicate this information at the intern's critical developmental moments, are better models for interns. However, some interns are able to master these strategies without a strong model. These are often interns with a clear sense of purpose, an ability to assess individual student learning, and who see 'the relationship between the task and the purpose and structure of peer learning. They learn from peers, the rich collaborative, coursework environment, and reflection. In contrast, those who struggle to make sense of classroom and curricular organization, have poorly developed abilities to use on-going assessment, and who are weak in disciplinary knowledge and thinking, tend to fall back on traditional approaches of teaching—*regardless* of the quality of the internship.

Year-Long Classroom Management Seminar

Another critical program factor that supports the intern's ability to implement collaborative and cooperative learning is the pacing of the classroom management course throughout the year. Effective management is fundamental to carrying out even the simplest of collaborative/cooperative learning strategies.

The classroom management course begins in the fall with a focus on how to establish norms for classroom cohesion and effective teamwork. Later, interns consider how to guide small group learning processes through data from observations, conferencing with students, and student feedback. The course continues through the early spring, culminating with the requirement to develop a full management plan that addresses the needs of special students and how to involve all students in ongoing academic and social learning. The faculty member who teaches the classroom management courses draws primarily from the Johnsons' (1987) conceptual approach for making decisions about using cooperative learning.

Collaborative and Cooperative Learning as Decision Making

Our experiences in teaching preservice and inservice teachers about effective groupwork strategies indicate that when teachers fail to understand the theory underlying a particular method they are likely to misapply the method and/or to abandon it when problems occur. Teachers also underestimate the need for the use of coaching and direct instruction for the teaching of social skills (e.g., basic communication skills), and content and task-specific skills necessary for students to learn complex information and processes (Meloth & Deering, 1999). If mentors or college teachers do not discuss the theoretical principles as they relate to different goals and purposes of the collaborative approaches they are using, the intern is left to discern these intuitively or serendipitously. Even when mentors have had cooperative learning training or have an extensive background in particular collaborative learning methods such as writers' workshops, their explanations for the use of peer learning are sometimes limited. Interns often struggle with how to selectively use certain forms of peer learning for different purposes such as mastering facts, peer editing in writing, or holding discussions to account for differing points of view.

LEARNING ABOUT COLLABORATIVE
AND COOPERATIVE LEARNING

Key ideas about learning, instruction, and assessment practices provide a framework for considering collaborative and cooperative learning as a set of decisions about how to best structure peer learning:

1. There are reciprocal effects between the learning goal, the task, and group characteristics;
2. The classroom is a social system and peers and teachers influence members' status, which in turn, affects students' ability to have access and learn;
3. Effective management plans cultivate norms of teamwork and a sense of community to support academic and social goals;
4. Collaborative and cooperative learning processes are best guided and managed through teacher-gathered data based on observations, conferencing with students, and other forms of student feedback. Good teaching involves careful notice of what is happening among students and thoughtful consideration about how and when to apply appropriate developmental or intervention strategies;
5. Reflection guided by a conceptual framework should provide insight into the questions: What did students learn? Did peer learning help or hinder academic or social learning?;
6. Meaningful assessment practices involve informal and formal authentic tasks that include a rich array of individual and group products and performances.

An example of how this conceptual framework weaves throughout the curriculum is the idea introduced in the "Child (or Adolescent) Development, Learning and Exceptionality" course in the summer which is, that classroom strategies should engage children in dialogue with other students, preferably those at different stages of cognitive and social development. This idea is supported through a series of literacy development units and courses in both the early childhood/elementary and middle/secondary programs. This same idea then progresses to the expectation that the intern develop curriculum through real-world problem-solving units (Nagel, 1996). In the middle/secondary program interns might be expected to devise group projects within curriculum units. Interns are expected to create opportunities for talk, tutoring, conferencing and students learning through self-initiated communication at different points throughout the year.

VARIATIONS IN TEACHING ABOUT COOPERATIVE LEARNING

Our interviews with faculty revealed that there is an ongoing tension between promoting general principles of good instruction and the need for specific, in-depth coaching and practice regarding certain instructional practices. With only a fifteen-month initiation period into teaching, faculty generally agree that it is more important to cultivate interns' capacities for good decision making than to be overly concerned with teaching specific techniques. On the other hand, interns must study, practice, and understand a variety of instructional approaches to create a basic repertoire for teaching. Cooperative learning is one practice that epitomizes this tension. The degree of emphasis on learning about specific forms of cooperative learning depends in part on the instructor's strengths and interests.

Program-Level Differences

There are different expectations for when and how peer learning processes are to be learned and applied in the classroom within and between the two program levels. In the middle to secondary program, much of the specific teaching about peer learning has shifted from the general methods courses to specific methods courses in language arts, social studies, foreign languages, science, art, music, mathematics and art. This shift occurred to improve the likelihood that interns will make a direct connection between disciplinary inquiry, the learning task, and the instructional method. Grossman and Stodolsky (1995) found that distinctive high school subject subcultures have significant—often negative—effects on teachers' willingness to adapt cooperative learning and other practices related to school reform. These subject subcultures are characterized by differing beliefs, norms and practices about the nature of knowledge, how it is organized and taught. Other studies of secondary teachers (Brody, 1998) suggest that secondary teachers tend to view cooperative learning as simply one of several competing views of good teaching and use it primarily for mastery learning and review. To counter the organizational pressure of middle and secondary school subject subcultures and to provide the strongest connection between content, task, instructional method and assessment practices, the program has shifted the focus on the relationship of peer learning and cooperative learning to the subject-area methods courses.

Language arts interns, for example, are expected to set up student-led literature circles and conduct writing workshops. Social studies interns use many of the same collaborative processes particularly in writing but they might conduct group investigations on a contemporary issue, or organize small group discussions. Foreign language interns need to understand the relationship between student-talk and both informal and formal structured tasks for practicing and expanding specific aspects of language learning. The science coordinator expects interns to learn how to conduct laboratories and to construct experiences that rely on both collaborative and cooperative learning approaches. Science interns focus on the value of complex tasks for student-directed inquiry and conceptual understanding.

The authors think that the effect of this shift from generic methods courses to specific methods results in less-common language among both interns and faculty about criteria for effective cooperative groupwork. On the other hand, there is a stronger connection between disciplinary content and the selection of an appropriate group work task and different purposes of talk and peer learning.

The treatment of cooperative learning in the early childhood/elementary-level program also varies among the courses due to the higher number of adjunct teachers. All interns complete a comprehensive literacy and language arts sequence of courses where they experience a number of collaborative learning approaches such as literature circles and writing workshops. In the science, math, social studies, and other methods courses, interns experience many variations of collaborative learning and create a curriculum that assumes they will apply these processes in the classroom as soon as they are able. Instructors tend to rely on self-reflective approaches (i.e., talking aloud while they are in the act of teaching in order to convey the rationale for what they are doing) to teach small group methods. The interviews with the elementary faculty raised the question about whether there is sufficient formal study of the elements of successful groupwork processes and where that study could best occur in the curriculum, so program coordinators are currently evaluating this.

College Curriculum vs. the Internship

Our preservice interns frequently find themselves navigating the conflicting territory between what they are taught in the college curriculum and what they observe in the schools. The gaps between our recommendations about best practice and actual school practice have increased in the last five years due to factors such as reduced funding and increased class size. In addition, the effects of the state's emphasis on standardized testing as measures for benchmarks have been devastating to the progressive practices including the use of cooperative learning in the schools. For example, middle school teachers and administrators in our state report that they have dismantled many integrated curriculum programs and instituted more seatwork because of a felt need to cover curriculum and to prepare for standardized tests in the eighth grade. Interns are finding it harder to observe good groupwork practices and are feeling more pressure to do these "correctly" the first time they try them in a classroom because they do not perceive that they have time to experiment and learn.

In preparing teachers, we often teach as if discrepancies between campus and schools are nonexistent. This widens the gap that preservice students must deal with in order to develop their own philosophy of collaborative learning and evaluate the different approaches to cooperative learning (Driscoll & Nagel, 1993). Unless we acknowledge these discrepancies, preservice teachers may ignore or devalue what is taught at the university (Applegate, 1986) and model their teaching based only on what they see in the classroom. We have fair to excellent success in the use of appropriate internships with greater consistency at the elementary level than with the middle/secondary levels. But because we are in a location with a number of teacher preparation programs, we vie for placements in schools and have only a few school partnerships that allow for more than four or five interns at one site. When school conditions are favorable the teaching by our interns can have a positive effect on the school culture, but this is a continual challenge in the current climate of retrenchment.

Due to the many different interpretations of cooperative learning, the discrepancies between what our students are taught and what they observe in the classrooms underscores the importance of discussing with the interns what minimum criteria constitute cooperative learning. Their own observations can provide a rich foundation for discussions and lay the groundwork for construction of a philosophy guided by collaborative learning with an understanding of the basics of cooperative learning and the range of peer-mediated learning processes they can develop.

Effective groupwork practices require interns to reteach or revisit expectations frequently for cooperative and collaborative work. However, elementary interns often assume that the process of groupwork was taught earlier by the mentor teacher or at a prior grade level. They frequently complain that students do not know "how to work in a group." Middle/secondary interns are finding that they too, must repeat this process in a compressed period of time with different groups of students. Although we, the authors, believe we need to give more thought to the sequencing and refinement of the teaching about cooperative learning, our interviews indicate that we must also engage our colleagues with these questions.

LIMITS OF A DECISION MAKING APPROACH
TO COOPERATIVE LEARNING

Our faculty would argue that cultivating a collaborative learning approach to peer learning with emphasis on the intern learning to make decisions, to think critically, and to raise questions about his or her practices is the best curriculum we can organize for students in the fifteen-month time period. We have been able to create conditions that might be enviable by other institutions' standards and they allow us a great deal of control of the explicit and implicit curriculum (e.g., the cohort experiences, the collaborative learning program philosophy and the year-long internship). Evaluating these factors over sixteen years gives us confidence that we can assist our interns to meet the challenges they are facing in schools. But these challenges also mean that we have to continually reassess our priorities. Teaching the specifics of cooperative learning has taken a back seat to the work of extending our understanding, for example, of how to prepare our students to teach an increasingly diverse student population with second-language learning needs—even as we acknowledge the importance of cooperative learning for second-language learning.

The authors recognize that our curriculum and faculty teaching practices may not be taking the process of learning the specifics of cooperative learning to a deeper level. We, the authors, believe that there are stages or phases in developing the groupwork capacity of students beyond the use of informal, short-term groups and these include teaching specific groupwork skills related to the task (see, for example, Baloche, 1997 and Webb & Farivar, 1998, for examples of progressions in supporting students' ability to use groupwork for more complex tasks.) Our experience also suggests that different approaches to cooperative learning may be more appropriate to be taught before others. For example, the use of simple structures as developed by Spencer Kagan (1993) couples well with a teacher's goal of building communication skills among students and using short time periods of peer learning for specific goals. Once interns have some experience structuring, observing, and evaluating informal groups, it is much easier to move to formal groups and the application of the Johnsons' conceptual approach (1987), a model favored by most of our instructors.

But novice teachers should also learn how to apply a sociological lens to the problem of status issues, which inevitably arise in groups. Cohen's (1994) interventions, in particular (see Lotan, Cohen, & Morphew, 1998, for a good explanation of this approach), instruct teachers in how they can treat inevitable status problems that occur in groups, including the teacher assigning competence on the basis of multiple abilities and by creating rich, ill-structured, group work tasks. We did not find any instructors in our interviews who taught about Cohen's research on status treatments so that interns could begin addressing early enough how to observe groups and intervene appropriately. On the other hand, understanding the significance of and developing complex, ill-structured tasks for integrating multiple abilities is well developed in several courses.

The Institutional Factor

We began this chapter with the assertion that Lewis & Clark College is able to develop novice teachers' abilities to step into complex, socially and economically diverse learning environments with the ability to use cooperative learning beyond simple, routine use. But our interviews suggest that there are some "next steps" in learning to implement cooperative learning at a more advanced level that are not clearly visible in our program. The first reason has to do with the typical institutional factors that create disruptions in program evolution and evaluation. Faculty who have expertise in certain areas leave, take leave, or change assignments and the result is that practices for teaching about cooperative learning that may have seemed well-integrated go by the wayside or are moved to other courses in a different form. And, other goals for teacher learning surface as counter-moves to prior shortcomings in program. At Lewis & Clark College, what allows us to move forward while maintaining strong connections to where we have been is our unusually robust, collaborative culture. However, lately we have been relying on more adjunct faculty for teaching in our preservice programs, which places a burden on the senior faculty to communicate and ensure the continuation of program goals and values as they run programs themselves. Because of these issues, we found that it is essential to rely on the six principles that guide our curriculum for teachers as decision makers, and reflective learning *through* collaborative and cooperative learning. We are continually shifting between emphasizing these larger ideas and the need for specific strategies and techniques that ground that theory. Maintaining commitment central to collaborative learning philosophy and working through these six principles provides a measure of coherence despite program challenges.

The Intern's Abilities

The second factor influencing our effectiveness of teaching students to implement cooperative learning processes effectively are the interns themselves and their stage of professional development. For example, if effective classroom management is difficult for an intern, the ability to work with cooperative learning groups is usually seen as formidable. Our experience suggests that we should continue to provide interns with the framework for understanding their limitations and strengths because this breeds a realistic sense of confidence and competence. By the beginning of full-time teaching in March, interns have had sufficient planning and implementation of informal groups for different instructional purposes and should be able to use these processes appropriately. And, if the classroom organization allows, they should be able to construct formal, groupwork tasks. When critical factors are not present, including the abilities of the intern, this expectation is adjusted for the particular intern through plans of assistance and more intense supervision. If, however, by the end of the internship, the intern is not able to integrate effective classroom management with purposeful curriculum and appropriate collaborative learning structures, the intern extends his or her internship in the fall of the next academic year. We have had good results with extending the internship. We have found that an intern's developmental challenges interplay with the placement itself and there is no "one best way" to ensure that interns will achieve a specific level of competency in teaching with cooperative learning.

A NEW OPPORTUNITY FOR ASSESSING INTERNS

Recently, a Continuing Licensure requirement was instituted in Oregon. All teachers are now expected to establish personal learning goals and to meet performance standards (and obtain a master's degree if they have not already done so) indicating advanced competency in eight areas of teaching and professional development. The consequences of this continuing educational commitment means that faculty will have an opportunity to work with program graduates and inservice teachers seeking the master's degree over the course of six years. This relieves some pressure from having to accomplish all of a novice teacher's preparation within fifteen months. It also requires us to do a thorough follow-up of our graduates through demonstration of these performance criteria.

The Teacher Education Program has aligned the Continuing License requirements to build upon those in the Initial (first) License. This will provide program continuity and an opportunity to develop longitudinal data on our graduates as to their use of cooperative learning and other instructional practices. Teachers will incorporate student work samples, videos of her classroom, narrative and evaluative reports based on classroom visitations, and other evidence that shows their understanding of the theory behind small group instructional practices. They must apply this in their classrooms at a level that goes beyond their proficiency at the Initial License. We hope to gain a more comprehensive picture of the factors that influence our graduates' abilities to develop their curricular and instructional capacities beyond a basic level of proficiency. From this knowledge base, we intend to develop better opportunities for our graduates to continue learning advanced instructional practices.

CONCLUSIONS

Our faculty rely on the collaborative culture of the programs and our accepted belief about collaborative learning to convey both the value of peer learning experiences and how to do cooperative learning. Our interviews with the faculty pointed out that they believe that cooperative learning is well integrated into the program and that interns will learn from the modeling and the self-reflexive strategies used by the college instructors. Our interviews also revealed that there is not agreement about an accepted standard for fidelity of use of cooperative learning in terms of theory-based application.

Over the last few years we have seen a shift away from teaching *about* cooperative learning as a generic strategy to an increasing reliance on the competence of the particular instructor to teach cooperative learning. The effect of this is that we tend to rely on the collaborative-learning context of the program and the modeling by the instructors of effective groupwork practices.

As faculty who developed and implemented the fifth-year program move to positions at other universities or retire, there must be a greater effort made to communicate and revisit our program philosophy and goals with our incoming faculty. It has became startlingly clear in the process of preparing this chapter that we must return to discussions about the challenges of relying on the "teacher as decision maker" approach for learning, when and how to incorporate cooperative learning in their classrooms.

REFERENCES

Applegate, J. H. (1986). Undergraduate students' perceptions of field experiences: Toward a framework for study. In J. D. Raths & L.G. Katz (Eds.), *Advances in teacher education*, Vol. 2. Norwood, NJ: Ablex.

Baloche, L. A. (1997). *The cooperative classroom. Empowering learning*. Upper Saddle River, NJ: Merrill Prentice Hall.

Brody, C. (1998). The significance of teacher beliefs for professional development and cooperative learning. In C. Brody & N. Davidson (Eds.) *Professional development for cooperative learning. Issues and Approaches*. Albany: State University of New York Press.

Brubacher, M. (1991). But that's not why I'm doing it. *Cooperative learning magazine, 11* (4), 2–3.

Cohen, E. (1994). *Designing groupwork*, 2d ed. New York: Teachers College Press.

Driscoll, A. & Nagel, N. (1993). Discrepancies between what we teach and what they observe: Dilemmas for preservice teachers and teacher educators. *The Professional Educator, 16* (1), 1–12.

Grossman, P. L. & Stodolsky, S. S. (1995). Content as context: The role of school subjects in secondary teaching. *Educational Researcher, 24* (8), 5–11.

Holmes Group. (1986). *Tomorrow's teachers: A report of the Holmes Group.* East Lansing, MI: Holmes Group.

Johnson, D. W., Johnson, R. T. & Holubec, E. (1987). *Circles of learning.* Edina, MN: Interaction Book Company.

Kagan, S. (1993). *Cooperative learning: Resources for teachers.* San Juan Capistrano, CA: Kagan Cooperative Learning.

Lotan, R., Cohen, E., & Morphew, C. (1998). Beyond the workshop: Evidence from complex instruction. In C. Brody & N. Davidson (Eds.), *Professional development for instructional leaders. Issues and approaches.* Albany: State University of New York Press.

Meloth, M. S. & Deering, P. D. (1999). The role of the teacher in promoting cognitive processing during collaborative learning. In A. M. O'Donnell & A. King (Eds.). *Cognitive perspectives on peer learning* (pp. 235–256). Mahwah, NJ: Lawrence Erlbaum Associates, Inc.

Nagel, N. (1996). *Learning through real-world problem solving: The power of integrative teaching.* Thousand Oaks, CA: Corwin Press.

Webb, N. & Farivar, S. (1998). Preparing teachers and students for cooperative work: Building communication and helping skills. In C. Brody & N. Davidson (Eds.), *Professional development for instructional leaders. Issues and approaches.* Albany: State University of New York Press.

CHAPTER 3

EDUCATING TEACHERS FOR SOCIALLY CONSCIOUS COOPERATIVE LEARNING

NANCY SCHNIEDEWIND

Cooperative learning is a powerful approach to learning because it is both an effective pedagogy and a compelling philosophy and worldview. Through teacher education programs we can provide professional training that educates teachers both to effectively implement cooperative learning in their classrooms and to develop a more reflective consciousness about cooperation as an idea and value and its application to schools and society. This chapter describes socially conscious cooperative learning, an approach that emphasizes both the instructional and social aspects of cooperative learning, as it is taught in one teacher preparation program. Data from program graduates is analyzed to determine the influence on teachers' practice of instruction that integrates cooperative learning pedagogy and philosophy. Implications of this study for teacher education are discussed.

SOCIALLY CONSCIOUS COOPERATIVE LEARNING

Socially conscious cooperative learning is an approach that introduces educators to cooperative learning pedagogy and teaches about cooperation as an idea and value. It links cooperative learning in the classroom to the broader goal of building a more cooperative and just society (Schniedewind & Sapon-Shevin, 1998). This term has two meanings. First, adults and young people become aware of how competition and cooperation in our schools, culture, and institutions affect their lives and examine how their classroom practices maintain or challenge this. Secondly, educators and students develop a heightened social conscience and take advantage of opportunities to become responsible for making changes in existing competitive, inequitable social structures.

This approach reflects the values inherent in cooperation itself; democracy, shared power and participatory decision making, respect for diversity, and working for the common good. Strategies used in this approach to cooperative learning mirror these values and the broader goals of social justice and equity within a democratic society. It asks for thoughtful reflection and practice at three levels: (1) the implementation of cooperatively structured learning activities, (2) the commitment to cooperative classrooms and schools, and (3) the goal of a society that is cooperative and socially just.

In a teacher preparation program or the classroom itself, socially conscious cooperative learning asks teachers to question three major areas:

1. *Content.* Are we teaching students to become more conscious of the effects of competition and cooperation on their own learning, their schools and society through the content that they teach?
2. *Process.* Is the process of cooperative learning being implemented in a way that builds an inclusive, cooperative classroom community?
3. *Vision.* Does our approach to cooperative learning articulate a vision of more democratic and equitable classrooms, schools, and society, and does it support learners and educators in working toward this vision in their lives? This chapter will focus on a teacher education program that provides a context for teacher inquiry in these three areas.

TEACHER PREPARATION AND COOPERATIVE LEARNING

Master's Program in Humanistic Education

The master's program in Humanistic Education at the State University of New York at New Paltz is a 36-credit-hour program for those seeking K-12 teacher certification. In New York State a candidate obtains an initial teacher certificate that becomes permanent with a master's degree. Therefore, most graduate students in this teacher education program are employed, beginning teachers working toward their permanent certification.

This degree program prepares teachers with the knowledge and skills to create humanistic, student-centered, democratic educational environments that foster intellectual, social, and emotional learning for all students. The program focuses on cooperative learning, multicultural/ gender-fair education, active learning, conflict resolution, curriculum development, group process, action research and teacher leadership for innovation and school change. Emphasizing reflective and critical teaching, the program provides teachers with an intensive study of the pedagogical skills necessary for fostering inclusive classroom communities that meet the educational needs of diverse learners.

The program values cooperation as an idea and value. One course focuses explicitly on cooperatively structured learning, but cooperative learning is sometimes used as a method in other courses. The values implicit in cooperative learning, such as respect for diversity and shared decision making, are norms throughout the program. Among the competencies expected of students graduating from the program, the following are directly related to socially conscious cooperative learning:

- Understanding cooperation as an idea and value, they will work collaboratively with others, create inclusive classroom communities, and use cooperative learning as an instructional approach;
- With an understanding of experiential learning principles, they will employ participatory pedagogies in the classroom;
- With awareness of principles of effective group process, they will democratically participate in groups and use creative problem-solving approaches and conflict-resolution strategies both with students and among peers;
- Practiced in reflective, critical thinking and questioning, they will integrate critical analysis into all aspects of their educational work;
- Understanding the linkage between personal, institutional, and social change, they will take leadership as ethically and socially responsible citizen educators in their schools, communities and society.

Students who share values that are consonant with socially responsible cooperative learning are often attracted to this program. Students with a particular interest in cooperative learning can register for an elective in the program called "Cooperatively Structured Learning." Data from students who have taken this course will be the focus of this study.

The Course: Cooperatively Structured Learning

The Cooperatively Structured Learning course reflects a socially conscious perspective. Class composition is a mix of students in the master's program in Humanistic Education and students in other graduate programs in the School of Education who take it as an elective. The course aims to enable students to:

1. Plan and implement well-designed cooperatively structured learning activities that include positive interdependence, individual accountability, teaching social skills, and processing.
2. Experience pedagogical skills and processes that they can transfer to their own classrooms;
3. Reflect on cooperation and competition as ideas and values; consider cooperative alternatives to competitive practices in classrooms and schools; examine curricular approaches to teaching about cooperation and competition as ideas and values;
4. Articulate their visions of democratic, cooperative, and equitable classrooms, schools and society and consider how their teaching practice contributes to making that vision a reality.

Course readings reinforce these objectives. David and Roger Johnsons' book, *Learning Together and Alone* (1999) provides research, rationale, and a coherent instructional framework for implementing cooperative learning. Kohn's *No Contest: The Case Against Competition* (1992) makes a compelling case about the negative effects of competition on our lives, schools and society. And *Cooperative Learning, Cooperative Lives: Learning Activities for Building a Peaceful World* by Schniedewind and Davidson (1987), in addition to providing a framework for thinking about why cooperative alternatives to competition may be beneficial, offers teachers cooperatively structured learning activities that integrate cooperative pedagogy and content. These activities help young people reflect on the costs and benefits of cooperation and competition in their schools, communities, and society.

The course sequence begins with activities that create an inclusive, cooperative classroom community. Only when educators feel they are in a nurturing environment are they able to grapple with the often difficult, value-related issues raised by a socially conscious approach to cooperative learning. The teachers-students engage in teacher-planned community-building activities at the outset of the course. In later weeks student partners teach the class a cooperative warm-up at the beginning of each class. *Cooperative Sports and Games Book* (Orlick, 1982) and *The Manual on Non-Violence and Children* (Judson, 1984) are valuable resource books that students use for this purpose. Cooperative groups provide practicing teachers on-going support for classroom-based work such as book discussions and peer editing.

A primary goal of the course is to enable teachers to understand the five essential elements of cooperative learning, that is, positive interdependence, individual accountability, face-to-face interaction, teaching social skills and processing (Johnson & Johnson, 1999). Teachers must be able to use that conceptual framework to structure and implement their own cooperative lessons. In a consistent effort to integrate theory and practice, teachers plan and implement a cooperatively structured activity in their classrooms every few weeks. They reflect on its strengths and weakness in a support group the following week. As a large class we discuss a few of these lessons each week, analyze them for the presence of the five essential elements of a cooperative lesson, and brainstorm solutions to problems that arose in implementation. Using the knowledge gained from such reflection, teachers return to their classrooms to implement a new activity. In this way graduate students become reflective practitioners, gaining a habit of mind that hopefully will influence their future practice.

Cooperative activities that graduate students engage in during the course are multicultural and gender-fair, and model both cooperative processes and content. Students experience a wide variety of formats for structuring cooperative learning. We begin with simple formats such as partners, and work toward more complex ones such as interdisciplinary, thematic learning centers (Schniedewind & Davidson, 1998). At the same time, the content of the activities enables students to think about cooperation as an idea and value. For example, in an introductory lesson, paired students interview one another to reflect upon their personal and professional life experiences that have been cooperative. A later activity that models the Jigsaw method is taught through a story about Harriet Tubman, containing content related to issues of both race and gender. As part of the processing of the content of this lesson, students consider the way in which the underground railroad necessitated the cooperation of many people. Teachers experience a variety of other activities that combine cooperative pedagogy and content throughout the course.

Activities and discussions about ways to address the needs of diverse student populations are integrated throughout the course. Teachers acquire methods for differentiating learning within cooperative lessons so that all young people are challenged at their various levels of preparation. They discuss how they can apply such approaches in their classrooms. They plan for the inclusion of a student with a disability as part of a cooperative activity that they develop. They learn to observe the gender and racial interaction patterns in the cooperative groups in their classrooms and consider means to foster equitable interaction. They discuss ways to help young people become more conscious of these patterns and to consciously change those that aren't fair. These beginning teachers learn to recognize ways to make heterogeneous cooperatively structured groups effective.

Throughout the course teachers are encouraged to reflect on the benefits and costs of competition and cooperation on schools and society. Toward the conclusion of the course, they analyze their teaching practice and consider the extent to which it contributes to transforming their classroom, school, and society or maintaining the status quo. They discuss a series of school-based case studies in which an educator meets a learning objective using competitive practices. They are asked to develop a cooperative approach to meet that same objective.

For example, one deals with a teacher who wants his students to become able spellers. He uses a spelling bee with extrinsic awards. Teachers then brainstorm a cooperative alternative for learning spelling that would also build intrinsic motivation.

These case studies often motivate teachers to alter practices in their own classrooms. For example, one teacher recently changed her system for motivating students to do homework. Formerly, she had a monthly pizza party for those students who did not miss a homework assignment all month. Some students did not get pizza. She changed that practice to one in which cooperative groups were responsible for devising a system to help all group members remember to bring in their homework. Since the homework would be used in cooperative group activities the next day, students were motivated to remember their homework; it had a practical purpose. They strove for success in doing homework as a class, not as individuals. On occasion the teacher would plan a celebration for their efforts. Only sometimes did the celebration include food. These types of classroom changes emerge from course-based reflection.

Some teachers will follow-up such reflection by using activities from *Cooperative Learning, Cooperative Lives* with their students. These activities not only enable students to become more conscious of the effects of competition and cooperation on their lives, but aid them in taking action to foster more cooperative practices in their school, community, and broader society. In these ways both teachers and their students are supported in becoming socially conscious and socially active.

THE STUDY

This study is based upon data obtained from practicing teachers after they completed the Humanistic Education program. About twenty-five teacher certification candidates are admitted into this program each year. Students typically finish the program in three years, taking one or two courses each semester. Not all elect to take Cooperatively Structured Learning.

Program graduates who had recently taken the Cooperatively Structured Learning course were invited to participate. Twelve of the thirty graduates contacted volunteered to respond in writing to a detailed questionnaire. Six were primary or elementary teachers, five secondary teachers, and one a special education teacher in a self-contained program. Most had graduated from the program within the past four years. Teachers were sent a detailed, four-page questionnaire. The data was collated and analyzed to determine how well their preparation in the program enabled them to implement cooperative learning pedagogy and bring a broader cooperative worldview into their classrooms, schools, and lives.

Pedagogy

Initially I wanted to know what effect the Cooperatively Structured Learning course had on teachers' implementation of cooperative learning, including why, and to what extent, they used cooperative learning in their teaching. When asked what in the course helped them implement cooperative learning in their classroom, the majority (eight) of the teachers cited the fact that they constantly *experienced* cooperative activities in the graduate course. A fourth-grade teacher wrote, "Experiential learning was best. We role-modeled 'how to' in class and were then able to carry our work and activities to our classrooms back at school." A majority of respondents also appreciated being introduced to a variety of concrete formats for structuring cooperative learning that they experienced, discussed, and then implemented. A number of teachers also mentioned the value of our class discussions. In particular they valued the time that was set aside each week for them to share cooperative activities they had tried with other teachers at their grade level, and in turn, get feedback and new ideas. A couple of respondents also mentioned how the course increased their own self-awareness, which improved their teaching.

Teachers were asked what was limited or missing in the course that would have assisted them in implementing cooperative learning. Six teachers indicated that more subject-specific resources and curriculum would have helped. One teachers wanted ideas for encouraging more of her school faculty to buy into cooperative learning. Another would have appreciated a follow-up program that included site visits to classrooms of other teachers using cooperative learning. Overall, teachers felt their preparation had served them well.

Since cooperative learning is a complex instructional strategy and teachers need support to persevere with this approach, educators were asked a series of questions about support. Initially they were asked how, if at all, the course provided support. Most teachers indicated that they felt considerable support from their classmates and the teacher in the course itself. "The course atmosphere allowed individual expression. People felt safe to express their fears concerning cooperative learning." The majority of respondents mentioned that the support of the instructor and other classmates was very important. An elementary teacher wrote, "The opportunity to design and implement activities to use for our own classroom at a time when we could then get constructive feedback on results was most helpful. I was able to get support on results from other teachers who were learning this." A primary educator responded, "I had support from my colleagues. The course created a very loving supportive environment, as it grew and as all got close, trust built." A couple of teachers reiterated the importance of attention to process in the course as supportive for their work in the classroom. "The interaction among students in our class provided support and insight regarding enhancing positive interaction among my students."

When asked what other support they received, four teachers noted other graduate students in the Humanistic Education Program. One mentioned support from staff at school, and two noted the course readings. In response to a question asking what would have been helpful that they did not get, two educators mentioned support-related suggestions. One suggested setting up small groups or pairs to observe each other using cooperative learning in their classrooms. Another recommended a support group for Humanistic Education graduates who were teachers in his field.

Subsequent to understanding the effects the course had on teachers' implementation of cooperative learning, I was eager to know how, to what extent, and why teachers used cooperative learning in their teaching. All of these practicing teachers integrate cooperative learning into their instruction. For a significant majority, cooperative learning is an ongoing, essential part of their teaching. An elementary teacher recorded, "I use it everyday, usually several times a day— somedays, all day long. I wouldn't consider teaching without it." A middle school teacher noted, "Ninety percent of the time work is completed in cooperative groups." Generally secondary teachers use cooperative learning less, typically twice a week, as this high school English teacher suggested. "I use cooperative learning one or two times a week to discuss literature, for peer editing, or as a review for tests."

When asked what encouraged them to use cooperative learning, teachers articulated academic, affective, and value-based reasons. While a majority of these educators pointed to academic gains young people made, none of them articulated those as the only reason for using cooperative learning. They were always linked to the effects of cooperative learning on classroom atmosphere and interaction, improved social skills, or increases in cooperative values. One teacher said, "Results! Also the children learn to care for each other, care for others outside school, and problem solve."

The educators articulated benefits of cooperative learning that are value-based as well as academic. A high school teacher communicated, "It is effective for review, it engages the students and allows more individual interaction between me and my students." An elementary teacher noted, "Cooperative learning provides an opportunity for *all* levels to help, not just the more advanced students. I use completely heterogeneous groups. I love hearing the more advanced kids thank others for good ideas and for information."

A few teachers pointedly focused on affective results as a source of motivation to use cooperative learning. A high school teacher responded, "Students enjoy it and they become closer friends as a result. It makes for a more comfortable environment." A special education teacher in a self-contained classroom of very challenging students noted, "The students *must* learn to accept each other, respect others, and tolerate behaviors. They must be taught these skills." Other teachers mentioned their goals for heterogeneity, equality and gender equity, as motivating their use of cooperative learning.

No consistent patterns emerged in teachers' experiences of what discouraged them from using cooperative learning. Two teachers mentioned the significant amount of planning time needed for effective cooperative lessons. Three others commented on time constraints in the classroom, among them are two high school teachers who worried about covering their curriculum. One wrote, "Forty-two minute classes make some lessons difficult to facilitate and it takes a longer time to cover the required material."

Other discouraging factors reported by individual educators were a lack of adequate physical space, the competitive spirit students bring from home and from competitive sports, and parental objections. One high school teacher wrote about his fears. "I fear students complaining to their parents and or the Board of Education. I fear administrators if my final exam results are poor." Thus institutional constraints contribute significantly to what discouraged these teachers from using cooperative learning.

Nevertheless all teachers responded that they have continued using cooperative learning ever since taking the course. Most, in fact, are very committed to it, as this elementary teacher's comment reflects. "Now cooperative learning is the foundation of my teaching." An elementary teacher who is the only one in her building using cooperative learning wrote, "Occasionally I think it might suit certain classes to teach in the 'command' approach because the rest of their day is based on this approach. Then I keep reminding myself that if I'm the *only* cooperative experience they get, I have to make it good for them." These teachers care about the whole person, and see the value of cooperative learning in educating children, cognitively, socially and ethically.

Consciousness about Cooperation as an Idea and Value

Our hope is that a socially conscious approach to teacher preparation in cooperative learning will heighten students' consciousness about cooperation and competition as ideas and values and that they will then take steps to support comparable reflection and action with students. Similarly, we hoped it would broaden educators' perspectives of these dynamics in their community and society as well. Questions asked of these graduate students explored these issues, as well as the extent to which they saw connections between the values implicit in cooperative learning and the MPS in Humanistic Education as a whole.

Teacher Consciousness. The Cooperatively Structured Learning course sought to introduce cooperative learning as a teaching strategy and to encourage educators to consider a broader perspective about cooperation and competition in schools and society. Teachers were asked how this dual approach helped them and in what ways it hindered them.

None felt hindered by this approach. Almost all teachers, for various reasons, found it helpful. Many appreciated the opportunity to reflect on cooperation and competition as ideas and values. "I do enjoy competition in terms of playing sports, but I realized that all individuals are different and when teaching physical education I try to keep all things equal, and most of all, fun. Your approach was very helpful in that it offered both perspectives and allowed us to discuss our place within it." A high school English teacher wrote, "It made me think more about the downside of competition—something I had previously given little thought to. I still find it difficult to eliminate competition from my life and work altogether. Sometimes I still think its necessary in certain situations."

Four teachers indicated that because they entered the course already valuing cooperative ideas, the course served to reinforce these beliefs. One high school teacher became even more motivated to use cooperative learning. He noted that his increased consciousness of a broader perspective of cooperation and competition, "established an urgency to using cooperative learning. It's not just about getting the curriculum done."

In response to a question about how they developed consciousness about the effects of competitive and cooperative teaching and learning, five teachers mentioned the readings, particularly *No Contest: The Case Against Competition* (Kohn, 1992) and also *Cooperative Learning, Cooperative Lives* (Schniedewind & Davidson, 1987). Other teachers mentioned the class activities and discussion.

Teachers were questioned about how this consciousness has affected what they do as a teacher and faculty member. Six teachers described changing classroom practices. A physical education teacher wrote, "I introduce cooperative games and do not keep score. K–2 grades do not play competitive games. Playing cooperative games with no winners is rewarding. Students are getting excited about *how* they are playing, rather than *who* is winning since there are not winners. Instead of quantitative scoring, students spell something or get pieces of a puzzle or picture to celebrate successful skills."

A fourth grade teacher noted, "There is now a lovely feeling of 'we will all get where we are going.' Students help each other find resources, they ask each other questions rather than give answers." A high school teacher wrote, "I try to encourage the notion that tests are diagnostic and that everyone can get an A. I avoid activities that have 'winners' and 'losers.' I try to discourage competitive behaviors in students. I conducted a qualitative research study on the effect of the class ranking system on students and the school."

Two teachers also indicated the effect of this consciousness on themselves as faculty members. For example, a middle school teacher noted, "I work harder for the good of all—rather than for myself or only my students. I try to raise awareness as much as I feel comfortable doing." The majority (nine) of teachers have, in fact, taken steps to lessen competitive activities and increase coopera-tive practices in their classrooms and schools.

Student Awareness. In what ways have teachers helped their students reflect on the effects of competition and cooperation on their lives both in and outside of school? Four teachers, most from the high school, did little. One earth science teacher wrote, "I only discuss this during cooperative groups. Outside of this I do not have time to expand on this—I wish I did." Time constraints were cited as an issue for many of these teachers. Eight teachers, on the other hand, worked intentionally with students to encourage them to reflect on competition and cooperation as ideas and values. Primary teachers' approaches varied. One uses role playing, another opens discussion.

Two elementary teachers described engaging students in two experiences, one individual and one cooperative, to enable them to articulate, compare and reflect on their experiences.

> In the beginning of school, I give several involved projects for students to work on. After a while I ask if they would like to be able to work cooperatively. After the projects are completed, we discuss how it was to work individually verses cooperatively. We have detailed discus-sions about the two approaches. This processing is crucial for success.

The second teacher adds an additional component.

> At the end of the year students write two paragraphs, one about work-ing competitively and one cooperatively. This goes in their permanent portfolio.

Several primary teachers also help students reflect on their experiences with cooperation, and in this case, compare them to competitive ones. Both have children play a game competitively and then cooperatively and then ask the children to share how they felt in each situation. One describes other simi-lar types of discussions where children reflect on the effects of competition on their lives. For example, "I talk with children about how it feels when one person says, 'My picture is better than yours'."

At the middle school level one respondent noted that she raised issues par-ticularly relevant to emerging adolescents. "We have discussed competition and cooperation a lot. Students feel the pressure of competition in grades, money, peer acceptance, and so much more. We have kept reflection journals and share them from time to time."

Few teachers, however, reported helping students put this consciousness into action in their lives. Teachers were asked what they have done *with* their students to develop cooperative alternatives to competition. Most responded by discussing cooperative alternative practices they had implemented *for* students. For example, one elementary teacher wrote, "If there is a negative experience on the playground, I invite the child into our classroom and provide the child a positive experience. I don't punish, but include the child in our cooperative classroom."

Another elementary teacher, however, described working *with* children to develop cooperative alternatives to competition.

> We overtly discuss what it feels like to be in a competitive verses cooperative situation and plan how we can shift activities around to be more cooperative. I am amazed at what wonderful problem solvers my students are—they come up with better solutions than I do alone.

More attention in the graduate course to ways to support young people in applying their heightened consciousness about cooperation to their lives might encourage other teachers to facilitate the combination of reflection and action that we see in these fourth graders.

A Broader Perspective. Educators were asked how the Cooperatively Structured Learning course affected the way they view competition and cooperation in themselves, their community, and society. All the teachers commended that their broader perspectives were affected and many cited actions they had taken based on that changed consciousness.

Three teachers noted that the course bolstered a perspective they had when they entered. "It reinforced my belief in the value of cooperation for our society," a male high school physics teacher wrote. "It had a significant impact. I am very aware of my own competitive feelings and I'm sensitive to practices that I, as a teacher, implement. I feel that cooperation is a word that is understood, but rarely practiced." A male secondary teacher also articulated a personal change. "I play softball in a men's league and find myself less competitive than I was as a child. I enjoy the game for the game."

Some teachers described areas beyond their classrooms in which they have implemented cooperative practices since the course. One special education teacher in a self-contained class catalyzed a change in another program in her school. "I worked to change the physical education approach used in our school! We no longer have a crisis after or during each physical education class because the kids are working *together* not competing." Another described adding cooperative games to her summer camp program. A third respondent proudly described a major cooperative event she helped initiate in her children's school.

I worked with a group at my children's school to produce a theatrical show in which everyone who showed up to try out got it! The school thought it couldn't be done. We raised over $10,000! Next year the school is considering entering such a production into the curriculum!

Two teachers reflected even more broadly. One elementary teacher articulated how her new perspective affected her whole life.

My shift in thinking has been from what would I do to what can *we* do, in every facet of my life. Family and school decisions are routinely made by the group—the solutions work better because everyone was part of the product and buy into the outcomes more sincerely.

A middle school teacher further extended her understanding of this broader perspective. "I have learned that cooperation is important when working for democracy." This is the hope for socially conscious cooperative learning—that educators will come to see that by building democracy in our classrooms, and talking with students about its value base, they can develop the consciousness and skills that will help foster democracy in our institutions and in society.

Relationship to Humanistic Education Program. Finally, I was curious to understand how students perceived the relationship between cooperative learning and the Humanistic Education Program. When asked about the connection between the values implicit in cooperative learning—democracy; sharing power and participatory decision making; respect for diversity; and working for the common good—and the Humanistic Education Program, most saw a strong connection. A special education teacher wrote, "All the courses I took in the MPS program stressed these values. Cooperative learning gave me a format to present these values in my classroom." A secondary teacher articulated it this way, "Simply put, I feel that cooperative learning is the MPS: Humanistic Education's philosophy in action. Not that cooperative learning is the sole outlet for the program's philosophy, but cooperative learning is extremely congruent with most of the program's precepts."

These educators also pointed to the connections between the values implicit in cooperative learning and the creation of a socially just society. A primary teacher wrote, "Cooperative learning strategies help to honor diversity as well as our interconnectedness. The value of both helps to strengthen individuality and raise consciousness of the power of unity—a beautiful duality indeed." Educators also highlighted the connections to social justice. An elementary teacher wrote, "When the school functions as an equal opportunity community, then students are more prepared to enter society." A secondary teacher shared, "Cooperative learning, when instituted and successfully practiced, creates a microcosm of equity in a group. When striving to teach students to create, monitor, and evaluate the equity in their cooperative group, teachers teach them how to begin to create a just society."

CONCLUSIONS

Teacher Outcomes:
The Three Levels of Socially Conscious Cooperative Learning

We have proposed that socially conscious cooperative learning asks for thoughtful reflection and practice at three levels: (1) Implementation of cooperatively structured learning activities, (2) commitment to cooperative classrooms and schools, and (3) encouraging a society that is cooperative and socially just. To what extent did these teachers address cooperative learning at these levels?

All teachers mentioned the value of the course in helping them effectively implement cooperative learning in their classrooms. For example, a high school English teacher wrote,

> I've added tools to my teaching that help me challenge students more. It makes my classroom more enjoyable for me and my students. Students learn more, remember more, build relationships, and learn group skills that they can use outside of the classroom. I really get to know my students because I interact with them, instead of lecturing to a sea of faces.

A number of other teachers mentioned learning to structure lessons cooperatively and the particular importance of attending to process. Some respondents mentioned their commitments to cooperative classrooms and schools, as exemplified in this teacher's comment. "I learned how to share responsibilities, to trust the ability of others and to share decision making. This is a profound lesson to learn—it leads to sound decisions!" More than half of the teachers also mentioned ways they've developed a more reflective consciousness about cooperation as an idea and value and its applications both in and beyond the classroom. For example, an elementary teacher responded, "I also like to share my cooperative spirit with faculty and staff. If a staff sets the example, the students should follow."

A few teachers articulated their commitment to building a society that is cooperative and socially just in their summary statement. A secondary teacher shared that what he had taken away from the course that was most important to him was, "The belief that cooperation is humanity's strongest asset and hope. This belief encourages me to devise ways to shed competitive practices in my classroom and school."

Analysis

The teachers' responses indicate that through teacher education programs we can provide professional training that educates teachers *both* to effectively implement cooperative learning in their classrooms and to develop a more reflective consciousness about cooperation as an idea and value and its applications for schools and society. Rather than detract from educators' implementation of cooperative learning, a broader perspective may motivate teachers to use cooperative learning even more. What are some of the factors that make this possible? What are some of the constraints that limit its potential?

Reflection/Action. The structure of the teacher certification process in New York State helps these teachers get the support they need to implement cooperative learning through their course work. Since teachers with a temporary certificate can begin teaching before they get their masters degree, many graduate students enroll in the Cooperatively Structured Learning course while they are beginning teachers. They can easily integrate theory and practice by applying what they are learning in the course to their classroom practice. This suggests that, wherever state regulations and certification procedures allow it, it is desirable for teacher education programs to be structured so course work in cooperative learning allows for such integration of theory and practice. That way much of the support beginning teachers need as they learn to implement cooperative learning can come from the course and the program.

Do models of teacher certification that enable students to begin teaching before completing the certification process, in fact, allow for more effective teacher education in cooperative learning? In a future research study I would like to compare the MPS students with the State University of New York at New Paltz's MAT/MST programs in which students are not teaching, but pursuing an intensive year-long master's degree. My observations of these students who take the Cooperatively Structured Learning course suggest that they have much more difficulty understanding and working with cooperative learning than students who are concurrently teaching. A study comparing how effectively teachers from both groups implement cooperative learning in their second or third year of teaching would be instructive in this regard.

Support. Educators need support for implementing cooperative learning, especially when they are first learning this pedagogy. The data suggests that because the Cooperatively Structured Learning course provides opportunities for students to receive support, they find less need for it in their schools. In this course students share cooperatively-structured lessons they've implemented in their classrooms and get feedback; cooperatively generate solutions for problems they face implementing cooperative learning; and have the ongoing encouragement of their instructor and peers. They also are in a teacher education program that provides an inclusive community of support. While on-site support and supervision is ideal, many of these teachers did not articulate the need for it.

What ongoing support over time do teachers need to continue to implement cooperative learning well? How can we build models of support into teacher education programs that will be useful to them in their practice over time? To answer these questions I would like to continue to follow these teachers over time. Will teachers have found other sources of support in their schools or elsewhere five years from now? Will they feel a greater need for support once their experience in the program and course is farther behind them? Will they still use any models of support they learned in the MPS Program in their futures? Interviewing these teachers again a few years will help answer these questions.

Cohesive, Value-Based Teacher Education Program. The experiences of these educators point to the strength of cooperative learning training when it is part of a teacher education program with a strong philosophical perspective that is congruent with the values implicit in cooperative learning. In such a program they get support for their efforts to implement cooperative learning not only from instructors and peers in the Cooperatively Structured Learning course but from those in other courses as well. For example, in a course called "Issues of Racism and Sexism in Education," students develop consciousness about equity and social justice. The strategies for creating multicultural and gender-fair classrooms and schools gained in this course support the emphasis on the Cooperatively Structured Learning course in building inclusive classroom communities. Similarly they become sensitive to issues of difference and understand the need for differentiation within cooperative learning activities and are eager to try the strategies suggested throughout the course to meet the needs of diverse learners. Conscious of equity issues, they can observe inequities based on social-group membership in cooperative groups, discuss these with students, and assist students in changing their behavior.

We believe that a teacher education program that articulates a clear philosophical perspective makes a difference. Since students in various master degree programs take the Cooperatively Structured Learning course, it would be possible to compare students in the MPS program and other programs to determine the importance of the program's common values in influencing both their pedagogy and consciousness about cooperation.

Consciousness about Cooperation as an Idea and Value. This study suggests that this teacher preparation experience in socially conscious cooperative learning has encouraged development of a heightened consciousness of cooperation and competition as ideas and values among teachers in a variety of ways, affecting both their teaching practice and their broader lives. What was particularly intriguing was the statement of one teacher that his increased awareness of the need for greater cooperation in all areas of life established an urgency for him to use cooperative learning in the classroom. If development of such consciousness can actually encourage educators to use cooperative learning, the effect of socially conscious cooperative learning may be mutually reinforcing of both pedagogical and broader social goals.

This experience in teacher preparation for socially conscious cooperative learning was less successful in catalyzing what we define as "social conscience," making reforms in existing competitive social structures. While some teachers reported making such changes, this was not as consistent among teachers as the development of pedagogical skills and social consciousness. In particular, few teachers had worked with students to assist them in putting their consciousness about cooperation as an idea and value into action to create change. Many teachers noted that constraints to moving beyond pedagogy included lack of time and the need to cover the curriculum.

One venue for addressing this is in the course. More emphasis is needed on highlighting what some teachers have done to change competitive and inequitable practices, programs, or policies into more cooperative and equitable ones. With such concrete examples, teachers could then reflect on similar possibilities for their lives. For example, if the account of the special education teacher who influenced her physical education department to change its program to a cooperative one was shared, teachers could be asked to identify a competitive practice or program in their school that was negatively impacting students or teachers and think about what might be done to change it. Similarly, more attention must be given to ways teachers can support students' developing social consciences.

Secondly, our collective action will be needed to further the development of greater social conscience of educators. These teachers have reported that they'd like to work more with their students on development of social consciousness and conscience, but lack of time and rigid curricular demands get in the way. Respondents gave examples of cooperative reforms they've brought about in after-school activities, camps, and in their lives in general. However, the current structures, expectations, and practices of schools constrict their potential to encourage similar changes there. As long as agendas of politicians and corporate executives are allowed to dictate educational priorities and practices, teachers will feel the ever-constricting limits on the practice of their craft from standardization and test-driven educational mandates. They will have less and less time to encourage students to reflect, to think critically, and to engage in creative problem solving and action for change—all essential to social conscience. Our collective energies are needed to challenge the prevailing, conservative educational ideology.

In the moment, the experiences of these teachers provide us inspiration. If the graduate students in this study have developed an effective cooperative pedagogy and social consciousness through a teacher education program—something that originally seemed ambitious—why doubt our collective creativity to do more! With a broad vision of a just and equitable society fueling our efforts, we can maintain our motivation to face this challenge by remembering the words of one of our respondents, "Cooperation is humanity's strongest asset and hope."

REFERENCES

Johnson, D. & Johnson, R. (1999). *Learning together and alone: Cooperative, competitive and individualistic learning.* Needham Heights, MA: Allyn and Bacon.

Judson, S. (1984). *A manual on non-violence and children.* Philadelphia: New Society.

Kohn, A. (1992). *No contest: The case against competition.* New York: Houghton Mifflin.

Orlick, T. (1982). *The cooperative sports and games book.* New York: Pantheon.

Schniedewind, N. & Davidson, E. (1987). *Cooperative learning, cooperative lives: A sourcebook of learning activities for building a peaceful world.* Dubuque, Iowa: W. C. Brown.

Schniedewind, N. & Sapon-Shevin, M. (1998). Professional development for socially conscious cooperative learning. In C. Brody & N. Davidson (Eds.), *Professional development for cooperative learning: Issues and approaches.* Albany: State University of New York Press.

CHAPTER 4

COOPERATIVE LEARNING IN TEACHER EDUCATION

A Four-Year Model

JOELLEN HARRIS AND BOB HANLEY

From the pressures of raising national standards to the complex demands of increasingly diverse classrooms, the teaching profession faces great challenges in the twenty-first century. The preservice education of teachers must equip them to meet effectively these competing demands. Fortunately, cooperative learning is a proven strategy that, when used properly, has increased the academic success of students as well as promoted social growth. For this reason, the teacher education program at Anderson College (Anderson, South Carolina) has integrated cooperative learning throughout the academic program for preservice teachers.

For insight into our use of cooperative learning, we provide a description of the cooperative learning program and the concept of a developmental approach that utilizes four models of cooperative learning—the structural approach (Kagan, 1990), the conceptual approach (Johnson & Johnson, 1987; Johnson, Johnson, & Holubec, 1987), Student Teams Achievement Divisions (STAD) (Slavin, 1983, 1989), and the complex instruction approach (Cohen, 1994). We also identify the challenges for each model and provide an overview of the management of the cooperative learning system. In addition, we conclude with insights gained from our experiences as well as recommendations for teacher educators who want to include cooperative learning as an integral part of a teacher education program.

At Anderson College, cooperative learning has become integrated into the philosophical foundation of our teacher education program. This interest in cooperative learning began several years ago when Dr. Joellen Harris was named head of the teacher education program. She had received formal training in student team learning developed through Johns Hopkins University and in the Johnsons' "Learning Together" approach of cooperative learning; she had studied both complex instruction developed by Liz Cohen, and the structural approach originated by Spencer Kagan. Because of her strong beliefs in cooperative learning's academic application, she began to promote this strategy as a theoretical framework to guide classroom management and instruction. Her enthusiasm and success in utilizing cooperative learning have led seven other Anderson College professors to participate in a semester-long course on cooperative learning in order to be able to use it in their classrooms and to help them to prepare teacher candidates with basic concepts and strategies. As a result, cooperative learning has become a significant teaching strategy for both our education faculty and our teacher candidates.

Its influence is readily seen in the conceptual framework that guides the teacher education program. With the central metaphor of *teacher as builder*, the program strives to produce teachers who are competent builders of knowledge, committed builders of community, and caring builders of values. We believe the teacher who utilizes cooperative learning as the foundation for instruction taps into a powerful vehicle for fostering student learning. As a committed builder of community, a teacher promotes collaboration within the classroom and stimulates the growth of learning communities. Through the application of the principles of cooperative learning, teachers are able to perform these roles effectively. By implementing cooperative learning, teachers also help students to develop values as they build classroom communities characterized by respect, responsibility, discipline, service, and grace. Such attitudes are marked by actions of recognition, respect, and acceptance. By enlisting the dynamic power of cooperative learning, teachers may foster patterns of behavior that lead to recognition of the importance of self and the recognition of the importance of others that are essential for the multicultural classrooms of today.

OVERVIEW OF THE FOUR-YEAR MODEL

Beginning as simply a small component within one course, cooperative learning currently serves as a major component of each of the four years in the teacher candidates' program. The particular structure of our cooperative learning program has developed from insights gained from earlier experiences. One important key is that we see progressions at work in our program for cooperative learning. First, the college students enter their education courses as freshmen with little or no knowledge of cooperative learning strategies and often unfairly label them. For example, some freshmen have had teachers who were not sufficiently trained and used cooperative learning incorrectly. A common complaint here is that student work resulted in group grades without individual accountability. Kagan (1995) identifies seven reasons that he opposes group grades, including their unfairness, their tendency to weaken motivation, and their failure to hold the individual student accountable. Such misuse of cooperative learning has led to strong opposition from parents where they see possible negative impacts on class rank and scholarship opportunities. This bias, and sometimes lack of knowledge, continues with the freshmen college student.

As a result, we have developed a four-year cooperative learning model where college students must go through a developmental progression while they acquire knowledge and skills of the theories of cooperative learning and skills in carrying out its strategies. In addition, teacher candidates are asked to utilize specific cooperative learning strategies in lessons they produce in the field experience setting, as well as in microteaching opportunities within the college classroom. As the candidates grow in skills and experience, as well as knowledge, they are better equipped to understand, utilize, and appreciate cooperative learning. In other words, the senior education major, through growth over time, has a broader and deeper understanding of cooperative learning than the freshman who experiences cooperative learning for the first time in an introductory education course.

A DEVELOPMENTAL MODEL

Of great importance is the introduction of different cooperative learning models in a sequential and incremental way. The logic of presenting the structural approach (Kagan, 1990), the conceptual approach (Johnson & Johnson, 1987), STAD (Slavin, 1983, 1989), and complex instruction (Cohen, 1994) in this order grows out of the amount of skill development needed for each for successful implementation. In this approach, the student learns one model then practices it in simulation with peers and/or in actual field placements. Each subsequent model requires more planning and higher levels of critical thinking in order to apply the model in teaching situations. (For example, teacher candidates find it easier to apply Kagan's simple structures; however, they find each subsequent model more challenging.) Thus, our program seeks to take advantage of the natural development of candidates from freshmen to senior and into the first year of teaching by matching the cooperative learning models on the basis of skill development needed to master and use each model.

From our experiences, we have developed a program that takes advantage of all four years of the teacher candidates' educational experiences in college. Similar to the progression where teacher candidates advance sequentially and incrementally in their developing and teaching lessons, we also provide experi-

ences with cooperative learning that increase in complexity and skill requirements for the teacher candidates as they move through the four-year model. In
Level 1, the freshman year, we introduce students to the basic concepts in cooperative learning. In a course called "Introduction to Education" students focus
on components of the structural model. Kagan's simple structures are easy for
students to learn. For example, teacher candidates at the freshman level easily
comprehend activities such as *Numbered Heads Together* and *Roundtable* and are
able to use them in working with students. Here, in the freshman year, teacher
candidates first work with the structured strategies with their peers. This experience is the hook that gives the teacher candidates the desire to continue the
study of cooperative learning. Then the teacher candidates are placed in a field
experience in the public school classroom with a cooperating teacher who successfully uses cooperative learning. With the cooperating teacher's permission,
the teacher candidate sets up and engages the classroom students with a structured activity such as *Roundtable* or *Inside-Outside Circle*. The earlier experiences
with their peers provide evidence of their ability to use cooperative learning
strategies, and they are usually successful.

At Level 2, the sophomore level, we emphasize the conceptual approach
(Johnson and Johnson, 1987). In the second field experience, teacher candidates
must teach a lesson in their public school setting, which utilizes the conceptual
approach. This model is more process-oriented, and, because of its open-ended
qualities and its direct teaching of social skills, it makes an effective second step
after Kagan. With the conceptual model our teacher candidates learn the value
of positive interdependence as the classroom students realize that they all have
a vested interest in achieving success. In addition, students learn that in cooperative learning there is both individual and group accountability, which helps
them to understand that there is much more to cooperative learning than just
putting people into groups.

At Level 3, junior year, teacher candidates are expected to develop more
complete lessons and put into practice the pedagogical skills learned in their
courses. Here, in "Elementary Methods or Secondary Methods," teacher candidates learn about STAD and Slavin's model of cooperative learning. The strategy fits naturally in the junior year as students now have a stronger pedagogical
foundation through courses and field experiences. Also, they learn Jigsaw II and
utilize this strategy as part of a teaching lesson. These components of the model's
strategies require extensive planning of instruction and monitoring, and they
match the development levels of these students. In addition, at the junior year,
teacher candidates are expected to design and implement more complex and
comprehensive lesson planning that details how they will integrate cooperative
learning into the unit format required.

During Level 4, the senior year, teacher candidates must demonstrate
advanced knowledge in lesson planning, classroom management, and the con-

tent knowledge and dispositions needed for teaching. Again, we expect the teacher candidates to demonstrate increasing abilities to integrate cooperative learning into their lesson planning. In addition, in the courses labeled "Directed Teaching," teacher candidates are introduced to Cohen's model of complex instruction. For Cohen, the success of cooperative learning must be built on "(1) the development and use of new curricular materials, (2) the ability to treat problems of status that inevitably develop within small groups, and (3) the availability of collegial relationships and strong support for classroom teachers who use cooperative learning" (1990, p. 135).

At the senior level, teacher candidates are best equipped to fulfill the expectations of this model. Here during their semester of student teaching, teacher candidates develop appropriate activities for their students that tap into the student's self-motivation. Teacher candidates learn the concept of status and its relationship to group dynamics. Cohen notes that "(academic) and peer status are the most important status characteristics," including "social class, race, ethnicity—and among older students, gender" (1998, p. 19). Students are made aware of these characteristics and their potential impact on student interaction and performance. They also learn the importance of avoiding the pitfall of "[confusing] status problems with personality characteristics of individual students, such as assertiveness, shyness, low self-esteem, or low self-concept" (1998, p. 19). They learn to treat status problems within groups so as to raise the status of those excluded from the intersection of the group. When forming teams, they learn that they should take into account student skills so that status issues are kept to a minimum as much as possible. For example, teacher candidates are taught to look for the different strengths classroom students may have in areas such as speaking, writing, drawing, and organizational skills, to name a few. Teacher candidates also learn to communicate to the classroom students that no one has all the skills needed but everyone has some of the skills and will be able to contribute to the success of the team. Therefore, during the student teaching semester, teacher candidates are expected to incorporate Cohen's cooperative learning model into their teaching. In particular, they must utilize her intervention strategies of "multiple-abilities treatment" and also "assigning competence to low-status students" as a way to encourage students to accept each other and to allow each team member to contribute positively in reaching the team goal. Cohen and Lotan (1995; 1997) state that the more often these two intervention strategies are utilized the more often low-status students participate in the class. As a result, teacher candidates are expected to make Cohen an integral part of their teaching strategies when they graduate and have classes of their own.

In the program model just presented, the four-year setting plays a highly significant role. By engaging students at the various levels (freshman, sophomore, junior, senior), we are able to introduce the cooperative learning models in both an incremental and sequential fashion. The four-year setting provides an excellent framework where cooperative learning concepts, models, and activities may be examined in depth and over time while teacher candidates are also advancing in their knowledge within their specific content area as well as developing skills in planning and implementing lessons. The various cooperative models may also be compared and contrasted each year to identify relative strengths in relationship to classroom usage. Thus the knowledge base and the pedagogical skills necessary for successful utilization of cooperative learning are more parallel and more effectively integrated.

THE STRENGTHS OF THE FOUR COOPERATIVE LEARNING APPROACHES

All four cooperative learning approaches (Kagan, the Johnsons, Slavin, and Cohen) bring strengths to a teacher education program. For Kagan, minimum training is needed to implement the model. Along with ease of implementation, the model may be applied with all ages and subject areas. In particular, students enjoy the game-like elements of Kagan and the opportunity for relationship building that crosses over traditional boundaries.

The conceptual approach also provides benefits. It emphasizes the importance of processing and notes the higher performance of teams who process more effectively. In addition, social skills developed in using the conceptual approach are highly important. Learning to work together cooperatively to enable processing to be productive helps students develop important skills that are essential for the work world. Also, the conceptual approach focuses on building the self-esteem of all team members; it seeks to improve the individual while, at the same time, utilizing the strength of the group, which makes it a valuable part of any cooperative learning program.

Slavin (1994) notes that many children give up on school early because they are unsuccessful. With the use of improvement points, he, in a way, "levels the playing field" so that weaker students still may contribute to the overall team score. With improvement points, a student is rewarded for demonstrating growth in understanding. Another strength of Slavin's approaches comes in his emphasis on public recognition to stimulate learning. Teacher candidates are urged to recognize publicly the achievements of their students. Whether it is by posting names on a bulletin board, notes to parents, or announcements on the public address system, teacher candidates must include public recognition in order to reap the full benefits of cooperative learning, according to Slavin. Such recognition spotlights academic achievement, builds an atmosphere of pride in successful performance, and establishes a level of high expectation for all students. Because of the improvement point system, students across the range of academic achievement enjoy improved self-esteem, which in turn leads to higher academic performance.

With complex instruction, Cohen has developed a powerful model for cooperative learning. The benefits of positive interdependence and increased student-to-student interactions are significant. An important added benefit comes in the enjoyment of students in productive activities. Time-on-task increases as students become more interested in their own learning and invest themselves in the learning tasks given to them. This active learning again builds stronger academic performance and higher self-esteem. Because of the emphasis placed on utilizing multiple abilities and on expectations for each student to make different intellectual contributions for the tasks assigned, emphasizing complex instruction helps the teacher tap into the strengths of all students while promoting mutual respect and team-building.

Another strength of complex instruction comes in the recognition provided for low-status students. Because teachers are required both to identify strengths for all students and to find ways to utilize each student's strength in completing tasks assigned, low-status students have opportunities to be recognized for personal achievement. Such recognition promotes stronger performance and improves team relationships. As a contributing member to the group's project, low-status students become more empowered and, having experienced such success, are more likely to participate and contribute to the group on future tasks. As group members begin to hold higher expectations for competence for them, low-status students begin to have higher competence expectations for themselves.

In addition, complex instruction emphasizes the specific learning of new norms for behavior with skill builders. Students who successfully utilize these skill builders will acquire new norms, will expand interpersonal skills, will deepen their subject knowledge, and will develop strong critical thinking skills. Productive dialogue will be stimulated that is essential for developing problem-solving skills as well.

THE CHALLENGES OF EACH APPROACH

While each of the four approaches have strengths, each one also poses certain challenges. The structural approach takes a very structured approach in cooperative learning, which for many students is helpful. Yet in some strategies, key problems may emerge. For example, certain strategies ask students to work together and then to share with the larger group. In this process, the student's curiosity promotes engagement with learning. However, in some instances generating initial curiosity within the classroom student is extremely difficult.

The structure called *Co-op Co-op* takes its group investigation strategy from Yael and Shlomo Sharan (1992). Here the overall goal is to develop higher-level critical thinking skills. The strategy divides the students in the class into groups, uses multifaceted learning tasks, and includes multilateral communication among the students. In addition, group investigation involves processing through six consecutive stages. The complexity of this particular strategy sometimes proves difficult for both the teacher candidate and the classroom students. Since the Sharans (1992) recommend a year of teaching before implementation of group investigation, the challenge posed by this strategy for teacher candidates is understandable.

With respect to the conceptual approach, teacher candidates do not always give sufficient attention to implementing the processing component of the Johnsons' approach. Instead, teacher candidates, under the pressure of classroom time constraints, may eliminate or cut down drastically the amount of time given to processing. Fad, Ross, and Boston (1995) agree with the Johnsons that processing is necessary for success. For them, "[a] crucial step in teaching social skills is processing at the close of the activity" (p. 33). Another problem, when using the Johnsons' approach, may emerge in the face-to-face interaction component. The Johnsons' stress the opportunity for students to interact with the absence of physical barriers. Hence, desks and other items located within the classroom may negatively impact what Johnson would consider an ideal room arrangement.

In STAD, certain problems may surface as well. For some teacher candidates, maintaining accurate records and keeping up with improvement points becomes difficult. Teacher candidates also may fail to capitalize on the team recognition component of the model through giving public attention to students and thus weaken the positive effects of cooperative learning. In addition, some teacher candidates allow the competitive element of STAD to override the strategy as a whole. Teacher candidates who overemphasize competition risk the detrimental aspects that come with competition, as Cohen (1990) has noted. When competition receives too much attention, the dominant students (the winners) tend to take over, leaving the slower students to disappear into the group.

For complex instruction, the two major challenges are (1) designing materials that focus on an intrinsically motivating task and utilize multiple abilities to accomplish the task and (2) identifying the strengths of each student, particularly low-status students, in order to help them to grow in engagement and participation in the task and to develop more academically. In *Designing Groupwork* (1994), Cohen notes that simply establishing cooperative learning groups that get students to participate is not enough to insure that all students benefit in the learning experience. Tasks should be structured to require the use of multiple abilities to promote the inclusion of students from a wide range of talents and skills. In addition, the low-status students have a particular strength publicly identified. If not, the low-status students will not have their ideas valued, and thus they will participate little and learn less than the high-status students. The challenging part for many teacher candidates is persevering to find the individual strengths of particular low-status students. Bracey (1995), citing the work of Cohen and Lotan, states that a key factor is in the teacher's [emphasizing] that no one has all these abilities [to complete the task] but that everyone has some of them (p. 727). Also, careful observation will allow the teacher candidates in their first full year of teaching to identify the strengths of all the classroom students and thus be able to encourage the students to capitalize on their abilities and contribute to the success of the whole group. As we continue to monitor and evaluate teacher candidates at all four levels in the teacher education program as well as graduates from the program out in the teaching field, we will be able to identify more clearly which cooperative models are used more frequently, why these models are used, and the relative strengths and challenges of the different approaches.

MANAGEMENT OF THE COOPERATIVE LEARNING SYSTEM

When using cooperative learning within the classroom, implementation problems may occur. From our work with teacher candidates and graduates, we have identified issues for the teacher candidate as well as for the first-year teacher. For the teacher candidate, the beginning challenge is to develop the knowledge base in cooperative learning that is necessary for success. The stronger the pedagogical foundation, the higher the confidence the teacher candidate has in these strategies. Thus, in each year of the program, teacher candidates receive theoretical grounding in the cooperative learning model under study (structural, conceptual, STAD, and complex instruction). We have subsequently seen a sharp rise in the positive perception of the strategies as a useful tool. Experience of cooperative learning only in the first year generated little confidence among teacher candidates. Since we introduced it in each of their four years in the program, teacher candidates at the senior level have voiced a 90 percent approval rate of cooperative learning as an important pedagogical strategy in formal surveys (thirty-three out of forty-two seniors surveyed). Fifteen of the seventeen current teacher candidates during the spring of 2000 indicated they intend to use it as an essential component of their teaching.

Another implementation problem lies in potential differences in teaching philosophies between the teacher candidate and the cooperating teacher in the public school classroom. Usually, the cooperating teacher's resistance can be traced to misconceptions about cooperative learning as merely allowing students to work together on a task with no individual accountability. In addition, because of the planning time needed for quality instructional use of this strategy, teacher candidates may become overwhelmed by the demands of the field experiences and fail to employ cooperative learning. Teacher candidates also often have classroom management problems. Because of lack of experience, they encounter challenges in handling student behavior issues. For example, how to handle the increase in noise level, how to avoid domination by certain students, how to keep students on task, and how to monitor the teams effectively are tasks that put pressure on the teacher candidate. Teacher candidates lament that the classroom students "think they are broken into play teams when they go into groups," "talk too much about topics off the subject," and "do not follow the established rules." As a result, they sometimes resort to the traditional teacher/ lecture format to manage behavior more efficiently since direct supervision is often easier for the beginner.

Both teacher candidates and first-year teachers combat a challenge when the administration of a school does not support cooperative learning. Some principals expect a "quiet" classroom and expect the teachers to be always "teaching" for learning to occur. Also, in implementing cooperative learning, both sometimes encounter conflicts generated by the accountability movement. The great emphasis on standardized tests and the scores themselves push teachers into a constant test preparation mode, which often translates into traditional teacher-dominated classes and a neglect of cooperative learning.

Other implementation problems may emerge with the classroom students themselves. Where they have not been exposed to this model, classroom students may view cooperative learning as manipulative, where the teacher, in their view, is devising a way to shift the work to the students. Some classroom students see themselves as "guinea pigs," the victim of experimentation by "college kids," and therefore they do not take the work seriously. In addition, some have been conditioned to perform with worksheets and, when cooperative learning expands their level of responsibility for learning, they respond negatively. Most significantly, classroom students have been taught competition rather than cooperation as the means to achievement. Dillon, Flack, and Peterman (1994), Johnson, Johnson, and Smith (1998), and many others cite the great emphasis placed on competition within the educational system. Thus, getting the students to value cooperation becomes a great challenge.

To illustrate, in a recent visit to an eighth grade language arts classroom, the college supervisor observed a teacher candidate conducting a lesson utilizing cooperative learning. At one point, one classroom student became very agitated when he thought another group got help with an answer from the teacher. He stated, "You can't help them win!" In this case the classroom student still saw competition and winning as the aim of the task. By demonstrating the value and power of the team, the teacher candidate will be able to change the culture of the class from competition to one of cooperation.

THE ROLE OF THE COLLEGE

The college must recognize these and other implementation issues and seek to address them through programming and support services. During the teacher candidate's progress through the teacher education program, the college should seek to match the teacher candidate with site-based teachers who are receptive to cooperative learning. The college should offer a system of practice and feedback that is sequential and incremental. In addition, specific courses and field experiences should be linked to insure adequate opportunities for implementation. Such a system provides the organization and structure necessary for teacher candidates to understand and put into practice these cooperative learning approaches.

Then, too, once in the field, the college should provide first-year teachers with continued support. Because of the challenges of the first year of teaching, keeping cooperative learning alive and viable is aided by strong mentoring by the college teachers with their graduates. By having this resource, first-year teachers are able to receive help in determining the appropriate time frame for implementation during the year and also have constant communication with professionals who are able to support and encourage when problems emerge.

Most importantly, we have found that for a successful cooperative learning program, we must invest in a sound evaluation and assessment system to provide the feedback necessary for continued improvement. As a result, we have identified sources for assessment data needed and have established both a schedule for data collection as well as a formal system for evaluation of data and use of results for improvement. We use surveys to seek information from teacher candidates, first-year teachers, cooperating teachers, public school administrators, college faculty, as well as other constituents. Interviews (both individual and focus groups) are also conducted. The following section shares some assessment results.

Insights Gained from Experience

We have accumulated much data to support the value of cooperative learning. We gather assessment data in a variety of ways. Teacher candidates complete surveys on their use and views on cooperative learning at the freshmen, sophomore, junior, and senior levels. Teacher candidates must also include reflections on their use of cooperative learning in their cumulative portfolio that is part of their formal entrance into the teacher education program as well as their successful exit from the program.

The state-mandated assessment and evaluation system for teachers ("Assessing, Developing, Evaluating Professional Teaching"—ADEPT) emphasizes the use of strategies that promote cooperation and teamwork. As a result of this mandate, the college supervisor and cooperating teacher in the public school who observe the teacher candidate must evaluate the use of cooperative learning within the lessons taught. To this point, we have gathered assessment data from over 250 teacher candidates. Six of the education faculty regularly take part in collecting assessment data.

During field experiences from the freshman through the senior level, college supervisors evaluate the teacher candidates' cooperative learning lessons. From an analysis of these evaluations, certain patterns have emerged. Results include the following: (1) success is linked closely to effective classroom management skills; (2) success improves with experience; (3) the teacher candidate who develops a strong foundation in the relevant theoretical constructs is more likely to be successful in utilizing cooperative learning on a long-term basis; (4) beginning users often fail to educate classroom students sufficiently in the function of groups or in building team identity; and (5) continued use is often hindered by management problems and perception that the required investment of time cancels out the potential gains from this strategy. (In future assessments by college supervisors, we plan to develop assessment instruments that will allow for more quantifiable statistical data regarding use and effectiveness.)

From students in their first experience in their freshman year to the teacher candidates in their student teaching experience as seniors, a majority view cooperative learning as a powerful pedagogical strategy that may be used in a variety of ways within the classroom. To illustrate, in a survey of freshmen who took "Introduction to Education," forty-four of the forty-five students responding indicated that cooperative learning was highly useful. Teacher candidates completing student teaching in the spring of 1999 were surveyed as well. Fifteen of these seventeen seniors strongly support the use of cooperative learning. The following quotes illustrate their views on its benefits:

> *Anna:* "I saw that students can learn from each other better than from a teacher sometimes."
> *Carrie:* "You can tell that every child gives 100 percent in order to not only be the best team but also to make the team members proud."
> *Jonathon:* "It helps low achievers improve with the high achievers."
> *Bruce* (senior): "Students don't pick on each other about ability levels and the best students feel good when they help someone else."
> *Gail* (senior): "Cooperative learning gets students excited about learning."
> *Amy* (senior): " I found that my low-level students were encouraged by my average and high-level students. I saw real results."

Most significantly, 100 percent of the teacher candidates in student teaching in spring of 1999 (seventeen of seventeen) responding to the survey indicated their intent to use cooperative learning in their own future classrooms. Surveys of teacher candidates in student teaching in the fall of 1999 showed similar results. Sixteen out of the seventeen teacher candidates see great value in cooperative learning and plan to use this strategy in their teaching.

Data from the sixteen graduates in their first teaching job show mixed results in implementation. Some have used cooperative learning but have become overwhelmed by the many demands placed on a first-year teacher and have not been able to integrate it fully into their teaching. Some first-year teachers cite a lack of confidence in their ability to implement this learning strategy and therefore were reluctant to use it their first year. Only a few (two out of sixteen) describe themselves as frequent users. We plan to study our first-year teachers more closely to determine the factors that lead to a teacher's effective implementation during the first year. We plan to modify the teacher education program to address their needs and to help them develop the skills and confidence to use this productive strategy.

Using the insights gained from the assessment review, we offer some suggestions for programmatic changes. First, in the field experiences prior to student teaching, teacher candidates should utilize cooperative learning in their teaching opportunities in the public schools. However, they are often not in the same school setting for a long enough period to realize the full benefits of cooperative learning. It takes time for students to learn the procedures and to grow to trust one another in group situations. To address this concern, we are lengthening the time for students in the public school setting in the semesters prior to student teaching. By allowing more time for the students to employ cooperative learning within the public school classroom, the students should reap more success in such efforts.

Second, our teacher candidates sometimes do not understand that the use of cooperative learning effectively means one must make it a fundamental part of the class. To accomplish this task, one must prepare thoroughly for the lesson and structure the class, the time, and the activities carefully. Instead, some teacher candidates give their students under-developed lessons and try to use cooperative learning. Then they spend days and sometimes weeks working through a poor lesson. The classroom students get frustrated and feel they are wasting their time, and in this case, they are. Our teacher candidates must realize that cooperative learning lessons must be rich in content and encourage students to dig deeper and continue to expand their thinking. As Cohen (1990) notes, tasks must be intrinsically motivating to get students interested in the learning process for the task. In a programmatic change, we have added a course in curriculum and instruction this year to provide more experience in lesson planning and development for all secondary content areas.

Third, our teacher candidates, when using cooperative learning, encounter problems in the real world of the public school classroom when individuals clash. Some students just do not like each other. Such dislikes may be based on personality differences, social and/or cultural biases, or any of number of factors. Our teacher candidates see as a basic challenge (in utilizing cooperative learning effectively) the goal of helping students to respect and appreciate each other and value the contributions that each student makes. We plan to address this issue through a greater emphasis on diversity training and team-building skills for our teacher candidates.

Back on the college campus, we need to bring more of the college faculty as a whole on board as believers and practitioners of cooperative learning. To move in this direction, we are planning and giving workshops on campus to promote the value of cooperative learning for all disciplines. We are also considering some team-teaching possibilities that would pair experienced faculty with those who would like to learn.

There are many benefits of having a wide spectrum of faculty involvement in the implementation of cooperative learning within the college classroom. If teacher candidates experience cooperative learning not only in their education classes but also in courses in general education and their content areas, then they are able to see these strategies successfully at work in multiple contexts. Moreover, the validation of the method by faculty outside of education improves the teacher candidate's level of trust in cooperative learning as a vehicle for teaching.

Similarly, if we place teacher candidates with site teachers who use cooperative learning, they will acquire more practical experience in the actual use of these strategies in the public schools. In other words, the more experiences teacher candidates have within the college classroom and within the public school setting, the richer the student becomes in understanding and in the ability to implement cooperative strategies successfully.

Despite concerns and issues that demand our attention, we are confident that cooperative learning is extremely valuable as a component of the teacher's pedagogical tools. We would strongly encourage other teacher education programs to consider its inclusion as a fundamental part of their teacher candidates' experiences. Most importantly, the concepts and practical application of the various cooperative learning models should be systematically embedded within courses and field experiences throughout the program.

Before incorporating cooperative learning within a teacher education program, we offer the following recommendations:

1. The teacher education program should provide adequate training of faculty in the approaches to be used that reflect their pedagogical philosophy.
2. The faculty should link the various cooperative learning approaches to specific courses and field experiences.

3. The faculty should utilize a systematic approach that is incremental, developmental, and embedded within various program elements.

4. The teacher education program should identify appropriate evaluation and assessment instruments that will identify strengths and weaknesses of their use of cooperative learning. Data gathered should be reviewed systematically in order to address weaknesses and to continue to improve the program.

5. The teacher education program should form a support group for their own teacher candidates to help them cope with problems and concerns they may have in using cooperative learning within their own classrooms.

These recommendations follow our best advice in designing a program implementing cooperative learning as an integral part of a teacher education. At Anderson College, we are at various stages of addressing these issues. One new addition we are considering is a comprehensive portfolio, which could help us to identify more clearly and systematically our teacher candidate's knowledge and skills in cooperative learning. We have proposed this four-year portfolio model that teacher candidates would keep from their freshmen year to the end of student teaching and graduation. The portfolio has within it a core set of questions that ask students to respond to their understanding of the various models and their successes and challenges in implementing the models. At the end of each year students would be required to review their responses and to write a reflective paper including their views on cooperative learning. Each year, the portfolio would be reviewed by the student's education advisor who would identify student growth and address student needs. Although many components of this portfolio have been operating for several years, we have proposed to begin requiring this four-year portfolio in the coming year. We believe by having such a record-keeping system, we will more effectively note the growth of students in their understanding of cooperative learning (as well as other components of the program) and identify areas we need to improve within our program.

THE FUTURE OF COOPERATIVE LEARNING AT ANDERSON COLLEGE

In all, cooperative learning (in both its theoretical foundation and pedagogical principles) has a major influence on the development of teacher candidates in the teacher education program at Anderson College. By equipping graduates with the knowledge of the tenets of cooperative learning as well as an array of implementation strategies, our student teachers have acquired a powerful source to aid them in successfully delivering instruction, managing the classroom, promoting student learning, improving student self-esteem, encouraging development of values, and indeed building the classroom community that makes learning both challenging and exciting. We have both quantitative and qualitative data over the last three years confirming both the teacher candidates' love for cooperative learning and their belief in its power to develop a dynamic learning community within the classroom. Indeed, we at Anderson College believe in the value of cooperative learning and its power as well. Faculty are actively studying and employing these methods within their classrooms. Not only has cooperative learning become a foundational principle of the teacher education program, but it is also finding application in the general education curriculum as well. English, math, history, and education professors are joining together with a common goal—to make learning a lifelong pursuit and to make friends while learning. Last, we hope the insights and experiences we have shared will aid others in their efforts to include this valuable learning approach within their teacher education programs.

REFERENCES

Bracey, G. W. (1995, May). Status and expectancies. *Phi Delta Kappan*, 727–228.

Cohen, E. G. (1990, October). Continuing to cooperate: Prerequisites for persistence. *Phi Delta Kappan*, 134–138.

———. (1994). *Designing groupwork: Strategies for the heterogeneous classroom* (2nd ed.). New York: Teachers College Press.

———. (1998, September). Making cooperative learning equitable. *Educational Leadership*, 18–21.

Cohen, E. G., & Lotan, R. A. (1995). Producing equal-status interaction in heterogeneous classrooms. *American Educational Research Journal, 32,* 99–120.

Cohen, E. G. & Lotan, R. A. (Eds.) (1997). *Working for equity in heterogeneous classrooms: Sociological theory in practice.* New York: Teachers College Press.

Dillon, K., Flack, M. & Peterman, F. (1994, November). Cooperative learning and the achievement of female students. *Middle School Journal*, 48–51.

Fad, K., Ross, M., & Boston, J. (1995, Summer). We're better together: Using cooperative learning to teach social skills to young children. *The Council for Exceptional Children*, 29–34.

Johnson, R. T. & Johnson, D. W. & Holubec, E. (1987). How can we put cooperative learning into practice? *Science Teacher, 54* (6), 46–48, 50.

Johnson, D., Johnson, R. & Smith, K. (1998, July/August). Cooperative learning returns to college: What evidence is there that it works. *Change, 30* (4), 26–35.

Kagan, S. (1990). The structural approach to cooperative learning. *Educational Leadership, 47* (4), 12–15.

———. (1995, May). Group grades miss the mark. *Educational Leadership,* 68–71.

———. (1996, January/February). Avoiding the group-grades trap. *Learning, 24* (4), 56–58.

Sharan, Y., & Sharan, S. (1992). *Expanding cooperative learning through group investigation.* New York: Teachers College Press.

Slavin, R. E. (1983). *Cooperative learning.* New York: Longman.

———. (1989). Cooperative learning models for heterogeneous classrooms. *Pointer, 33* (2), 12–19.

———. (1991). Group rewards make groupwork possible. *Educational Leadership, 43* (5), 89–91.

———. (1994). *Using student team learning.* Baltimore: Johns Hopkins University.

CHAPTER 5

Cooperative Learning in Preservice Teacher Education at the University of Maryland

FRANK LYMAN AND NEIL DAVIDSON

Cooperative learning represents a paradigm shift for many classroom teachers. Although the advantages seem obvious to some teachers, others see the complexities of implementation as forbidding. Particularly at the secondary level, there is a reluctance to incorporate cooperative learning into a repertoire of strategies. Given this reality, colleges of education should make a special commitment to teaching both the rationale and technique of cooperative learning to undergraduate and graduate students.

To have a chance of future implementation, cooperative learning must be modeled for the preservice teachers and experienced by them as learners. The student teachers should use cooperative learning in connection with tools for reflection, practice it repeatedly with feedback, see it as a part of a constellation of allied strategies and techniques, and understand its relationship to dependent variables such as social and academic outcomes. Finally they should value it as an adult learning strategy.

Using this philosophy of instruction, the Curriculum and Instruction Department at University of Maryland, College Park, has for many years emphasized the importance of cooperative learning. This chapter gives examples of programmatic elements and outcomes of this emphasis. Examples come from the campus-based "Principles and Methods of Teaching" course (elementary and secondary) taught by Neil Davidson and colleagues, and the field-based Teacher Education/Professional Development School Center coordinated by Frank Lyman.

COOPERATIVE LEARNING IN BASIC COURSEWORK

Elementary and secondary methods courses systematically address cooperative learning. These courses are designed partly around a "models-of-teaching" approach including selected information-processing, social, behavioral, and personal models (Joyce & Weil, 1980). Richard Arends and his colleagues, Neil Davidson and Rochelle Clemson, developed the models-of-teaching approach in these elementary and secondary methods courses at the University of Maryland in the mid-1980s. A frequently used text is *Learning to Teach* by Richard Arends (1998).

Cooperative learning is the main social model in these methods courses. Relevant elements of both courses included:

Rationale and research base for cooperative learning;
Definition of critical attributes of cooperative learning;
Climate-setting through class-building and team-building;
Social skills development;
Classroom implementation issues such as roles of the teacher and group members, group formation, classroom assessment and evaluation, conflict resolution, managing the classroom, etc.;
Simple cooperative structures many of which are described by Kagan (1992) including interview, Think-Pair-Share and its variations, Round Robin and Round Table, Numbered Heads Together, Pairs Check, and Group Brainstorming;
More complex cooperative procedures such as Jigsaw (Aaronson, Blaney, Sikes, & Snapp, 1978), group investigation (Sharan & Sharan, 1992), constructive controversy (Johnson & Johnson, 1987), and Student Teams Achievement Divisions (STAD) (Slavin, 1986).

In order to foster classroom implementation of varied models of teaching, prospective teachers present several minilessons in a microteaching lab setting, with videotaping, peer feedback, and constructive critique. In the cooperative learning minilesson, preservice teachers employ one or two simple cooperative structures in teaching their classmates a small content segment appropriate for either elementary or secondary school students. At first, the instructor leads critiques of lessons in all models with student participation. Later, students lead these sessions using criteria sheets for the specific models. They follow guidelines for constructive written and oral critique, making sure to point out positive aspects of the lessons and to provide alternative approaches and constructive suggestions for improvement. Students have the opportunity to revise their lesson plans based upon the feedback they have received and upon their own personal reflection, both of which they submit along with the revised lesson plan.

After students learn and present minilessons with simple cooperative structures, they participate in lessons with the more advanced procedures. The jigsaw method demonstrates an alternative method of presenting and learning with a topic such as De Bono's "six hats for thinking" (1985). The technique of constructive controversy centers on a controversial issue such as tracking. All class members participate in a major group investigation of some aspect of either multicultural education or mainstreaming, making group presentations to the entire class. Students experience Student Teams Achievement Divisions, another strong example of the research base for cooperative learning in improving student achievement, motivation, and inter-group relations in urban, culturally diverse school settings and in settings where special education students have been mainstreamed.

This generic undergraduate course is the first methods course in the elementary or secondary education program. Following this experience, the program calls for curriculum methods courses in language arts, social studies, science, mathematics etc. Curriculum methods courses vary in the extent to which cooperative learning is incorporated.

COOPERATIVE LEARNING IN STUDENT TEACHING

The University of Maryland places student teachers in schools that function as teacher education centers (now having evolved into professional development schools), mostly in five surrounding school districts. The coordinators of the centers are familiar with cooperative learning and encourage students to experiment with its implementation. Student teachers experienced modeling, practice, reflection, and peer collaboration in the program of the Howard County Teacher Education Center coordinated by Frank Lyman—a program that three times received national recognition from the National Association of Teacher Educators.

Cooperative learning in field-based teacher education has three related dimensions: the repertoire of and rationale for cooperative learning for students; the methods used in the student teaching seminar that are often models of cooperative learning; and the collaborative, reflective interaction between student teachers/interns, cooperating teachers, and university supervisors. Each of these dimensions occurred in the teacher education collaboration between the University of Maryland College of Education and the Howard County Schools. Along with some evidence of effectiveness, this section will focus on what principles and techniques might improve upon what was done.

When undergraduate and masters program teacher candidates arrived at their orientation seminars in Howard County for student teaching, they received as their only textbook, Spencer Kagan's *Cooperative Learning* (1992). The Center's coordinator reviewed with the students the content of the book and told them that cooperative learning should be a central strategy in their instructional repertoire. Cooperative learning is one of several allied elements in an overall model designed to give every student the opportunity to respond. Other elements include wait time, metacognition, cognitive mapping (visual organizing), bonding (interpersonal relationships), curiosity as a motivation (discrepant events), theory making (constructivism), and transition cueing. Thus placed in context, cooperative learning is to be understood as a means rather than an end, and is most effective when combined with other techniques and their underlying principles.

Student teachers were then encouraged, as were their cooperating teachers, to try several of the structures from Kagan's text and to videotape where possible. The second of two student teacher videotapes was to be as state-of-the-art as possible, including "wait time" and other allied techniques. Additionally, in weekly observation/analysis conferences with the Center's coordinator, student teachers discussed logistical issues such as grouping and role setting, and also learning/social outcomes of cooperative learning.

In retrospect, students could acquire a more extensive repertoire. Besides the emphasis on Jigsaw and varieties of Think-Pair-Share, the program could focus on three or four other structures; such as: structured investigation, Round Table, Numbered Heads Together, and Pairs Check. It sometimes happened that a student teacher would not go beyond two or three structures, particularly if these were favorites of the cooperating teacher or coordinator. Student teachers often wrote that they were hesitant to use some structures because of inability to manage them. Having studied with different campus professors, the student teachers came to the Center with varied preparation for cooperative learning. In general, a more careful assessment of prior knowledge could strengthen the ability of the staff to work successfully with these student teachers.

Seminar Methods

All student teachers attended bimonthly or weekly seminars in the public schools. There was a concerted effort to align the methods of teaching in the seminar with those being prescribed for the classroom. For instance, rather than having to answer questions on the spot in the seminar, the student teachers responded in writing to most questions presented for discussion. This was an adaptation of the heavily researched "wait time" variable. Only after written response and often interaction of pairs, did the discussion in the whole class begin. The results of this collective process produced less shared ignorance and more powerful discussions than when one or two extroverts dominated the discourse. Each individual gained a voice.

Besides Think-Pair-Share, Think-Pair-Square, and varieties thereof, instructors used Jigsaw to process complicated aspects of teaching/learning. One example of this was the formation of expert groups to gain deeper understanding of teaching principles such as those related to "bonding" or "wait time." Visual aids, called "Teaching/Coaching Wheels," provided a common system of principles, concepts, and techniques for the observation and analysis of teaching and learning. Jigsaw was also suitable for problem solving on such topics as diversity and classroom dynamics.

The student teaching seminar was a forum for causal analysis of the difficulties and successes related to cooperative learning. Classroom and societal benefits of cooperative learning were a focus, particularly as they related to the complex demographics of today's schools.

Using videotape models of strategies such as cooperative learning, the coordinator was able to teach generic analytical and collaborative peer coaching skills. For example, the student teachers wrote down teaching/learning events and connected concepts and principles to these events by classifying and analyzing cause and effect. Student teachers then reflected collaboratively on the teaching, using their observational notes. They would analyze the effects of Structured Pair Retell on test scores. From an analysis of improved test results, the student teachers could derive a principle that immediate cooperative response improves recall.

The dilemma in designing student teaching seminars is how to apportion emphasis among pressing pedagogical questions, philosophical issues, repertoire building, and reflective activities. Whereas more modeling of cooperative learning in the Professional Development School Center setting is important, it is not possible, nor should it be necessary, to teach directly all of Kagan's key structures. The combination of the "Principles and Methods" course on campus, the Kagan textbook, and knowledgeable cooperating teachers should be enough to cover all the relevant strategies.

Collegial Cooperation and Use of Reflective Tools

There were four combinations of professionals who acted as collaborative units for preservice education in the Howard County Schools setting. These were: cooperating teacher/student teacher; university coordinator/student teacher; university coordinator/cooperating teacher (clinical mentor); and student teacher/student teacher. Adult collaboration can be a learning experience and an opportunity for joint problem solving. Crucial to the success of such collaboration is a common language, in this case a set of principles and associated concepts or techniques upon which all participants could focus. A theory/practice template of theory and practice (The Principle-Based Teaching/Coaching Wheel) provided this common language. The template links together in a visual display several theoretical principles with relevant courses of action. In each cooperative pairing, participants were able to discuss teaching/learning in reference to the principles, concepts, and techniques of the template. Instructors tried to connect every teaching/learning event to a concept or principle, thereby facilitating transfer to a similar event students might experience in the future. For instance, the concept of "bind" meant allowing students to learn cooperatively, and helping to build cooperative relations among children. For each analysis of a cooperative event, students used this concept. Thus, the cognitive path was from practice to theory to practice to future practice. The spirit was one of joint inquiry rather than one of experts instructing novices.

Center participants used several other common language tools, among which was a problem-solving/action-research heuristic (See figure 3) and a specific design for comparison of videotaped lessons. This design included the cause and effect analysis from the problem-solving/action-research heuristic. The student teachers wrote up their analysis and comparison of two videotaped lessons. They used models of earlier student teachers' quality written work and learned how to make connections between theoretical constructs and classroom events. They made this comparison of videotapes after they had analyzed the tapes with a partner. In some semesters, the Center coordinator monitored the collegial peer conference by audiotape.

The research literature was a main source of concepts making up a common language; and careful field-tests evaluated the student teachers' use of the language. Providing a common language and cognitive paths for reflection made collaborative work more productive than it otherwise might have been.

EVIDENCE OF EFFECTIVENESS

In the past twenty years there have been several doctoral studies of programmatic aspects of the Howard County/University of Maryland Teacher Education/Professional Development School Center. One study focused specifically on the uses of cooperative learning in the classroom, while seven others dealt with collaboration among professionals.

Journals, self-evaluations, and video comparisons written by student teachers provided other evidence of effectiveness of these methods for teaching cooperative learning. Also, audiotapes of peer conferences and action-research

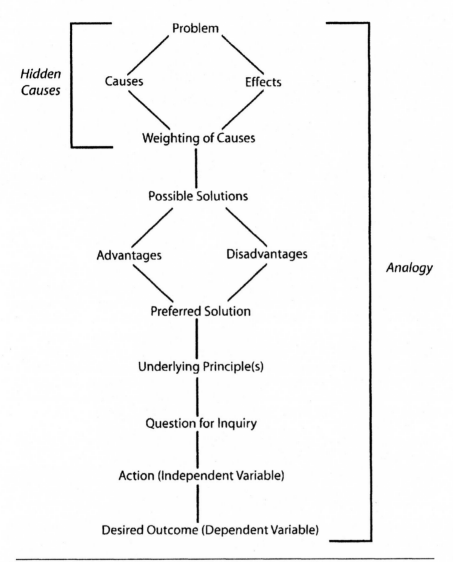

Figure 3. *Problem Solving/Action Research Thinking*

studies by student teachers revealed both effective collegial cooperation and evidence of the effect of cooperative learning on students. Much of this writing by students has been kept to provide data for future doctoral studies.

A doctoral study by David Morrocco (1992) compared graduates of the University of Maryland Masters Certification programs and undergraduates on their reported use of cooperative learning techniques. The respondents in the graduate group ($N = 30$) in this study were from other UMCP centers as well as the Howard County Professional Development School Center. The comparison group ($N = 26$) consisted of undergraduate students who were not placed in centers. Morrocco concluded that "data from this study suggest that teachers who graduated from the masters certification program and undergraduate programs were using cooperative learning strategies just about every day, possessed some repertoire of cooperative learning strategies, and used research-based reasons when deciding to use cooperative learning in their classrooms" (1992, p. 125). Think-Pair-Share was by far the most frequently utilized strategy. Differences between the graduates who had worked with the professional development centers and undergraduates who had not were insignificant, with the undergraduates having a slight edge in repertoire and the graduates being more aware of research.

In the years that undergraduate student teachers completed action research projects, about 60 percent of all the interventions were cooperative learning. In twenty of the summarized studies, interaction between pairs of children had positive academic results. In 1986, the Teacher Education Center received the Maryland Association Supervision and Curriculum Award for these action research studies. About 20 percent of the masters certification interns have done studies of cooperative learning as seminar papers. Some of the desirable outcomes of these twenty studies on cooperative pair interaction were: focused behavior (a willingness to participate), retention of information, organization of thought (clarity), elaboration, inclusion of a broader range of students, completion of work, and creative ideas (Davie & Lyman, 1986).

Another indicator of the use of cooperative learning during student teaching was the almost 100 percent use of cooperative learning in the videotaped lessons. The written cause/effect analyses demonstrated the student teachers' understanding of the efficacy of cooperative learning and the difficulties connected to its implementation. The following quotes are representative:

> "I had put a lot of thought into the pairs, thinking of who would be a good influence on whom."

> "When students are given a choice to work in pairs or individually, more tend to work in pairs; a few introverts or girls sitting with boys chose to work independently."

> "The three percent or so who seemed apathetic gradually joined in because their group needed them for the finished product. Plus, it's much easier to get students on stage when they know they'll perform in groups."

"Vagueness was at times apparent in my direction-giving and mode setting for Think-Pair-Share."

Using a common language of principles and concepts as a framework, every student teacher was required to write a self-evaluation on the midterm and final. One category of the evaluation was cooperative learning. The following quotes are organized thematically around four patterns of response: implementation issues, self-critique, rationale, and description.

Implementation Issues

"I had the opportunity to work with structured groups (using the Kagan approach) as well as unstructured groups, allowing the natural dynamics to decide roles."

"I want to know why I want to group the students, and how to group them effectively."

"My biggest struggles with cooperative groups seem to be in determining the best group structure . . . and also organizing so that the groups stay focused on their responsibilities. . . . I want 'happy hour' to be integrated into the learning."

Self Critique

"The Social Studies projects I described earlier were a good example of group investigation. . . . I kept wanting to jump in and straighten out everyone's lives . . . allowing children to figure out their own problems. . . . I need to work on . . ."

"I used cooperative learning effectively and can improve by varying the structures and modes, providing more prethinking, and using more peer-tutoring or teaching. . . . In math, I found that cooperative work improved with voluntary grouping."

Rationale

"I feel I have learned a lot about cooperative learning. The students seem to learn more information in a shorter period of time when they work in cooperative groups, even in groups of two . . . works well in all subjects, especially math, reading, and science."

"Techniques such as Think-Pair-Share and group activities worked extremely well in mathematics classes. Students really began to rely on one another to learn. . . . This was especially evident in the calculus classes. . . . This type of cooperation builds relationships among students and fosters a sense of interdependency."

"The students like to help fellow students. . . . This gives them the opportunity to develop patience and understanding for each others' differences."

"Through these [cooperative] activities, the children learn to explain their ideas . . . and feelings, and simply develop understandings with others while contributing to a positive classroom atmosphere. . . . As a result, I will continue to support and implement cooperative learning in many of my lessons."

"Our classroom glows with cooperative learning. . . . Our students work as a united front."

Description

"I have used Think-(Write)-Pair-Share, Stand and Share, Three Step Interviews, Group talk, Round table, peer editing, [pair] processing directions, and peer tutoring. . . . I plan to use Kagan's book . . . every week."

"At the middle school, I used groupwork much more often with labs, Think-Pair-Share, a Jigsaw on heat movement, a Jeopardy review game on heat, and various in-class partnerships."

As a final informal assessment, all the Center graduates with whom Frank Lyman is still in contact use cooperative learning in their classrooms. This number would be about one hundred of the perhaps eight hundred still teaching, and many of these are in Howard County. (The remaining seven hundred may also be using cooperative learning but those data are not available.)

Another indicator of the ongoing use of cooperative learning is membership on the Mid Atlantic Association for Cooperation in Education (MAACIE) Board. Six of the Board members are graduates of the Howard County Professional Development Center.

EVIDENCE FROM COLLABORATIVE REFLECTION

As mentioned earlier, common language templates and cognitive path flow charts were used as tools to assist independent and collaborative reflection. Each template has cooperative learning dimensions and provides the language for collaborative reflection. Researchers documented the use of language from these templates for analysis, problem solving, planning, keeping journals, video analysis, written self-evaluation, peer coaching, and supervision (Wuestman, 1997; Livingston, 1990; Winitsky, 1987; Winitsky & Arends, 1991; Hosford, 1992; DiGiaimo, 1994).

Figure 3 shows the heuristic we used to represent how a teacher's mind can work to solve a problem. After proposing a solution to the problem, student teachers created an action research design to gather data on the effectiveness of the solution. In seminar, students worked in cooperative groups using the flow chart to solve instructional problems. The action research studies mentioned above used problem-solving thinking for project design (Eley & Lyman, 1987).

Roxie Watson, a student teacher, wrote in her journal, using the problem-solving heuristic to deal with the problem of high school juniors who groaned when she asked them to participate in groupwork. Among the causes she considered were: "Students aren't used to working in groups and are apprehensive about changes; roles aren't well defined"; "most of these students are grade hounds and don't want others to play a role in their grade for fear that someone else's input might have an adverse affect on their grade," and " students don't understand why I want them to work in groups; they don't see the logic or advantage of the process." She then gave weight to these causes and determined that the most powerful cause was when students did not understand why they were being asked to participate in group learning and had negative preconceived notions about cooperative learning. After considering the advantages and disadvantages of each of a set of five possible solutions she determined that a preferred solution was to ask students for a written response concerning their thoughts as to why she wants them to work together followed by another explanation using real-world examples of cooperation. She specified the principles underlying her preferred solution. Finally she selected a question for her action research: "If the teacher asks students to create a written rationale for cooperative learning, what will be the effects on their willingness to work cooperatively?" The desired outcome, her dependent variable, was the absence of moaning and groaning among the students when asked to work cooperatively.

An experienced teacher, Mary Koback, who graduated from the Center and won the NEA's Student Teacher of the Year Award for work with Think-Pair-Share, believed that the problem-solving heuristic was the most valuable tool she had acquired. She said she had the flowchart "branded" in her mind and used it frequently to solve her problems.

A common language made collaborative peer coaching possible. The student audiotapes of the peer conferences contain a striking degree of honesty and instances of connecting principles and concepts to examples. The students observed each other's video lessons and took notes. They connected teaching/ learning events to concepts and principles, analyzed cause and effect, sought analogies, and prescribed solutions. It is unlikely that they could have had such high-level discourse without a common pedagogical language, as well as practice in using that language.

A REFLECTION

In review, the crucial program elements that lead to the desirable outcomes noted above are: modeling for preservice teachers, experiencing cooperation as learners, practicing along with feedback, connecting cooperative learning with allied strategies and techniques, relating strategies to social and academic outcomes, and collaborating with other adults. For cooperative learning to have reliable roots in the university experience, professors, field supervisors, classroom teachers, and preservice teachers must themselves cooperate. A professional development center is the best context for this collaboration in which all participants focus on student teachers becoming expert at teaching and reflection.

Cooperative learning is a centerpiece of the partnership of the University of Maryland and the Howard County Schools. When cooperative learning is emphasized in the "Principles and Methods of Teaching" course and reinforced in the field experience, it is more certain that cooperative learning will be a permanent part of the experienced teacher's repertoire. Furthermore, the combination of collaborative reflection with a common language for discourse can accelerate a teacher's development from novice to expert.

REFERENCES

Aaronson, E., Blaney, N., Stephan, C., Sikes, J., & Snapp, M. (1978). *The jigsaw classroom*. Beverly Hills: Sage Publications.

Arends, R. (1998). *Learning to teach*. Boston: McGraw Hill.

Davie, A., & Lyman, F. (1986). *A summary of action research reports*. Unpublished manuscript. University of Maryland.

Di Bono, E. (1985). *Six hats for thinking*. Boston: Little Brown.

DiGiaimo, S.(1994). *A study of pedagogical thinking as evidenced in student teacher analytical writings*. Unpublished doctoral dissertation, University of Maryland.

Eley, G., & Lyman, F. (1987). Problem solving and action research for beginning teachers. *Maryland A.T.E. Journal, 3*, 16–19.

Hosford, K. (1992). *A study of factors related to teaching efficacy of student teachers.* Unpublished doctoral dissertation, University of Maryland.

Johnson, D. W., & Johnson, R. (1987). *Creative conflict.* Edina, MN: Interaction Book Company.

Joyce, B., & and Weil, M. (1980). *Models of teaching* (2nd ed.). Englewood Cliffs, NJ: Prentice Hall.

Kagan, S. (1992). *Cooperative learning.* San Clemente, CA: Kagan Cooperative Learning Co.

Livingston, C. C. (1990). *Student teacher thinking and the student teaching curriculum.* Unpublished doctoral dissertation, University of Maryland.

Morrocco, D. (1992). *Comparison of the use of cooperative learning by graduates of an alternative and of traditional teacher preparation programs.* Unpublished doctoral dissertation, University of Maryland.

Sharan, Y., & Sharan, S. (1992). *Expanding cooperative learning through group investigation.* New York: Teachers College Press.

Slavin, R. (1986). *Using student team learning* (3rd ed.). Baltimore: Johns Hopkins University, Center for Research on Elementary and Middle Schools.

Winitzky, N. E. (1987). *Applying schema theory to educational demonstrations of cooperative learning in pre-service teacher education.* Unpublished doctoral dissertation, University of Maryland.

Winitzky, N. & Arends, R. (1991). Translating research into practice: The effects of various forms of training and clinical experiences on preservice students' knowledge, skill, and reflectiveness. *Journal of Teacher Education, 42* (1), 52–6.

Wuestman, R. T. (1997). *Student teachers' reflections on theory practice relationships.* Unpublished doctoral dissertation, University of Maryland.

CHAPTER 6

PREPARING SECONDARY TEACHERS TO USE COOPERATIVE LEARNING STRATEGIES

CHANDRA J. FOOTE, PAUL J. VERMETTE,
JENNIFER WILSON-BRIDGMAN, THOMAS J. SHEERAN,
ROBIN ERWIN, AND MARY MURRAY

A problem plaguing high schools has been that too many teachers teach in only one way, that is by the lecture method—the same way they were taught. They often feel that lecturing is the most expeditious method for covering a large volume of material.
—National Association of Secondary School Principals, 1996, p. 22

This quote reflects the commonly held belief that secondary teachers instruct primarily using the models they have personally experienced. If there is no cooperative learning in typical secondary classrooms, we cannot expect the graduates of secondary teacher education programs to implement these strategies in their own classrooms. A cycle begins with secondary teachers, is perpetuated by professors in higher education, and is then carried back into the classroom by novice teachers who have primarily experienced lecture-oriented teaching models.

The burden of breaking this cycle falls upon the faculty in teacher education programs. As John Dewey suggested many times over, we learn by doing. When faculty members prepare teachers by lecturing about cooperative learning, there is no real impetus for change. However, if our secondary teacher education classes utilize cooperative learning, students will learn what to do and will feel encouraged to practice such techniques with their own students in the future. If they do not experience it during teacher preparation, where will they ever learn it?

A MODEL OF SECONDARY TEACHER PREPARATION

Niagara University is a small private institution situated on the border of the United States and Canada, just outside the City of Niagara Falls, New York. Niagara prepares teachers for service throughout Western New York and Southern Ontario. In a typical school year, approximately 125 undergraduate and 75 full-time graduate students enroll in the secondary teacher preparation programs. Four full-time faculty members serve as primary advisors and instructors for these students.

The backbone of a quality teacher preparation program is its philosophical framework. The education programs at Niagara University are dedicated to three philosophical ideals. First, we embrace a *process-product* orientation implying that there are many forms of effective practice. Educators should be encouraged to continuously examine and implement a wide range of effective research-based practices. Second, we hold a *constructivist perspective* on learning, wherein developing professionals must build upon their present knowledge through meaningful exploration. Finally, we emphasize *reflective practice*, instilling the skills of self-assessment as well as examination and improvement of one's own practice.

Cooperative learning is both a philosophical position and a set of teaching strategies. We find that cooperative and collaborative teaching and learning strategies are compatible with each of the tenets of our philosophical framework. Within the program, faculty members instruct students in the philosophy and strategies of cooperative learning, and subsequently model these elements in the instruction provided in every course in the program. Cooperative learning allows our candidates an opportunity to explore their own knowledge in meaningful ways, and it provides the impetus for self-exploration and reflective practice. Additionally, we hope that by emphasizing cooperative learning from a reflective and constructivist orientation, our graduates will carry these ideals into their own classrooms.

Beginning in the mid-eighties, the faculty serving the secondary teacher education programs began to examine the research on cooperative learning. We studied approaches such as Jigsaw (Aronson, et al., 1978), STAD (Slavin, 1983), and Learning Together (Johnson & Johnson, 1989) and found them to be both useful teaching methods, and promising in their potential to change school teaching which was then conceptualized and dominated by Madeline Hunter (1994). Over the years, individual faculty members embraced one or another approach encouraging students to read certain works including those of David and Roger Johnson and Holubec (1994), Cohen (1994), Clarke, Wideman, and Eadie (1990), and Slavin (1990). In their courses, future teachers discussed the practices and techniques advanced by various proponents and were required to emulate and reflect upon them in their own field experiences. As faculty continued to explore the works of others, notably, Sharan (1994) and Kagan (1992), it became clear that there were many ways to effectively implement cooperative learning. Rather than endorsing any one particular method, we needed to encourage teacher candidates to explore the essential components leading to "best cooperative learning practice."

The faculty has not subscribed to a single "blueprint" of cooperative learning. Throughout the program candidates learn about and participate in variations of a number of cooperative learning approaches including Jigsaw II (Slavin, 1986), group investigation (Sharan & Sharan, 1976), elements of the structural approach (Kagan 1990), academic controversy (Johnson & Johnson, 1992) and complex instruction (Cohen, 1994). Each instructor models a few of these approaches using content material from his or her own course. At some point in the lesson, the instructor will indicate the cooperative learning approach used and identify its components. At the conclusion of the instructional segment, the instructor will query candidates as to the advantages and disadvantages experienced as a part of using the particular approach. In this manner, candidates visit and revisit a variety of cooperative learning methods and learn about their characteristics and appropriate applications.

As candidates experience the many approaches of cooperative learning, we invite them to reflect upon best practice issues related to *grading, governing,* and *grouping*. Later in the program, candidates are taught about and expected to generate, construct, and evaluate learning activities based upon these three issues.

In his book *Making cooperative learning work: Student teams in K-12 classrooms*, faculty member Paul Vermette (1998) identifies issues related to grading and accountability in cooperative learning settings. According to this text, the teacher must carefully balance a mix of individual and group-graded works and emphasize that each student should contribute to the learning of others. One unique element of this eclectic grading approach is an emphasis on positive interdependence in which students focus on assisting other members of their group as a means to assist themselves.

As they work in cooperative teams throughout their program, candidates experience first-hand the issue of accountability. These experiences are often in direct contrast to their typical university classes where negative interdependence is typically both emphasized and promoted. Candidates reflect upon these personal experiences and develop lessons for their field experiences that effectively balance mutuality and individual accountability.

Early in their programs, candidates also explore issues related to team governance. Vermette (1998) describes governance as it relates to classroom management and opportunities for students to develop interpersonal and social skills. The teacher must ensure that students understand these expectations and have opportunities to assess their own performance and growth and that of their teammates. These objectives are accomplished through a series of introductory exercises that explicitly instruct students in those skills needed to succeed in a collaborative learning environment. Students must also have the chance to compare their own perceptions with those of the teacher. Teacher candidates, in their very first preparation courses, experience these introductory exercises and learn the social skills expected of them as members of class teams. As they progress to their methods and student-teaching field experiences, instructors remind candidates of the necessity to act in a proactive fashion when introducing cooperative learning. They explore methods of classroom management that facilitate effective cooperative learning and review the social skills that their students are expected to demonstrate.

Finally, Vermette (1998) examines the research on group design. He notes the benefits and drawbacks of various team sizes, the issues related to heterogeneity in team construction, various methods of assigning members to teams, and dealing with individual students who present challenges in teams. Teacher candidates in Vermette's own secondary methods class must participate in semi-permanent teams to complete the requirements of the course; and they must design and teach cooperative learning lessons and units in the associated field experiences. Following these lessons, candidates must reflect upon their effectiveness in relation to the three issues of grading, governing, and grouping presented in their methods course.

In all courses, teacher candidates are placed in four- or five-person teams that are relatively permanent for the duration of the course. Instructors compose these teams along the lines of salient diversities to foster understanding of differences based on personal experience. For example, to build heterogeneous teams, they use demographic factors, including gender, age, nationality, subject specialty, university standing (graduate or undergraduate), as well as personal factors such as personality, religion, and interests. Instructors provide teams with learning activities to complete in class and hold them responsible for one or more projects to complete outside of class time over the duration of the semester. Some, but not all, of the products are evaluated with a group grade. Teacher candidates also assess their growth and that of their teammates in areas of interpersonal and social skills. In this manner, teacher candidates learn about cooperative learning from academic study and application, as well as from personal experience.

To examine implementation of cooperative and collaborative strategies, it is helpful to hear directly from those faculty members who teach in our program. The next section provides some detail on the incorporation of these strategies into coursework in each phase of the program. In addition, students in these courses provide insights gained from direct experience.

Foundational Level

"Cultural Foundations of Education," the very first course taken by all candidates, includes a number of course requirements related to cooperative learning. Within this course, prospective teachers must demonstrate that they are able to:

Work effectively with people from diverse populations;
Implement strategies that reach all learners;
Collaborate to solve problems;
Understand and establish a community of learners.

The course instructor has the following to say about the use of student collaboration within the course:

> Cooperative learning is built into the course in several ways. First of all, students begin to understand it conceptually as part of the content of the course at an introductory level. Students are not taught specific approaches of CL such as Slavin's STAD or Johnson's "academic controversy," although in some cases they experience these approaches as part of the method of delivery of content. Secondly, students interact with one another as a central focus of every class. Groupwork and Pair-Share' are regularly utilized. In addition, the requirements for the course include team projects, and there is an expectation that certain course projects will be completed in teams that I construct. Finally, because reflection is an expected practice throughout the program, students frequently examine and assess their own performance as team members. I find that this reflective practice drives students towards even more collaborative analysis and that the work at this phase of the program serves as a precursor for the intensive analysis demanded at the Methods level.

Methods Level

During the phase of the program immediately preceding student teaching, prospective teachers must complete two methods courses: "General Methods of Secondary Education" and "Methods in the Content Areas." These courses are taken simultaneously and include a significant field component. At this level, students are expected to demonstrate a number of skills and abilities with respect to cooperative learning. Most importantly, they must utilize the concept of multiple intelligence (Gardner, 1993) and cooperative leaning theory in lesson and unit plans, they must act professionally in collaborative relationships with fellow teacher candidates, and they must demonstrate other affective qualities of good teachers (Goleman, 1995; Foote et al., 2000).

The fundamental structure of these critical courses, both philosophically and practically, is cooperative learning. Students are expected to learn the strategies associated with cooperative learning (especially the grouping, grading, and governing tenets described above). They must also demonstrate that they can work effectively with others and move toward the conceptualization of the "community of learners" desired by school reformers (Darling-Hammond, 1997). The faculty member who has instructed the general methods class for the past ten years has the following to say about cooperative learning within his course:

> I do not expect them to be proficient in the ability to work coopera-
> tively and to use cooperative learning at the onset of the course and I
> make certain that they understand that it is not yet a norm in the sec-
> ondary field. I believe that the early part of the course is the most
> important in establishing a secondary teacher's motivation and desire
> to effectively use cooperative learning in future secondary classrooms.
> I establish several conditions at the outset to facilitate this. Within the
> opening moments of the course, students are randomly paired and one
> partner in each pair is given a concept to "teach" to their designated
> partner in three minutes. Before beginning, I instruct pairs to shake
> hands (unless it is culturally inappropriate) with each other and say
> "(Name), I don't have to like you, I just have to work with you and
> show you respect." I point out to them that many secondary teachers
> don't use cooperative learning because teens say they don't want to.
> Teenagers often dislike cooperative learning because they are heavily
> peer-bound and interacting with members of the "wrong crowd" has
> social costs. Students greet each other in this way repeatedly through-
> out the course and it begins to be met with laughs, a knowing smile,
> and a spirit of community. This disclaimer is also successfully used in
> school-based practice and helps groups in normal secondary classrooms
> get started. An interesting caveat to the first use of this greeting is that
> preservice teachers who balk at the activity are presenting evidence
> that they may have selected the wrong profession. What teacher can
> refuse to show others respect and/or pick the faculty members or stu-
> dents they want to work with?
>
> Approximately 50 percent of class time is spent in collaborations
> of various formats. Students often perform informal problem solving
> together. Formal heterogeneous teams are created early in the semester
> and students remain in the team throughout the semester to perform
> required activities of analysis or synthesis. At certain points, these
> teams use the Jigsaw technique with other teams to share views across
> groups. As the course draws to a conclusion, teams collaborate on
> formal projects during class time. To me, the second biggest mistake
> made by secondary teachers (and college instructors) experimenting
> with cooperative learning is the "sending home" of all collaborative
> work. This virtually assures that the hardest working members will be
> abused and that some students will reap benefits without effort. More-
> over, the instructor never gets to offer assistance and/or assess the con-

tribution of individuals. The first fatal flaw, by the way, is letting students pick their own teams (see Vermette, 1994).

In addition to the many other ways in which cooperative learning is addressed within this course, I am currently experimenting with a new twist on the weekly reflective journals that I require students to submit. I am attempting to integrate technology into cooperative teaming by having students e-mail their reflections to one group member who synthesizes the group's collective ideas and forwards the new product to me and back to their team members. (I rotate this leadership role each week.) I then respond to the collective synthesis. While it is too early to tell how valuable this strategy is, the fact that teams can "virtually" meet outside of class time allows the students to experience the thoughts of their peers in a manner they might not otherwise have used.

The "Methods in the Content Areas" courses, taken simultaneously with general methods, are designed to introduce prospective teachers to teaching strategies related to their discipline. These courses explore approaches to cooperative learning that are most conducive to individual content areas. Due to the many subject matter disciplines in which Niagara prepares secondary teachers, and to the small number of students completing the program each year, the courses on specific content methods have low student enrollment—about five to ten students enrolled in any given semester. Practicing secondary teachers from local schools teach the content methods courses thereby helping to integrate coursework and fieldwork. The course instructors have commonly found it inappropriate to use lecture strategies in these small classes and prefer to create a few cooperative teams. Typically the largest of these has been "Social Studies Methods," taught for the past seven years by a veteran high school social studies teacher from a local city school. Her perspective provides a unique examination of the integration of cooperative learning into secondary preservice teacher preparation.

In my course, cooperative learning is the prevailing philosophy from which all of my planning operates. Groups are carefully selected over time with a focus on diversity. This includes ability, knowledge, gender, race, and attitude. In this, I model a "way of being" that works for social studies instruction at every level. Candidates learn about gaming and simulation through gaming and simulating. Candidates learn about curricular decision making by making decisions with their groups. They create classroom policies, homework policies, and unit plans; and they critique each other's work within and between teams. The use of microteaching in groups decreases anxiety and increases confidence before entering the field for the required experience that introduces prospective teachers to instruction in secondary social studies settings.

The structure of the "Social Studies Methods" course appears to be working. Candidates produce high-quality products. They are able to use their special talents in each setting. They develop discipline and are highly accountable both on an individual and on a group level. Our professional responsibility is to model good teaching strategies to future teachers. We must show by example that cooperative learning works. Students learn that way and carry the torch to the young people they will teach. It is not enough to talk the talk . . . we must walk the walk.

A graduate student enrolled in both the general and content methods courses had this to say about his cooperative learning experiences during the methods coursework:

I found that many of the people in my classes had a lot more experience in schools than I did. When we worked together in teams, we were able to share professional insights. The teamwork unconsciously eliminated competition and allowed us to support each other. I also found it surprising how often the professors used cooperative learning. Each professor did it a little differently and I have now seen a number of models that I think I will use in my own classes.

Student Teaching Experience

A standard aspect of teacher preparation is the student teaching semester. Accompanying this experience is a seminar designed to provide the opportunity for students to come together with the expressed purpose of sharing insights, reflecting on experiences, and gaining support for and assistance with problems that are an inevitable aspect of student teaching. The full-time faculty member responsible for instructing the seminar provides insight into the way that this course incorporates cooperative learning strategies.

The student teaching seminar provides an ideal opportunity for the professor to organize candidates into cooperative learning groups based either on the certification area (science, math, etc.) or on the level of assignment (high school or middle school). Creating cooperative learning groups in these ways provides heterogeneity that allows cross-content insights, permitting candidates the opportunity to "steal" methods and techniques found successful in other curricular areas. In addition, heterogeneity provides cross-age-group experiences that encourage reflection on the age-specific behaviors that need to be addressed for a student to succeed.

One particularly successful element of the seminar is an analysis of each candidate's "best lesson." After forming cooperative base groups in the initial seminar meeting, all subsequent interactions during the seminar are organized around these cooperative groups. One such interaction involves having candidates identify their single most successful lesson and prepare this lesson for discussion with their base group. Candidates have guidelines as to how to prepare for this discussion and provide copies to each base group member, and to me as the instructor. The net effect of the interaction among base group members is an increased feeling of efficacy on the part of each teacher candidate and a higher level of support by base group members to corroborate and affirm the successful teaching of their peers.

A candidate currently completing her student teaching semester made the following comments about her cooperative learning experiences throughout her program:

I can specifically remember being in cooperative learning groups in almost every course in the program. I think I will be a much more effective teacher from those experiences. I know that when I am applying to schools for a job I will capitalize on my knowledge of cooperative learning. My experiences during student teaching have shown me how important cooperative learning is in promoting responsibility and leadership among learners. The only suggestion I would have for the program regarding cooperative learning is that inevitably some students will carry more weight than others in a group project. There is a need to make certain that each student does his or her own part.

A cooperating teacher who has had many years of experience with Niagara University student teachers was asked about his opinions of the results of the program:

The graduates of your program are absolutely prepared for using cooperative learning, and the field experience serves as a good means to practice that preparation. In student teaching we expect that. They must build groups, manage, and teach using cooperative learning. When my student teachers use cooperative learning, I require them to do much more specific plans than if they were using traditional methods. They have to break down the lesson plan into detailed bits, and it is more difficult to plan. I also feel that the informal dialogue that takes place between cooperating teachers and student teachers helps them to learn from each other. The only thing that might help future teachers to use cooperative learning more effectively is more practice in the field. They need lots of practice, the more the better.

A first year teacher, and recent graduate of the secondary program had this to say about her experiences with cooperative learning:

I find that I am more prepared to use cooperative learning than some of my fellow teachers. I distinguish between cooperative learning and regular groupwork. In cooperative learning, I plan the groups, looking at a variety of factors. It is an activity that students look forward to, and students help each other. I think that having my professors incorporate the strategies into our courses got us to buy into it, which is important because when people don't really understand it, they see it as a waste of time. Cooperative learning is a great teaching and testing method, a great motivator. I use it and give extra points when students work well together. It helps to bring all students up to a higher level. If I had to recommend anything to the program about how to encourage teachers to use cooperative learning, it would be to emphasize that they should use it at least once a week; caution them not to withhold cooperative learning as a punishment for their high school students; and caution them that if it didn't work the one time you tried, try again. When it's set up and done correctly, it works.

ISSUES AND CONCERNS

Despite our great efforts to instill in candidates the ability and desire to implement cooperative learning strategies, several issues and concerns have surfaced and fall into two arenas. Some concerns are related to how we operate on campus. Other concerns arise within the local secondary schools that our students enter. In examining each we hope to offer insights so that these concerns might be less prevalent in similar programs hoping to include a cooperative learning focus.

On campus the majority of our full-time faculty members in the Education Department use cooperative learning to some degree in teaching their classes. Those who began using it years ago have experienced positive results, have kept up with the literature, and are comfortable teaching their students how to implement it in their future classrooms. However, several faculty members, both full-time and adjunct, have not had these experiences to draw from and probably did not experience cooperative learning themselves as students. These faculty members are less confident about addressing many of the concerns preservice teachers have about cooperative learning and therefore may weaken the link in promoting its use.

Further, faculty members from the arts and sciences teaching our students generally conduct their classes using a lecture-oriented approach (though we have evidence that they are moving toward more active learning strategies) and have been known to ridicule the education faculty for over-emphasizing groupwork. Although our preservice teachers seem to overwhelmingly favor the use of cooperative learning in the education classes they take at Niagara University, research suggests that they are likely to teach their discipline in the manner they were taught (NASSP, 1996). If the instruction they receive in their discipline follows a lecture-driven format, they are likely to believe that although cooperative learning is effective in some courses, it must not be effective in their subject area. Otherwise, why wouldn't their professor be using it? For this reason it is to our benefit to have professors in other departments use cooperative learning in their classes.

We have taken several steps in the past to encourage dialogue among faculty members, both full-time and adjunct. Each summer the Dean of the College of Education has called a meeting with full-time and adjunct faculty for the purpose of examining our past progress and future goals. At these meetings faculty review our philosophical framework and explore the relationship between the framework and our own teaching practices. In discussing strategies such as cooperative learning, faculty help one another develop as instructors by sharing successes and concerns. Another means of encouraging dialogue about cooperative learning has been through classroom observations. For full-time, untenured faculty, these observations take place twice in the first year of teaching and at least once in the following years. Part-time faculty members are observed each year as well. Conferences following these teaching observations often reflect upon the effectiveness of strategies for cooperative learning.

We have recently begun working on several other ways to improve our program. We are creating an adjunct handbook in which we will share our philosophical framework and our commitment to cooperative learning. With the urging of many new faculty members, we intend to build time into our regular meetings for professional development and sharing so that we can learn together and from one another. Several new faculty members have taken the opportunity to observe classes of professors who use cooperative learning. We intend to do more of this. Team teaching, which frequently occurs in the summer, provides us with further learning opportunities.

To address our concerns about faculty outside the Education Department who work with our education students, but who use a lecture approach to teaching, we are developing a grant to establish a Center for College Teaching. This center, currently being planned by four of our institution's recipients of Outstanding Teacher Awards, will provide a forum for dialogue about effective teaching practices, including cooperative learning. It is our hope that cooperative learning will eventually become common across all disciplines so that our education students will see that it can be effective in their content area and as a result, will use this approach in their own future classrooms.

Off campus, in the secondary schools, we want our students to be in classrooms where the teachers share our philosophy and utilize effective teaching practices including cooperative learning. In reality, this does not always occur. Each district has its own policy on selecting cooperating teachers and because we need to place all of our students, we must take the available placements.

When our students enter their teaching placements, it is often the case that their cooperating teacher does not use cooperative learning. Candidates who believe that their cooperating teachers are not supportive of these methods may be less likely to use it for fear of receiving a poor evaluation. If the student does attempt to use these strategies, the lack of teacher support may be detrimental to its success. In fact, in a survey conducted with the supervisors of our student teachers, we found that the main reason that student teachers did not use cooperative learning in their placements was the classroom teacher's negative attitude. Classroom teachers who are graduates of our program were using cooperative learning in their classrooms and were encouraging and supporting our student teachers in doing so as well. Obviously, we hope that the new graduates will also supervise our student teachers in the future.

Classroom management is another concern for our student teachers attempting to use cooperative learning in their placements. Secondary students whose regular teacher does not use cooperative learning may act out because of the novelty and unfamiliar freedom they experience with the new method, and this may further discourage the preservice teacher from experimenting with the strategy. Survey responses from our supervisors indicated that the second leading reason our candidates avoided using cooperative learning strategies was the lack of effective management of the classroom.

This issue of classroom management, an area in which novice teachers generally feel least prepared, is also pertinent to first-year teachers. These new practitioners are often overwhelmed by the many demands of having their own classroom. If they do not have a firm grounding in the philosophy, structures, and practices of cooperative learning, they may feel powerless. As a result, they may easily resort to classrooms of silent students sitting in rows. Unfortunately, this type of classroom is often preferred by school administrators who view them as more productive, and the teachers of such classrooms as more effective classroom managers. As graduates become part of the teaching force, institutions must increase support for cooperative learning by helping to establish networks. This often occurs as graduates return to their undergraduate institution for advanced studies.

We are currently implementing several steps to address concerns about student teaching placements. One step is to update the student teaching handbook to include information about the program's philosophical framework (including explicit information about cooperative learning) and our expectations for our student teachers. Another step is to meet with cooperating teachers to share this information verbally and to address any questions or concerns. In the past, a few of our professors have provided workshops for various districts on cooperative learning. It would be beneficial for us to offer these once again.

As a department, an institution, and a partner with local schools, we should engage in an open dialogue about our concerns related to implementation of cooperative learning. We must cultivate strong relationships with effective cooperative learning teachers in the field and on campus and use them to mentor our preservice teachers. We need to share ideas, our successes and failures, and supportive materials. We should open our classrooms to one another for feedback in a nonthreatening, supportive manner and actively pursue in-service training to develop a common understanding of this highly effective approach to teaching and learning.

CONCLUSION

Although we paint a rosy picture of the benefits of cooperative learning, we realize that there are many challenges to its effective implementation. As a faculty, we readily admit that candidates do not always enjoy working in the groups we design. In many situations, certain candidates carry much more of the workload then others. We find ourselves playing the role of group therapist more often than we would like. Finally, we understand that students are experiencing a serious disparity between their preparation courses and the reality of their experiences in secondary classrooms, leading to a loss of confidence in the ideals presented in their education program.

In spite of these challenges, we must keep three things clear if we are to bring about true change in the way secondary students are educated. First, if we don't create reflective experiences with cooperative learning, future secondary teachers are unlikely to ever use them and thus they will perpetuate the failure to reach standards. Second, the job of today's teacher is not just that of knowledge transmitter (Darling-Hammond, 1997). Teachers are problem-solvers, motivators, challengers, and counselors, and they need to have the in-depth knowledge of others that can only come from intimate experiences with other human beings. Lastly, the adolescents of the future will be knowledge-workers and human managers, working frequently in teams and groups and they need to be prepared for this reality. If we as secondary teacher educators do not initiate the establishment of a community of learners wherein students, teachers, administrators, and professors work together to generate, examine, and reflect upon learning we do nothing to resolve the problem. As Franklin D. Roosevelt once said, "People acting together as a group can accomplish things that no individual acting alone could ever hope to bring about."

REFERENCES

Aronson, E., Blaney, N., Stephan, C., Sikes, J., & Snapp, M. (1978). *The Jigsaw classroom*. Beverly Hills: Sage.

Clarke, J., Wideman, R., & Eadie, S. (1990). *Together we learn*. Scarborough, Ontario: Prentice-Hall Canada.

Cohen, E. G. (1994). *Designing groupwork* (2nd ed). New York: Teachers College Press.

Darling-Hammond, L. (1997). *The right to learn*. San Francisco: Jossey Bass.

Foote, C. J., Vermette, P. J., Wisniewski, S., Agnello, A., & Pagano, C. (2000). The characteristics of bad high school teachers reveal avoidable behaviors for new teachers. *Education, 12*, 128–135.

Gardner, J. (1993). *Multiple intelligences: The theory in practice*. New York: Basic Books.

Goleman, D. (1995). *Emotional intelligence: Why it can matter more than IQ*. New York: Bantam.

NASSP. (1996). *Breaking ranks: Changing American institution*. Reston, VA: National Association of Secondary School Principals.

Hunter, M. (1994). *Enhancing teaching*. New York: MacMillan.

Johnson, D. W. & Johnson, R. J. (1989). *Cooperation and competition: Theory and research*.Edina, MN: Interaction Book Company.

———. (1992). *Creative controversy*. Edina, MN: Interaction Book Company.

Johnson, D. W., Johnson, R. J., & Holubec, E. J. (1994). *The nuts and bolts of cooperative learning*. Edina, MN: Interaction Book Company.

Kagan, S. (1990). The structural approach to cooperative learning. *Educational Leadership, 47*, 12–15.

———. (1992). *Cooperative learning*. San Clemente, CA: Kagan Cooperative Learning Co.

Sharan, S., & Sharan, Y. (1976). *Small group teaching*. Englewood Cliffs, NJ: Prentice Hall.

Sharan, S. (Ed.) (1994). *Handbook of cooperative learning methods*. Westport, CT: Greenwood Press.

Slavin, R. E. (1983). *Cooperative learning*. New York: Longman.

———. (1986). *Using student team learning* (3rd ed.). Baltimore, MD: Johns Hopkins University, Center for Research on Elementary and Middle Schools.

———. (1990). *Cooperative learning: Theory, research and practice*. Englewood Cliff, NJ: Prentice-Hall.

Vermette, P. J. (1998). *Making cooperative learning work: Student teams in K-12 classrooms*. Upper Saddle River, NJ: Merrill/Prentice-Hall.

———. (1994). Four fatal flaws: Avoiding the common mistakes of novice users of cooperative learning. *The High School Journal, 77*, 255–265.

CHAPTER 7

COOPERATION AND COLLABORATION IN A FOREIGN LANGUAGE TEACHER TRAINING PROGRAM

The LMR-Plus Model

CLAUDIA FINKBEINER

This chapter focuses on collaborative and cooperative learning in the context of foreign language teacher training in the European dimension. Teaching foreign languages has become one of the most pressing goals in the European educational context (Finkbeiner, 1995) and foreign language teacher training is being redefined and restructured. I will describe my approach to the redefinition of English as a Foreign Language training through the use of the Learner-Moderator-Researcher-plus (LMR-plus) Model of foreign language teaching. The LMR-Plus Model is a method employed at the university level primarily with teachers studying to become EFL (English as a Foreign Language) instructors. It has been developed and influenced by my own research, the research of Legutke (1998), and by many years of practical experience in the school and university settings. After describing the German university and school context, I will explain the LMR-Plus Model and will provide practical examples. The last part of the chapter is a report on a study of the implementation of the model.

The Campus

The model is used in teacher training classes offered in the Department of English and Romance Languages at the University of Kassel, Germany. The university has 18,000 students, 1,087 of whom study English; approximately 240 students study English for the primary school level, 80 for the secondary level one (*hauptschule* and *realschule*), and 228 for the secondary level one and two (grammar school), 20 for the vocational school level, and 220 for the master's level, and 196 for the diploma degree in business.

The University of Kassel is, as is every other German state university, tuition-free. The academic year is divided into two semesters of thirteen and fifteen weeks, respectively. Students spend the five months lecture-free time in school internships, exam preparation, paper writing, and living abroad to practice their foreign-language skills. They also hold part-time jobs to pay for living expenses during their studies. We advise students to plan for a stay of at least half a year at one of our partner universities in the English-speaking world.

One of our major goals is to make the foreign language a regular and normal tool for all our students. Studying in our department prepares them for using the language with native-like proficiency. We believe that teaching a foreign language successfully requires teaching it in the target language itself. Thus, English is our official classroom language and the required language for written papers. Cooperative learning offers a wonderful possibility for our students, not only to practice their teaching and learning strategies but also to practice the foreign language in small groups (Finkbeiner, 2002).

The German School System

Those university students qualifying for the teaching degree will work at one of the following levels of the German school system: primary (ages 6 to 10), secondary level one (ages 10 to 16), which includes *hauptschule* and *realschule*, gymnasium and comprehensive schools (integrating all three tracks), secondary level two gymnasium (ages 16 to 19), and vocational school (16-plus). Kindergarten (ages 3 or 4 to 6) is regarded as part of the preschool program.

At the end of a child's participation in primary school, parents have to decide together with the child and the teacher which one of the three secondary tracks the child will attend. *Hauptschule* is the first track, *realschule* the middle track, and *gymnasium* the third (highest) track. Students leaving *hauptschule* or *realschule* usually attend vocational school for at least three more years. Vocational schooling parallels an apprenticeship on the job. *Gymnasium* qualifies students for college and university directly. Students leaving gymnasium with the *abitur*, the final exam, are 19 to 20 years old, and have had twelve to thirteen years of schooling.

Students qualifying at the University of Kassel will be teaching in Hesse, a state which has quite a large number of comprehensive schools at secondary level one. Kassel students will be teaching in one of the levels and one of the specific tracks. This is according to their qualification for each specific school type and track as a primary school teacher, or as a *hauptschul, realschul,* or *gymnasium* teacher.

The Importance of Learning English in Germany. Because of the stress on foreign languages in general and on English in particular, the LMR-plus Model requires the students to function in English within the class. Foreign language teaching had always had great importance in Germany, but has increased after the fall of the Berlin Wall in 1989. The significance of learning European languages is stressed in Article 126 of the Maastricht Treaty, and, in addition, article 128 declares intercultural competence as an important goal (Finkbeiner & Koplin, 2002).

English has become the *lingua franca* of business, industry, commerce, trade, publishing, and of all computer-related fields (Finkbeiner, 1995). Other languages have to be taught as well. With a population of more than 320 million people, Europe has become the biggest labor market in the world. In order to make use of these new opportunities, Europeans have to become more mobile, both in their thinking and in their language proficiencies.

Germany, a country the size of Montana with a population of 82 million people, has, geographically speaking, 10 direct neighbors: Denmark, the Netherlands, Belgium, Luxembourg, France, Switzerland, Liechtenstein, Austria, the Czech Republic, and Poland. Europe is culturally and linguistically highly diverse (Finkbeiner & Koplin, 2000, 2002). For many people living in Germany, cities in some of the European border states are closer than any city in Germany. For example, a person living in the northernmost part of the country in the city of Kiel might prefer a job in the south of Denmark to one in the south of Germany. Yet, these options are only realistic if job seekers speak and understand the languages of their neighbors. Language is the most important precondition for successful cooperation in Europe. Therefore, the European Union declared the year 2001 as the European Year of the Foreign Languages. Foreign-language learning was further enhanced and fostered in that year.

English has been a requirement in all German schools except primary and remedial schools. Recently, English or French have been made requirements in primary schools in an increasing number of states. Thus, children start learning English or French as a foreign language at the age of 6, 8, or 10. English is the language most frequently taught as the first foreign language. In 1998/99 according to the Statistisches Bundesamt of Germany (2000) over six million students were learning English as a foreign language in Germany. *Second* foreign languages are typically French or Latin, Ancient Greek, Italian, Russian, or Spanish. In addition, the languages of the European neighbors are taught. In some of the sixteen federal states, students study Turkish and Portuguese and Asian languages, such as Chinese or Japanese.

THE LMR-PLUS MODEL

The LMR-Plus Model focuses on higher mental functions developed through social interaction (Vygotsky 1962, 1978, 1982, 1983). Learning is viewed as occurring through social interaction that is closely connected to metacognitive processes related to the particular language use. This connection between social action and metacognition allows students to think in more complex ways.

Legutke's approach (1998) to professionalism in teacher training has had an impact on the development of model. Cohen's approach (1994) of complex instruction also influenced the LMR-Plus Model, particularly with respect to the creation of equal-status interaction in heterogeneous classrooms (Cohen & Lotan, 1997), and the power issues of discrepancies between students' mother tongue and the language of instruction (Cohen, Lotan, Scarloss, & Arellano, 1999). An understanding of teachers' professional development for cooperative learning has also informed this approach (Huber, 2001; Brody & Davidson, 1998).

What does LMR mean?

In this model, L stands for learner, M stands for moderator or teacher, and R stands for researcher. Legutke (1998) points out the necessity of a teacher always being a learner as well as a researcher. While the main focus of Legutke's model is on the changing role of the teacher, the LMR-Plus Model focuses on cooperation and collaboration among the changing and interchangeable roles of teacher and learner and researcher. As there are three different roles, students must acquire at least three different sets of competencies.

L as in learner. As a learner, one needs to develop learning strategies, learning techniques, and learning awareness. This set of competencies includes declarative ("knowing what"), procedural ("knowing how"), and situational ("knowing when") knowledge about learning (Garner, 1987, 1990), as well as appropriate use of strategies and learning techniques. Thus, learners need to know the facts about learning itself as well as how to make optimal use of these facts, and how, when, and where to apply them.

On the declarative level, students learn about the constituents of the model, such as learner, moderator, and researcher, along with examples of how to implement the model. For example, they learn different approaches to cooperative learning such as working with partners, developing expertise, solving problems cooperatively, and project learning (Huber, 2001). They also learn to articulate what they think about cooperative learning.

On the procedural level students then try to implement their knowledge in class, which allows them to simulate the real-life situation. Then they implement these strategies in their preservice teaching, learning to take different learner types into account and implementing a holistic and action-oriented method of teaching. Very often there is considerable discrepancy between what students have read and seemed to have understood and what they then do in the real teaching practice. Unanticipated and unpredictable events, such as not having enough worksheets for each group member, not having clarified the instruction enough, or not having calculated enough time for the groupwork evaluation phase can contribute to major chaos in class.

On the situational level, students have to learn how to apply and differentiate different approaches to cooperative learning, depending on factors such as homogeneity or heterogeneity of groups and learner types, age of the students, language proficiency level, gender, motivational status, and interest.

To build a metacognitive awareness about their own individual learning processes, it is very important that students relate to, reflect upon, and evaluate their own learning biographies and actions. This process demystifies professional conduct and attitudes and leads to a concept of professionalism that is no longer characterized by strict authority, control, and instruction but rather by democratic cooperation and collaboration. Students acknowledge expertise within learner groups, and acquire competence in self-directed and autonomous learning.

M *as in moderator*. As a moderator, one needs organizational skills, as well as strategies for presentation and moderation. Organizational skills include giving task and learner orientations and developing criteria for the appropriateness of tasks and topics. A metacognitive awareness of these techniques allows the individual to revise his or her theories on moderating and teaching groups.

R *as in researcher*. A researcher's profile contains an elaborate diagnostic competence, the ability to develop and use tests, and respect for specific standards of reliability and validity in tests and research results. For example, in this role, a teacher needs to make sure that test objectives are carefully defined. In using peer assessment, the researcher-teacher needs to make sure that peers know how to assess one another in particular situations.

LMR *as in learner, moderator, and researcher*. Each participant in the EFL classroom, as well as any other classroom, is regarded as all three: learner, moderator, and researcher. This, in turn, supports the idea of life-long learning. Being a member of an LMR group, one has to acknowledge the different roles and the expertise of someone cooperating as a partner on an equal basis. For teachers or professors, this means the capacity to learn to let go, recognizing that they might be novices in certain fields where their students might be the experts. This requires a certain attitude that allows for cooperative and collaborative learning.

Each participant has to develop a differentiated set of competencies depending on the situation-specific role one holds at the very moment of learning.

What is the "Plus" in the model about? The "Plus" refers to the fact that we use the foreign language as a vehicle for classroom communication. Using a foreign language involves knowledge about a different culture, empathy for others, the capacity to change perspectives and see the world through the other person's eyes, and the power to negotiate and give critical yet constructive feedback to peers.

When and How Often Do We Teach the Model?

On our campus, all classes on EFL teaching and on foreign language research are based on the LMR-Plus Model. The team responsible for the EFL teacher-training and foreign-language research consists of several doctoral students, three pedagogical assistants, one lecturer, approximately five student tutors, and a professor. As our team shares the same strong belief and appreciation for the underlying philosophy of the LMR-Plus model, it has become the essential teaching and learning approach in all our classes.

In the large (more than 120 students) introductory course in EFL teaching, students first become acquainted with the model and its practice. The LMR-Plus Model allows us to teach and manage very large classes. Specific class duties and assignments are distributed to different groups, thereby developing differentiated expertise in a range of topics and fields that are relevant for the introduction to EFL teaching methodology and research. Students must share responsibilities for the success of the learning outcomes and thus develop into more autonomous learners.

In the follow-up courses on EFL teaching and foreign-language research, the model and cooperative learning are not the topic of the classes themselves, but function as vehicles to transmit subject matter. These courses are seminars with topics such as "Learning Strategies and Learning Techniques in Foreign-Language Teaching," "Teaching Literature in the EFL Class," "Holistic and Action-Oriented Teaching of English," "Evaluation of the EFL Classroom," "Intercultural Learning" (Finkbeiner & Koplin, 2002; Schmidt, 2001), and "A Constructivist Approach to EFL Teaching."

Students must complete two school internships organized with direct cooperation of university and schools. They are assisted by highly qualified teachers and by our pedagogical assistants. The internships allow students to apply the LMR-Plus Model directly in class and to reflect on their practice. Before they apply the model in the school setting, they have many opportunities to practice it in team teaching in one of our classes on EFL teaching and EFL research.

How Do We Form Groups?

In each seminar permanent as well as temporary groups are formed. The temporary groups are newly formed in each session. The formation is open, semiopen, or structured. When it is open, we allow students to join each other in groups as they like. When it is semiopen we usually encourage students of the same teaching profile to join each other in groups with specific profile-oriented group tasks. When it is structured, we usually randomly assign students to groups.

All students must commit themselves to one permanent group (of three or four students) at the beginning of the semester. We form permanent groups according to the students' programs, for example, primary or secondary school, business, etc. We also try to form groups with equal numbers of male and female students, but given the higher percentage of women, this is not always possible.

Group Liabilities and Group Commitments

Each permanent group is fully responsible for conducting the whole class with cooperative activities for one session. The group plans the sessions together, with the professor giving major input during the planning phase. The students practice and usually improve their English during the phases of planning, presentation, evaluation, and writing the paper. The professor, as well as the students, has to adopt very different roles as indicated by the model. The professor also provides feedback on teaching style as well as linguistic proficiency.

Since we only use four-person groups, there may be more groups than sessions if the class is large. In this case, we give alternative tasks that are not presented in class but are just as challenging from a cooperative point of view.

Following the initial planning session, students divide the labor, each becoming an expert in a different part of the task. This phase includes individual reading assignments. The next planning session builds on individual work, preparing for the presentation, and developing instructions and tasks for the temporary groups. At this point, there is a second meeting with the professor who suggests material and forms of interaction. In a final e-mail to the professor, the group delivers a detailed timetable for the session along with plans for materials and classroom management. This is very important as it forces the students to structure their ideas precisely in written form. Following the presentation, there is a class and group evaluation, a written assignment, and a final reflection and evaluation. The professor, with an assisting doctoral student, meets with the group for one or two postevaluation session(s).

How to Become an Expert

For the cooperative team to function optimally we have to make sure that group members represent different fields and aspects of a particular task. Members bring their individually acquired knowledge to the group, sharing it, and making it public property, so that there is a high level of group synergy. This can only happen if, socially and emotionally, there is a "good feeling" in the group. Otherwise teamwork can become a scenario in which some students team and others work alone.

Mutual support, respect, and the acceptance of certain rules set by the group and class can create good feeling and group commitment. If we allow students to become experts, integrating their unique knowledge into the group work, we can establish respect and acceptance more easily. This is particularly crucial for students having status problems. We have observed that as soon as a student functions as an expert in class, the acceptance, respect, and appreciation of his peers towards him or her increase.

Groups are deliberately formed to encourage individual expertise. For example, a typical heterogeneous team is the following: Christine, studying English and sports for secondary level; Yeshim, studying English and math for the primary level; Peter, studying English and music for secondary level; and Polyxenie, studying English and German for the vocational school level. Their task is to prepare a session in a class on "Literacy Development in the EFL Class." Their topic is "Cooperative Practice for Creative Work with Multiethnic Literary Texts." The team chooses, as their overall goal, the production of creative, motivating, and authentic cooperative tasks relating to texts of bilingual and bicultural authors in North America. After analyzing the subject matter, they divide the labor so that each group member has an independent and specific task. In this group, the formation of experts is straightforward because each member represents a different teaching profile and has unique knowledge of the curricula as well as the developmental and psychological requirements of each age group. Thus, each member concentrates on multiethnic literature for children in a different age group.

After the group members complete their individual projects, they come together for intense evaluation and final planning of the class session. As bicultural members, Yeshim (Turkish-German) and Polyxenie (Greek-German) are experts on the bicultural point of view and contribute to a constructive exchange of ideas, evaluation, and feedback. A presentation of individual results enables constructive planning for the group presentation and implementation in the class. Following this planning phase, the group meets with the professor and works out detailed and specific tasks for cooperative practice in class.

This group chooses Sandra Cisneros and Toni Morrison as authors representing multiethnic literature in North America. They find texts by these authors for both adult and young readers. The group prepares four different tasks with a similar cooperative format according to the different profiles represented in our class. After their presentation, in which they convey important background knowledge on different models of cooperative practice that seem useful for the teaching of multiethnic literary texts in an EFL class, they divide the class into temporary groups.

One temporary group receives a complete set of materials on Sandra Cisneros, including her texts, her biography etc. Their task is to implement multiethnic literature in cooperative learning arrangements in grades 9 and 10 of secondary level. The temporary group decides to use the expert method also known as Jigsaw (Huber, 2001). This allows the secondary students to select portions of text from an array. Each member becomes expert on one textual portion. After the meeting of the expert groups, original groups are reassembled so that every individual member of the group alternately has the role of teacher explaining and presenting material while other students have the chance to ask questions. The temporary group must simulate this process by having each member become expert on one of the texts. They then reflect on their cooperation while evaluating their learning process.

Students are encouraged to use similar tasks not only in the laboratory situation at university but also in their internships and preservice studies at school. Data from case studies show that this indeed happens.

Challenging Factors

We have experienced a few difficulties in implementing the LMR-Plus Model. The first problem concerns the issue of feedback during the evaluation phase. Positive feedback is not readily accepted in the culture of the German educational system. The student receiving the positive feedback and praise from a teacher might experience extreme peer-group pressure and the derogatory label of *streber* (geek or nerd). In addition, our students' feedback in English is sometimes very simplified due to lack of vocabulary and is not sufficiently specific. They tell their fellow students whether their work is "good" or "bad," with nothing in between. To deal with the vocabulary problem, we have implemented an additional task for groups in which we ask them to create a glossary with a wide range of terms that could be used for more specific feedback.

A second difficulty arises from unique university conditions. In many classes there are no obligatory assignments for all students in class, only for those who wish to gain credits. These are acquired through papers and class presentations. Because German universities are tuition-free, many students attend but do not contribute actively to class. This, of course, undermines the principles of the LMR-Plus Model that relies on the active contribution of all participants.

The third difficulty is irregular attendance in a tuition-free university system. Class attendance is based on the free decision of each individual. In one session there might be fifty students present, and in another only thirty. I personally have resolved this problem by insisting on attendance as well as the active contribution of all. This does, of course, represent a contradiction between my insistence and the underlying democratic paradigm of the LMR-Plus model.

The fourth difficulty is the large, heterogeneous groups. We have a growing number of re-entry students with many years of work experience. Also growing is the number of students with young families in their care. A large percentage of our students work and go to school simultaneously. This means that the age of the participants, and the amount of time they can spend on their studies varies. Class members also vary in the amount of teaching experience they have had, as well as in their ability to speak English fluently.

OVERVIEW OF THE STUDY

In the final section of this chapter, I report some results of a study of EFL candidates in the introductory and advanced courses. An attitudinal questionnaire provides general responses to cooperative class activities. In analyzing the data, I compare beginning students with more advanced students in order to test the prediction that there will be long-term attitudinal effects of the cooperative practices of the LMR model as students advance through their studies. I also investigate whether there are gender differences in response to cooperative activities.

Following the results of this study, I present excerpts from one student's journal as she tries to use the LMR-Plus Model in her internship (see heading below, "Journal Entry from the Classroom"). These excerpts illustrate the successes and challenges of a beginner's use of the model.

Setting and Sample

The questionnaires were administered to EFL students in the summer of 1999. Of 200 questionnaires distributed, 104 were returned. The beginning and the advanced students constitute two subsamples. The sampling and method for distribution of questionnaires varied for the two different samples.

For the first sample taking the introductory EFL course, the testers handed out the questions to the students directly who filled them in during class and returned them immediately. For the second sample, the questionnaires were also given directly to the students. They were, however, returned within a week.

All students of the first sample (N = 54) attended our introductory course in foreign language teaching and had just become acquainted with the LMR-Plus Model for the first time. Thus, their experience with cooperative practice was based only on the short time they had attended the course and the probable prior knowledge that dated back to being a student at a secondary school themselves.

The second sample, Advanced EFL (N = 50), consisted of advanced EFL students attending different courses in the EFL section of our department. Students of the second sample were significantly beyond introductory level in their knowledge about and experience with the LMR-Plus Model.

Approximately two-thirds of both samples were women. Samples were also comparable in age although the average age of the advanced EFL sample was slightly higher. They ranged from nineteen to thirty-nine, with the majority under twenty-six years old. The two samples were also comparable in their teaching profiles.

Questionnaire

The questionnaire was developed on the basis of research conducted by von Saldern and Littig (1987), Huber (2001), and Eder (1996). I was the principal investigator and Kruswitz and Viehman (1999) served as student assistants. The questionnaire contained twenty items about negative and positive responses to cooperative learning, specifically students' attitudes and concrete behavior in different situations concerning cooperation. We wanted to find out how much students were willing to cooperate with one another and whether there were significant differences (a) between the Intro EFL and Advanced EFL groups; (b) between the different age groups and student profiles; and (c) between the two genders. We hoped to see the long-term effects of the LMR-Plus Model and cooperative practices employed. We posed the questions in German. Response options were the following: "I fully disagree, I partly disagree, I partly agree, I fully agree." Responses were coded in order of an increasing amount of agreement from 1 to 4. Sample items included:

> "During seminars I am only interested in my own success" (how one values one's own success at the expense of peers' success);
> "If we do groupwork, I try to work with my friend when possible" (students' social behavior concerning group formation);
> "I prefer to solve difficult problems alone" (whether students saw difficult situations as conflicting with the idea of groupwork); and
> "A student who knows more than others would be stupid if he gave up this advantage by working together with others" (students

willingness to share their knowledge with other students if it might interfere with their own success).

The statistics were calculated for the following subgroups: Intro EFL and Advanced EFL, Intro-EFL: Male and Intro EFL: Female, Advanced EFL: Male and Advanced EFL: Female, Intro EFL: Age and Advanced EFL: Age, and Intro EFL: Teaching Profile and Advanced EFL: Teaching Profile. The following statistics were calculated with SPSS: descriptive statistics (frequencies and mean values), multivariate analyses (factor analyses), correlation analyses, and Student's t-Test.

Results: Introductory Group Versus Advanced Group

On a number of the items, the more advanced students chose the responses more favorable to cooperative groupwork. For example, disagreement was the more favorable response on the item "I try to do my work better than the others." Although a majority of both samples disagreed with the item, 79 percent of the Advanced EFL group disagreed in comparison to 68 percent of the Intro EFL group. A test of the difference between means of the two samples yielded a statistically significant t value of 1.82 ($p = .04$).

The majority of students found that groupwork enhanced their ability to deal with difficult problems. For example, for the item "I can understand difficult problems better when I work them out with other students" the Advanced EFL group showed stronger agreement than the Intro EFL group. Forty percent of the advanced students fully agreed with this item while only 17.3 percent of the beginners fully agreed. The mean difference was statistically significant ($p = .04$).

A negatively worded item was "A student who knows more than others would be stupid if he gave up this advantage by working together with others." The majority of the respondents preferred sharing their knowledge with others rather than holding back in order to have an individual benefit. Comparison of the two samples shows that the more advanced students were more likely to disagree with this item than the beginners. The mean difference was statistically significant ($p = .04$).

There is strong statistical evidence that Advanced EFL students believe themselves likely to accept influence from others. On the item "I am very easily persuaded to change my opinion," 13.7 percent of the Intro EFL group partly agreed and none of the students fully agreed. In contrast, of the Advanced EFL group, 2 percent fully agreed, and 25 percent partly agreed with the item. In this case the Student's t-Test reveals statistically significant differences in the mean values of the two groups: $t = -2.92$; $p = .002$.

In summary, both groups were likely to choose the cooperative response. As predicted, advanced students consistently chose more cooperative responses than beginners. This was probably a result of their continuing exposure to cooperative practices in their classes at the university, and more particularly to the LMR-Plus Model. The consistency of response differences across positively and negatively worded items supports this interpretation.

Results: Gender Issue

On several questionnaire items, women gave more favorable responses to cooperative practices than men. For example, there was a marked difference in the average response to the following item: "During seminars I am only interested in my own success." Using two-tail probabilities, a t-test revealed that men were significantly more likely than women to agree with this item. When the t-tests were calculated separately for the beginning and advanced students, the direction of the difference was the same for both groups and the difference reached statistical significance for the Advanced EFL group ($p = .01$). I have observed, for example, that men are more likely to act as a speaker during presentations. Women in both groups are more likely to set their own success behind the success of the group.

There is a tendency for women to prefer to work with their friends during groupwork ("If we do groupwork I try to work with my friends when possible."). The difference in the means approached statistical significance with women more likely to agree with this item than men within each of the two groups.

On a final item, a majority of male students agreed that they prefer to solve more difficult problems alone. The t-tests show statistically significant differences in the mean values between female and male respondents within the advanced group ($p = .013$) and a borderline significant result for gender in the Intro EFL group ($p = .061$). This means that the female respondents are more likely to persist in groupwork even if the situation turns out to be difficult.

Journal Entry from the Classroom

As a part of ongoing case studies, I have followed a few students from their beginning in the program into their experiences as novice teachers. I asked them to what extent they implemented cooperative learning in their own classrooms. The excerpts of the following case study (Christine) underscore the willingness of a young teacher to try the model, the awareness she developed concerning cooperative practice, as well as the difficulties she faced.

Christine's role as a moderator.

In groups my students deal with a task helping each other and I am only the initiator of their work. So, while cooperating they learn, first of all, different ways of learning.

The issue of expertise.

They also take up different roles or positions according to their knowledge or skills. As I vary my tasks there is always an expert for something: if-clauses, rhymes, present perfect, etc.

Group feeling.

The task-based orientation of their cooperation makes it easier for the students to accept *themselves* as a group because it is not easy for them to accept a randomly assembled group or a group that I have designed.

Problems and challenges.

The challenges I have to face mostly have to do with the problem that students first have to get used to cooperative learning. Most of my students are in puberty so they don't want to cooperate with some other students. Also, they often don't start working in groups because they are used to exactly defined working steps by their teachers and they have to learn that they have to work out cooperative strategies to fulfill their tasks.

Another problem in my class is that with 33 students there is not much space for the groups and it easily gets very noisy. Since I am still in a teacher's training course I sometimes feel awkward because I know that there is a class next door that is working very quietly and can feel disturbed by us. In the school I am teaching at, some teachers prefer traditional teacher-centered classes because they feel that it is difficult to teach 24 lessons a week with 33 students in each class if you always have noisy lessons. I can understand this view and respect their opinion but since I am not teaching more than 10 lessons a week at the moment, I myself prefer lively lessons and feel more tense if I have to catch the student's attention for 45 minutes.

Self-reflection on critical role in groupwork phases.

It is difficult not to be the center of attention once you join a group. Of course, it is good that the students can ask me for help or I can give them advice if I see that they don't progress, but I don't like to interfere once they are working successfully as a group. I enjoy the chance to get to know individual students better and I get to know which positions they take up when working in a group or when presenting their results. I then know which tasks I can give them next time so that they might take up another position and, for example, have the important experience of once being an expert in something.

Changes in the role of teacher.

My role as a teacher has changed to that of a more relaxed and flexible moderator. In front of the whole class I have to respond to 33 impulses but when they are working in groups, I can concentrate on one group. I can give more individual feedback to individual mistakes or text productions. I also have the chance to have a look at their productions and thus I have a better overview of what they have understood or if there are still problems with a certain subject matter. I can join groupwork, but I can also retreat to remain the neutral moderator when they present their results. I like this role because it is more realistic: As a teacher I cannot make them learn something, I can only create suitable settings for learning. I think it is better to make the students aware of the fact that they are responsible for their learning process and success. It is more adequate to be the moderator and initiator and a helping hand for them because I cannot claim to be more.

CONCLUSION

The results of the questionnaire study illustrate the overall positive attitudes toward cooperative practices. The differences between the students who had only taken an introductory course and the advanced students suggest that the key to changing some negative attitudes toward cooperation is a long-term effort with continuing cooperative practice in the university classroom. As the students progressed they became increasingly more favorable towards cooperative practice.

The gender issue is one that requires further research. One can only speculate how gender differences are manifested in the predominantly female classes we observed. One wonders whether the differences in attitude cause problems in mixed-gender groupwork. For example, if the men feel that when the task has become difficult they will do better by themselves whereas the women prefer to persist as a group, one can imagine either withdrawal from active participation by the men or overt conflict. In addition, power and status problems are probably connected to these differences in attitude, making some men prefer individual performance. If the professor does not intervene, for example, male students will tend to present the group's work. "Game rules" for presentation teams can help overcome the problem. One can mandate, for example, that students have to take turns to present. One can also suggest, that each person in a team has equal time within each presentation. Additionally, one can conduct exercises with the goal of learning to share time fairly as a democratic principle (Cohen, 1994).

The case study clearly illustrates a high level of awareness about the issues and problems raised in the LMR-Plus Model and in cooperative practice in general. Christine, the young teacher, shows proficiency as a reflective practitioner in analyzing the context of teaching and the variables that enhance or hinder cooperative learning.

In conclusion, the importance of creating a high level of awareness about these issues within students becomes clear: What students perceive and learn on campus is formed into perception-expectation hypotheses. The students must not only experience cooperative practices consistently at the university, but they must move through a process of acquiring favorable attitudes toward cooperative practice to an expectation that they will try out these practices. Moreover they must develop a metacognitive awareness of what they are doing and why they are doing it. At minimum, if we do not consistently implement cooperative practice in classes on campus *today* and make it a regular and daily practice, our students will not apply cooperative practices *tomorrow*.

REFERENCES

Brody, C., & Davidson, N. (Eds.). (1998). *Professional development for cooperative learning. Issues and approaches*. Albany: State University of New York Press.

Cohen, E. G. (1994). *Designing groupwork* (2nd ed.). New York: Teachers College Press.

Cohen, E. G., & Lotan, R. A. (Eds.). (1997). *Working for equity in heterogeneous classrooms: Sociological theory in practice*. New York: Teachers College Press.

Cohen, E. G., Lotan, R. A., Scarloss, B. A., & Arellano, A. R. (1999). Complex instruction: Equity in cooperative learning classrooms. *Theory Into Practice, 38*(2), 80–86.

Eder, F. (1996). *Schul- und klassenklima. Ausprägung, determinanten und wirkungen des klimas an weiterführenden schulen*. Innsbruck: Studien Verlag.

Finkbeiner, C. (1995). *Englischunterricht in europäischer dimension. Zwischen Qualifikationserwartungen der gesellschaft und schülereinstellungen und schülerinteressen. Berichte und kontexte zweier empirischer untersuchungen*. Bochum: Dr. Brockmeyer.

————. (2002). Foreign language practice and cooperative learning. In C. Finkbeiner (Ed.), *Wholeheartedly English: A life of learning.* Berlin: Cornelsen.

Finkbeiner, C., & Koplin, C. (2000). Handlungsorientiert Fremdverstehen lernen und lehren. *Fremdsprachenunterricht, 44/53*(4), 254–261.

————. (2002). The ABC's Model: A cooperative approach for facilitating intercultural education. *Reading Online*, November. Retrieved October 30, 2002, from http://www.readingonline.org.

Garner, R. (1987). *Metacognition and reading comprehension.* Norwood, NJ: Ablex Publishing Corporation.

Garner, R. (1990). When children and adults do not use learning strategies: Towards a theory of setting. *Review of Educational Research, 60*(4), 517–529.

Huber, G. L. (2001). Kooperatives Lernen im Kontext der Lehr-/Lernformen. In C. Finkbeiner & G. Schnaitmann (Eds.), *Lehren und lernen im kontext empirischer forschung und fachdidaktik* (pp. 222–245). Donauwörth: Auer.

Krusewitz, U., & Viehmann, A. (1999). *The development of a research project concerning cooperation.* Unpublished manuscript, University of Kassel, Germany.

Legutke, M. K. (1998). The English teacher as learner and researcher. In H.-E. Piepho, & A. Kubanek-German (Eds.), *"I beg to differ." Beiträge zum sperrigen interkulturellen Nachdenken über eine Welt in Frieden* (pp. 153–167). München: Iudicium.

Statistisches Bundesamt (2000). *Allgemeinbildende Schulen. Schuljahr 1999/2000. Ergänzende Tabellen zur Fachserie 11 Bildung und Kultur, Reihe 1 – Allgemeinbildende Schulen.* Wiesbaden: Statistisches Bundesamt.

von Saldern, M., & Littig, K.-E. (1987). *Landauer Skalen zum Sozialklima 4.-13. Klassen, LASSO 4-13.* Weinheim: Beltz.

Vygotsky, L. S. (1962). *Thought and language* (E. Hanfmann & G. Vakar, Eds. and Trans.). Cambridge, MA: MIT Press.

Vygotsky, L. S. (1978). *Mind in society.* Cambridge: Harvard University Press.

Vygotsky, L. S. (1982). *Collected works.* In 6 volumes. Vol. 2. Moscow: Pedagogica.

Vygotsky, L. S. (1983). *Collected works.* In 6 volumes. Vol. 3. Moscow: Pedagogica.

CHAPTER 8

THE INTEGRATED SEMESTER

Building Preservice Teachers' Commitments to the
Use of Cooperative Learning as Essential Pedagogy

FRANCES SLOSTAD, LYNDA BALOCHE, AND DANIEL DARIGAN

West Chester University is a regional comprehensive university with a long history of teacher education. The Department of Elementary Education has the largest number of students in the university with approximately twelve hundred students seeking elementary certification. Over nine hundred of these students are undergraduates and, at the undergraduate level, students are required to complete professional education courses that are housed in ten separate departments.

Program coherence is a constant challenge. The notions of textbook adoptions by course and common syllabi are typically rejected by faculty and the "home department" has very little influence in decisions made about courses in the other departments. In spite of these constraints—or perhaps because of them—several small, innovative programs have developed within this large program of loosely coupled courses. The undergraduate professional program includes two pre-student-teaching, field-based courses, only one of which is housed in the Department of Elementary Education. The other field-based course, a six-credit reading practicum, is housed in the Department of Literacy. Students typically complete this course in their junior year.

This six-credit, field-based course has been one center for innovation within the program. For instance, some faculty have linked this course with other literacy courses and focused their field experiences in an urban area; other faculty have focused their field experiences in a poor rural area—using the field component of the course to help make a significant intervention in a rural district. A third innovation—the result of several semesters of experimentation before settling into its present form—links nine additional credits of coursework that are housed in Elementary Education to the six-credit practicum and develops a semester-long cohort of approximately eighteen students. All of these innovations have been well received by students and each has been designed by individual faculty members or faculty members working in small, self-selected groups.

When viewed collectively, one benefit of these innovations is that they allow faculty to develop their own passions, and to share these passions with students, within a professional program that must answer both state and national accreditation mandates. To extend the analogy first developed by Powell, Farrar, and Cohen (1985), these innovations represent well-crafted "boutiques" strategically placed within the larger shopping mall. When first developed, students learned about these boutique experiences through word-of-mouth and personal contacts; now each is carefully described or "advertised" on a department bulletin board and in the course schedule book. By encouraging faculty to develop these special experiences, and by advertising these experiences, it is hoped that every student will select a "boutique experience" at least once in their undergraduate curriculum and thus get the benefit of an experience that has been customized to maximize students' contact with the particular passions of the faculty involved.

In many ways, the approach towards innovation taken in this program seems to be the antithesis to the concept of institutionalization and, indeed, this approach does little to guarantee similarity of experiences. It does, however, provide students with choices and encourages them to make choices that will more fully develop their interests and relationships with selected faculty. In a large program that could be somewhat impersonal, we think this is important. In a program that has struggled for coherence, we think this has proven to be an effective strategy.

In this chapter, we describe and examine one innovation that has been developed within the context described above. In place for over six years, this particular boutique experience has become known as the "Integrated Semester." We analyze students' weekly journal entries for emergent themes and utilize "Stages of Concern" strategies (Hall & Hord, 1987) as well. Through analysis of journal entries, we create a preservice teachers' profile of expressed values and concerns; this profile provides valuable information for continuous improvement of the courses in the Integrated Semester and potential insights for other teacher educators.

DESCRIPTION OF INTEGRATED SEMESTER

The Integrated Semester consists of a fifteen-credit block of courses: a six-credit "Reading Practicum" plus three credits each of "Self and Group Processes in Diverse Classrooms," "Creativity in the Classroom," and "Classroom Management." Typically, three faculty share responsibility for the fifteen credits and "Self and Group" and "Creativity" are taught by the same faculty member. Students enrolling in the integrated semester commit to an intensive five-day-a-week literacy practicum and three evenings of additional coursework. In comparison, other practicum sections spend only two mornings a week in their field placements and the students' additional coursework is not specifically designed to emphasize the connections between theory and the students' practicum experiences.

All the courses in the integrated semester are designed to complement each other and to explore the potential for constructivist-learning theory and practice through a variety of lenses. The primary lens chosen in "Self and Group" is cooperative learning and, within this course, a conceptual framework for cooperative learning is carefully explicated. Since this chapter is focused primarily on how students develop in relation to cooperative learning, the course content and structure of "Self and Group" will be described in some detail while the other on-campus courses will be referenced primarily as they relate to this course.

Self and Group Processes in Diverse Classrooms

In "Self and Group," students study socially constructed learning in general, and cooperative learning in particular, through (a) reading and study of theory and models; (b) experiential activities and reflection on those activities designed to provide students with "here and now" experiences related to the concepts being studied; (c) discussion and analysis of scenarios and case studies; and (d) observation, teaching, and reflection in their field placements. To develop a basic understanding of the nature of "group," basic principles of group structure—values, norms, and roles—are examined and selected models of group development are examined, with special emphasis on Schutz (1966). The works of Cohen (1986, 1994a, 1994b) and Banks (1993, 1994) are used to focus a study of equity and status issues and to build understanding of the need for learning opportunities that are complex and appropriate for diverse groups of learners. The basic model for cooperative learning includes the elements of positive interdependence, simultaneous interaction, individual responsibility, interpersonal and small-group learning skills, and reflection and planning. These components, often associated with the Johnsons (D. Johnson, R. Johnson, & Holubec, 1992; Baloche, 1998), serve as an organizing base for the study of cooperative learning. Students join together in base groups, informal groups, and formal learning groups (Johnson et al. 1992; Baloche, 1998). Various cooperative learning structures, typically associated with Kagan (1992; Baloche, 1998), are used throughout the course.

In "Self and Group" students are required to maintain a reflective journal. Journal topics are sometimes assigned by a professor; at other times the class is asked to suggest a useful topic for reflection. In addition to responding to specific topics, students are encouraged to use their journals to "keep track of events and to reflect privately on the personal and public meaning of those events. What happened? Why did it happen? What was my role? What beliefs did my actions reflect? How should I act in the future on the basis of what happened?" (Posner, 2000, p. 25). The journal requirement in this course is one piece of a programmatic requirement designed to encourage reflective practice; it culminates with a student-teaching journal. It is the "Self and Group" journal entries, from two semester's cohorts—a total of thirty-six students, that are analyzed and excerpted in this study.

The Practicum Experience

In the Integrated Semester section of "Reading Practicum," the professor meets with the students for ten, three-hour, on-campus class periods during the first two weeks of the semester. This intensive period of instruction, plus conferencing with the other faculty in the integrated experience, helps the professor to know the personalities, strengths, and potential limitations of each student. During this on-campus time, the professor models a wide variety of literacy lessons that emphasize literature-based instruction and process writing in real and authentic contexts. The objectives for this segment of the course include (a) reinforcing learning presented in previous literacy courses; (b) allowing students to experience, plan, and critique the kinds of holistic lessons we will be asking them to develop and teach; and (c) providing students with opportunities to interact in many literacy-related whole-class, small-group, and paired situations.

Students in the Integrated Semester are typically placed in three suburban elementary schools. The students are assigned to their field-placement classrooms for approximately twenty hours a week. This time commitment represents about sixty percent more time in the classroom than other reading practicum classes and helps students to develop closer relationships with the children and a feeling of continuity with the classroom. Since the practicum professor has worked with these schools fairly consistently for the past five years, the majority of teachers in these schools are well known to him. The practicum professor determines all student placements. His familiarity with the schools and teachers, coupled with the intensive period of campus-based instruction and the extensive time students devote to their field placement, increase the potential for successful collaboration between the students and their cooperating teachers. This track record of success tends to make teachers eager to work with students enrolled in the program.

The three schools serve a diverse population of children. In School A, the children are primarily European American and African American; they come from a wide range of socioeconomic backgrounds. In School B, the children are primarily European American and typically come from economically impoverished households. School C is linguistically and culturally diverse; the children bring approximately eighteen different primary languages to the school. Field placement classrooms in these three schools range from a developmental-kindergarten-first-grade combination up through fifth grade.

The university professor of the literacy component visits the schools twice each week. In addition to informal coaching sessions, each student receives two formal observations, once before and once after the midterm. Students receive both written and audio feedback based on these observations and these observations are viewed as a coaching tool for the students' continued growth as teachers of children. At the conclusion of the semester, each student videotapes a lesson. The student and the professor view this tape together, critiquing teaching strategies, analyzing children's reactions and responses, and evaluating student/child rapport.

SIGNIFICANT JOURNAL THEMES

Group Values, Norms, and Roles

During the first week of the semester, students are asked to write descriptions of two experiences they have had in classrooms when they were children: one "great" experience and one "not-so-great" experience. In preparation for the second week of classes, students are asked to read some theoretical material about group structure and development. Using a simple cooperative structure such as Group Interview (Baloche, 1998), students are then asked to share their great and less-than-great experiences. Group members help each other sift through their personal stories and begin to articulate the values underlying these classroom experiences, the norms that shaped the interactions, and the teacher and student roles that were assumed in each situation. In each group, students are asked to create a composite chart of values, norms, and roles; intergroup sharing of this work is facilitated with the help of a structure such as One-Stay

Three-Stray (Baloche) or Gallery Tour (Kagan 1992; Baloche, 1998). To facilitate a focus on the present, students are typically asked to articulate what values, norms, and roles are beginning to develop within the Integrated Semester and to document the "evidence" by responding to such questions as, "How do you know we [the faculty] want you to help each other?"

Once students move into their field placement, they are typically asked to articulate what values, norms, and roles they see in their placements. Although they had been asked primarily to focus on values, norms, and roles, several students began to comment on specifics of the cooperative model, suggesting that goal interdependence can be used to help create positive group norms. For example, one of the values is mutual respect. The class is child-centered. The teacher reminds children of group roles. They discuss and find solutions to problems that occur when working in a group. She stresses individual responsibility within the group and helping each other. The children know their responsibilities.

Building Positive Interdependence

Using the Johnson and Johnson Learning Together model as a guide, students are taught that, in addition to building a sense of whole-class identity and community, direct planning for positive interdependence is necessary within individual lessons. During university instruction, video clips and scenarios are used to develop this understanding. Sample lessons are examined to determine what types of positive interdependence might "make sense" within the context of a given lesson. Students develop lessons that incorporate different types of positive interdependence and cooperative structures are examined so that students begin to realize that different structures emphasize positive interdependence in different ways.

Several students' journal reflections suggest their understanding of the importance of positive interdependence. For instance, one student noted that "positive interdependence gives students structure and responsibility." Another thought she might "post the nine types of positive interdependence on my desk as a helpful reminder when planning lessons." Several students perceived a clear relationship between developing a sense of positive interdependence and teaching interpersonal skills. As one student wrote: "Teaching positive interdependence and [teaching interpersonal skills] go hand-in-hand."

Students used their developing sense of the concept of positive interdependence to (a) identify types of positive interdependence that they observe teachers use in their field placements; (b) suggest the use of carefully structured positive interdependence as a way to solve problems that they observed during groupwork; and (c) suggest how they might plan to develop positive interdependence at a later time. For example, one student said, "I see goal interdependence all of the time. Children come together to discuss a goal, ways to obtain the goal, and ways to maintain the goal. Also, children are assigned roles. They are assigned different roles in varying situations."

Teaching the Skills of Cooperation

As Johnson and Johnson recommend, students are taught that direct teaching of interpersonal and small-group learning skills is needed for success in small-group learning. To develop this understanding during university instruction, a wide variety of experiences and materials are used. Students complete short instruments that encourage them to examine their task and maintenance orientation (Bales, 1950, 1970) and their orientation towards conflict; they participate in "Fishbowls" (Baloche, Mauger, Willis, Filinuk & Michalsky, 1993) designed to encourage further examination of these same orientations. They are asked regularly to reflect on their own use of interpersonal skills within their cohort experience. Video clips and scenarios of classroom life are studied. Sample lessons are examined to determine what skills might "make sense" within the context of a given lesson; students each develop a lesson that uses a picture book to help teach an interpersonal skill. Cooperative structures are examined so that students begin to realize that different structures require different skills and levels of skills.

In their journals, students often linked their observations about levels of interpersonal skill use to their understanding of values, norms, and roles. This was expressed quite simply by one student as, "Respect is taught." Students tended to express a belief that (a) children would need to use these skills throughout their lives and that learning these skills could not be left to chance; (b) direct instruction is important; (c) children need to be provided with many opportunities to practice these skills; and (d) teachers need to provide appropriate feedback and to assess progress frequently. Many journal entries suggested that students were beginning to address directly the teaching of important interpersonal and small-group learning skills.

Using Informal Learning Groups

Using the Johnsons' distinctions among formal, informal, and base groups as a guide, scenarios, sample lessons, and analyses of specific structures are used to help students begin to distinguish among different "kinds" of groups for purpose, duration, and level of complexity in planning. Students remain in the same base group for the three university-based courses and also experience formal and informal groups during instruction. Students are encouraged to try informal groupings in their field placements and to incorporate some "simple" structures.

In their journals, students expressed (a) a level of valuing the use of these groups; (b) concern about the random grouping that the use of certain structures seemed to imply; and (c) concerns about management issues, especially when they described their own use of informal groups during their field placements:

> I have attempted [informal groups] in my second-grade class. It was harder than I thought it would be. I did not know how to pair the students up correctly. I pretty much let it go and hoped for a good turn out. My other concern is [what to do if] the groups do not get along and have great difficulty working together. Is it all right to stop the lesson and change members of the groups? Would this disrupt the lesson too much?

Cooperating Teachers as Models

Even with the careful placement of students in the field, some students were in field placements in which the careful use of cooperative learning was not modeled. These students often expressed conflict between their university class experiences and knowledge of cooperative learning strategies and their observations in their classroom placements. Journal reflections focused on the lack of cooperative experiences for children and on observing their cooperating teachers' unsuccessful efforts to implement cooperative learning. In these entries, students tended to diagnose the impediments they saw to implementation within their field placements and frequently used language and concepts they had been taught; they often suggested the developmental nature of learning to work together as well. For instance:

> She [the teacher] tries to use it, but it doesn't work properly. I can tell she has not taught any positive interdependence skills or roles for cooperation.
>
> Children work in pairs, but no one explained how to work cooperatively. Often she will pair them, but they will continue to work alone but sit together. It seems to me that resource interdependence is necessary here. This forces the students to work together because they rely on each other for pieces of information or materials. I plan to try this with two of my lessons next week.

Other student comments reflected (a) a personal lack of freedom or "authority" to implement cooperative learning; (b) cooperating teachers who changed (or suggested changes to) the students' cooperative learning lessons to meet their (supervising teacher's) personal teaching style; and (c) no effort by the classroom teacher to implement base groups, teach interpersonal skills, or generally to use the cooperative learning strategies our students were anxious to demonstrate.

One student said her supervising teacher's comments about her cooperative learning lessons were that her lessons were "fine," however, frequently added, "No . . . that's not the way I would do it!" As other students wrote about their frustration, they reflected on the values expressed by their teachers—implying that their frustration may have come from a lack of shared values with their cooperating teacher. One student, for instance, said simply that, in her placement, "peer discussions were not valued."

A Missing Vocabulary

In "Self and Group," equity and status issues are examined; the need for learning opportunities that are complex and appropriate for diverse groups of learners is emphasized. Students view video—especially *Status Treatments in the Classroom* (Cohen, 1994b)—learn how to collect and analyze sociometric data, develop lessons for children that use picture books to facilitate discussions about different kinds of abilities, and analyze scenarios and lessons. This work is supported in the Creativity course with an examination of various models of intelligence as discussed in Gardner (2000) and Sternberg (1988), in "Classroom Management" with the study of the theories of Albert, (1996), Nelson (Nelson, Lott, & Glenn, 1997) and Kohn (1996), and during early, university-based instruction in the "Practicum" when holistic planning is stressed.

Although it is not an expectation that during the semester students will become highly skilled at recognizing status problems and making effective status interventions, they are encouraged to analyze classroom interaction through a lens that includes the concepts of status and equal access. Some students did include observations about levels of participation in their journals but they tended not to use the vocabulary of this more sociological lens that they had been encouraged to explore. One student, for instance, mentioned a concern with quiet and dominant students, but not in a way that would suggest she had considered possible, socially constructed reasons for these behaviors: "I am concerned about take-over children. The children do not see themselves as a group. The quiet ones let others walk all over them. It's hard to watch and not step in."

Positive Practice Opportunities

Many of the preservice teachers in the Integrated Semester had positive opportunities to plan and implement the use of cooperative learning in their field placements; they typically targeted fairly simple learning goals and used simple and appropriate strategies to match their goals. Several students, for instance, felt confident using Think, Pair, Share (Baloche, 1998; Lyman, 1992) during their lessons. One student wrote, "I use it every day, during read-alouds." Others incorporated strategies whenever they felt they were appropriate and their examples suggest that they had chosen the strategies they used quite purposefully. For instance, one student reported, "I used Inside-Outside Circle (Baloche, 1998; Kagan, 1992) with added paraphrasing because [the children] don't listen to each other." Some students' journals suggest that they have begun to view their planning and instruction within larger contexts than their immediate "lesson":

> I have used a lot of informal groups throughout my experience with my fourth graders. It does create such a change of pace and fresh perspectives for the work because the groups are always different.
> I'm creating a *Book of Experts* for a whole-class identity.

MANAGEMENT THEMES

In addition to an analysis for emergent themes, the journal entries from "Self and Group" were examined from the perspective of "Stages of Concern" to help develop a profile of preservice teachers' concerns related to cooperative learning. Stages of Concern is one dimension of the Concerns-Based Adoption Model (CBAM) developed by Hall and Hord (1987). Throughout their journals, students revealed the challenges they perceived when considering the implementation of cooperative learning in their classrooms. Management concerns tended to dominate.

Early in the semester, management of time and materials were primary concerns for our students, as were the selection of goals and appropriate activities for the implementation of cooperative learning. For instance, one student expressed the concern that "the lessons could be unpredictable. . . . What if one group completes the assigned task way ahead of or behind the other groups?"

As students began to teach, a second theme—"managing children"—began to emerge. In "Self and Group," the study of group development was used to contextualize the processes needed to develop a "community of learners"; in "Classroom Management," primary objectives included studying methods for developing the community of learners and for developing the democratic classroom. Many students remained focused, however, on the "management paradigm" and expressed anxiety about their personal competencies in managing the behavior of children. Several wrote about the need to "control" behavior, to be certain the children "get along" and "focus on the assignment." One asked what would happen if the students "get along too well and don't focus on the assignment." Another, reflecting on the concept of the democratic classroom, expressed an honest concern about her personal style of "wanting to dominate the conversation" and having concern about "giving up control to the children." These expressed concerns that reflected the need to manage may also have reflected what they thought was expected of them within the schools.

Toward the end of the semester, a third theme—larger time, concept, and lifestyle management issues—emerged. Students asked: "How will I fit it all in?" "When will I have time to consider everything when planning?" and "Will I have time for family and friends?" One student wrote a poem to express her concerns.

> How do I distinguish
> What will or will not work?
> I guess it's trial and error
> I've just lost my smirk . . .
> Where do I begin?
> What should I get rid of?
> What should I extend?

STUDENT ASSESSMENT OF THE INTEGRATED SEMESTER MODEL

The Integrated Semester provides preservice teachers with continuous opportunities to link theory to practice. Students' personal journals reveal enthusiasm for (a) the special connectedness and cohesiveness with other students, their university professors, and the teachers and students in their field placement; (b) the authentic and practical opportunities to practice their observation skills; (c) the opportunities to practice new knowledge and skills and to reduce personal fears related to their upcoming roles as student teachers and teachers; and (d) their experiences in reflective practice related to the planning, implementation, and evaluation of cooperative learning. As one would hope from a boutique experience, students began to share their professors' "passion" for this cohort experience in general, and for small-group learning in particular. Toward the end of the semester, their journal entries began to suggest that the cohort experience and intensity of the semester has begun to help them focus on professional collaboration. This focus is consistent with the developmental nature of the Stages of Concern theme. Journal entries that support this development include:

"I liked the small class size [in university classes] and the closeness of the professors and peers."

"By being part of a base group myself, I was able to experience it's effect first hand. We were really able to help each other along the way in the learning process."

CONCLUSION AND IMPLICATIONS FOR
PRESERVICE TEACHER EDUCATION

Journal data from this study suggests that students in the Integrated Semester value cooperative learning as essential pedagogy in their university classes, have begun to develop a vocabulary for the observation and implementation of this pedagogy, to see the application for this pedagogy in field-placement classrooms, and I have begun to realize that cooperative learning is not a simple one-size-fits-all set of strategies. The cohort experience, and the small number of students in the cohort, helps students get to know each other quite well and supports their developing understanding of the value of collaboration. This emphasis on the value of collaboration will be critical as students move into their professional roles.

For the professors, the advantages of working in the Integrated Semester boutique are many. We are able to know our students on a more personal level, to differentiate instruction to meet individual needs, to teach for more immediate application, and to teach more in alliance with our passions. The collective nature of this particular boutique also allows us to collaborate and problem solve with respected colleagues. Our collective experience provides us with a complex set of lenses from which to reflect on, and revise, our semester; and the kind of research presented in this chapter—which can be, and has been used to help determine course revisions and appropriate interventions—is more efficiently and effectively accomplished as a team. Also, our teaching is just more fun.

This study has reinforced for us the importance of extending field experiences for preservice teaching and linking supported practice to theory. Many, but not all, students had successful field experiences. Those who did not remind us that careful selection of cooperating teachers is always a critical element and that careful selection based on one dimension of instruction does not necessarily ensure compatibility in other dimensions. In an effort to make their implementation relevant and to encourage them to make careful and contextualized instructional decisions, students are typically given considerable freedom in how to plan their cooperative learning practice. More prescriptive expectations might give students some leverage to experiment in classrooms with reluctant cooperating teachers. The balance between prescription and decision making in the classroom context is, however, delicate.

To support all students in their implementation efforts, it appears that—in response to concerns expressed in journals—even greater attention, in the early weeks of the semester, should be given to management concerns as they relate to socially constructed learning. The university faculty member who visits students in the field focuses primarily on the literacy component of instruction. Ways need to be explored for students to receive more direct and immediate coaching, feedback, and encouragement about the cooperative learning aspects of their work with children.

When faculty design an experience that reflects their own passions, they tend to teach passionately. Passionate teaching tends to be both intricate and expansive and provides students with opportunities to experience both the depth and breadth of a discipline. Students, however, are beginners. The faculty are well aware of this and know that the students' implementation of concepts must, of necessity, begin simply. We encourage students to "start simple and start small" but we suspect that this encouragement must become even more explicit. Perhaps very deliberate and repeated examinations of the external and internal factors affecting their lesson may be helpful in learning that "change [and learning to teach] is a process . . . not an event" (Fullan 1993). Depending on the nature of their field placements, we may also need to explore further ways to help our students be effective "humane authoritarians" (Schmuck & Schmuck, 1996, p. 40) while we continue to help them move toward more interactional and democratic practice. It is essential that we remember that the regular opportunities we provide students for coplanning, sharing of successful experiences, and problem solving for lessons they perceive as unsuccessful are critical and that these opportunities not only help them address their concerns but support their apparent readiness for professional collaboration as well. Further use of reflective journals, perhaps focused on different aspects of emergent practice, may help to reveal—with greater intricacy—the instruction, practice, and support preservice teachers need to negotiate both the professional and personal aspects of learning to teach.

REFERENCES

We would like to thank our students at West Chester University for permission to quote from their journals.

Albert, L. (1996). *A teachers' guide to cooperative discipline* (revised ed.). Circle Pines, MN: American Guidance Service.

Bales, R. (1950). *Interaction process analysis: A method for the study of small groups.* Cambridge, MA: Addison-Wesley.

———. (1970). *Personality and interpersonal behavior.* New York: Holt, Rinehart and Winston.

Baloche, L. (1998). *The cooperative classroom: Empowering learning.* Upper Saddle River, NJ: Prentice Hall.

Baloche, L., Mauger, M., Willis, T., Filinuk, J., & Michalsky, B. (1993). Fishbowls, creative controversy, talking chips: Exploring literature cooperatively. *English Journal, 82*(6), 43–48.

Banks, J. (1993). Multicultural education: Progress and prospects. *Phi Delta Kappan, 75*(1), 22–28.

————. (1994). *Multiethnic education: Theory and practice* (3rd ed.). Boston: Allyn and Bacon.

Cohen, E. (1986). *Designing groupwork*. New York: Teachers College Press.

————. (1994a). *Designing groupwork* (2nd ed.). New York: Teachers College Press.

————. (1994b). *Status treatments in the classroom* (video recording). New York: Teacher's College Press.

Fullan, M. (1993). *Change forces: Probing the depths of educational reform*. Bristol, PA: Falmer.

Gardner, H. (2000). *Intelligence reframed: Multiple intelligences for the 21st century*. New York: Basic Books.

Hall, G. & Hord, S. (1987). *Change in schools*. Albany: State University of New York Press.

Johnson, D., Johnson, R., & Holubec, E. (1992). *Advanced cooperative learning*. Edina, MN: Interaction Books.

Kagan, S. (1992). *Cooperative learning*. San Juan Capistrano, CA: Kagan Cooperative Learning.

Kohn, A. (1996). *Beyond discipline: From compliance to community*. Alexandria, VA: Association for Supervision and Curriculum Development.

Lyman, F. (1992). Think-pair-share, thinktrix, thinklinks, and weird facts: An interactive system for cooperative learning. In N. Davidson & T. Worsham (Eds.), *Enhancing thinking through cooperative learning* (pp. 169–81). New York: Teacher's College Press.

Nelson, J., Lott, L., & Glenn, H. (1997). *Positive discipline in the classroom*. Rocklin, CA: Prima.

Posner, G. J. (2000). *Field experience: A guide to reflective teaching* (5th ed.). New York: Longman.

Powell, A., Farrar, E., & Cohen, D. (1985). *The shopping mall high school: Winners and losers in the educational marketplace*. Boston, MA: Houghton Mifflin.

Schmuck, R., & Schmuck, P. (1996). *Group processes in the classroom* (7th ed.). Dubuque, IA: William C. Brown.

Schutz, W. (1966). *The interpersonal underworld*. Palo Alto, CA: Science and Behavior Books.

Sternberg, R. (1988). *The triarchic mind: A new theory of human intelligence*. New York: Penguin.

CHAPTER 9

TEACHING DEMANDING STRATEGIES FOR COOPERATIVE LEARNING

A Comparative Study of Five Teacher Education Programs

ELIZABETH G. COHEN, DANIELLE BRIGGS, NIKOLA FILBY,
ELAINE CHIN, MARY MALE, SUSANA MATA, SUSAN MCBRIDE,
THERESA PEREZ, ROSALINDA QUINTANAR-SARELLANA,
AND PATRICIA SWANSON

This study of five campuses grew out of a long-term project centered at Stanford University in which Stanford collaborated with teacher educators at five campuses of the California State University (CSU).[1] The general purpose of the project was to find out what was necessary in order to "scale up" the successful strategies of the Program for Complex Instruction. Under the leadership of Elizabeth Cohen and Rachel Lotan over the last twenty years, this research and evaluation program has developed and evaluated a set of strategies to create equitable classrooms. In equitable classrooms, students use each other as resources in the context of equal access to a challenging curriculum and equal-status interaction in small groups. Central to this approach is the use of cooperative groups carrying out tasks that require multiple intellectual abilities. A major feature of the collaborative project was a planned intervention in the preparation of preservice teachers. Wherever possible, preservice teachers who had learned about complex instruction in their classes at the university were to do their student teaching in classrooms of teachers who were already accomplished in complex instruction.

To support this intervention, Lotan provided organizational support during the academic year and ran a faculty seminar every spring for CSU faculty who wanted to learn about the research and theory of complex instruction. The coordinators from each campus met regularly in a task force to discuss problems they were experiencing, develop solutions, and consider the implications of their particular experiences for long-term institutionalization of the knowledge and practice of creating equitable classrooms.

The five campuses represent a range from small to large programs of teacher education as well as a range from comparatively rural settings (CSU Stanislaus, California Polytechnic, San Luis Obispo) to decidedly urban settings (San Francisco State, CSU San Jose, and CSU Fresno). All the programs require a student teaching experience. Moreover, the classrooms to which student teachers are assigned all have diverse populations if for no other reason than the requirement from the state of California that students be prepared to work with linguistic and cultural diversity.

This chapter will present lessons learned from systematic data collection from 100 preservice teachers and experience with teaching this particularly challenging set of strategies for cooperative learning to preservice teachers at the five different campuses. In the project's final year (1998–99), 737 preservice candidates studied these strategies for cooperative learning. Teacher educators elsewhere who want their students to master similarly demanding methods of cooperative learning should find the lessons we have learned instructive. We start with an analytic tool that allows teacher educators to consider the implications for their educational program of the type of cooperative learning they want their teacher candidates to master.

MORE- AND LESS-DEMANDING STRATEGIES

Cooperative learning methods vary from simple to complex. When instructional methods are complex and demanding, they cannot be reduced to a recipe or to step-by-step instructions. Rather, teachers need to develop more general, theoretical ways to understand what their task has become.

In the less-demanding methods, groups are doing the same task and students proceed in roughly the same manner and at about the same pace. Frequently, these tasks are paper-and-pencil or reading-and-discussion; they come from textbooks or worksheets, and they do not require a variety of materials, sources of information, or manipulatives. The teaching objectives typically include comprehension of text, application of an algorithm, or mastery of factual material. Collaborative seatwork is an example of a relatively simple method; the teacher might ask groups of students to solve a math problem, to answer a comprehension question on a reading assignment, or to go over the material that has just been taught.

In contrast to these routine tasks, are intrinsically interesting, open-ended, discovery-oriented, investigative tasks—those that involve innovative problem solving, original and creative thinking, mechanical ingenuity, artistic refinement, dramatic poise, or musical delivery. When tasks are varied and open-ended, different groups proceed by different paths, using a variety of materials and a wide range of problem-solving strategies. These demanding, multidimensional tasks are true group tasks—one person would have difficulty in completing the job unassisted in a limited amount of time. With true group tasks, it becomes necessary for people to exchange ideas, propose alternatives, investigate possible solutions, and actively contribute to the work of the group.

Differences in characteristics of the learning tasks produce marked differences in the role of the teacher while groups are operating. When student tasks are less demanding, the teacher may act as direct supervisor, checking to see that all groups are completing tasks in a timely and efficient manner. In contrast, when the groups are working on more challenging and uncertain tasks, the teacher must delegate authority to the groups so that members can go about finding a solution to their problem in their own way. Even when the students make mistakes, there is no need for direct intervention—for the group learns from its mistakes. The teacher holds the groups accountable for their group products.

Instead of directly supervising, the teacher listens and observes, decides whether or not intervention is inevitable for groups that are floundering, looks at group behavior, and collects information on intellectual and social problems, as well as on ways in which the groups may have solved their problems. Based on what they see and hear in the groups, they may stimulate further thinking with a brief question or comment, or they may act to equalize the participation within the groups by using what are called "status treatments" (Cohen, 1994a). The purpose of using status treatments is to raise expectations for competence of those students perceived as low-status by helping students to understand that multiple intellectual abilities are relevant to the group task and by specifically pointing out the intellectual contributions made by low-status students. The teacher's decisions have become nonroutine—they cannot be scheduled in advance. The teacher must have a sufficient grasp of the underlying theory, sufficient control of the classroom, and sufficient powers of observation in order to play this new role well.

These analytical distinctions among methods do not imply that there are better and worse ways of doing cooperative learning. The approach teachers use depends on their teaching objectives; highly skilled teachers use different approaches at different times. Many versions of cooperative learning fall somewhere in the middle on the continuum of complexity we have just described.

COOPERATIVE LEARNING AND THE EQUITABLE CLASSROOM

Many of the preservice teachers at the five California State University campuses we are comparing were studying strategies for creating equitable classrooms. These strategies (referred to as complex instruction) involve cooperative learning with particular attention to tasks requiring higher-level thinking, and with a central emphasis on producing equal-status participation within the cooperative groups. The teacher who wishes to create an equitable classroom with the use of cooperative learning must master delegation of authority, the use of tasks that require higher-order thinking and many different intellectual abilities, and the direct treatment of unequal participation in the group, i.e., status treatments. (For a discussion of equitable classrooms, see Cohen, 1997.)

From the perspective of the foregoing analysis of more- and less-demanding approaches to cooperative learning, complex instruction is an especially demanding technology, requiring many nonroutine decisions. Rather than following a preformulated plan or set of directions, the teacher's actions depend on careful observation and consideration of multiple factors, including the underlying theory of what makes groups work; how students learn difficult new skills and novel ideas in group settings; how status problems operate to impede interaction and learning; and how to treat these problems.

FOLLOW-UP IN THE CLASSROOM

To achieve good implementation, teachers who are learning how to apply theory and how to make nonroutine decisions require systematic follow-up in the classroom. If this is the case for experienced teachers, the same should hold for preservice teachers. However, providing preservice teachers with the necessary practice, coaching, and feedback in the classroom presents serious practical problems.

More complex strategies of cooperative learning require close coordination between coursework or workshop and actual practice in classrooms. In a recent volume on professional development for cooperative learning (Brody & Davidson, 1998), a number of the contributors stress the importance for teachers of classroom assistance from experts (see chapters by Rolheiser and Anderson, and Schneidewind & Sapon-Shevin).

In the case of complex instruction, each teacher should ideally receive nine classroom observations based on a systematic observation instrument. In addition, the staff developer should provide three feedback sessions, using data from an average of three observations each. In actual practice, some teachers receive more visits than others. In a study of the relationship of feedback to implementation (Cohen, Lotan, & Morphew, 1998; Ellis & Lotan, 1997), the number of feedback visits proved to be a powerful predictor of the quality of the observed implementation of cooperative learning by the teachers as well as their conceptual understanding of the knowledge base. Those teachers who had more feedback visits and those teachers who saw the evaluations they received as more soundly based were better able to carry out the difficult and nonroutine strategies in the classroom.

We argue that this requirement of follow-up and feedback in the classrooms holds for preservice teachers as much as it does for inservice teachers. If accomplished teachers require extensive staff development including classroom observation and feedback, then there is no way to produce the same outcome for a preservice teacher by providing only coursework and limited opportunity to practice.

University Barriers

The structure of CSU campuses in many ways precludes intimate involvement of university teacher educators in classrooms of their students. The challenge has been to find a way around these barriers. We present some data on the extent to which these adaptations have been successful.

OVERVIEW OF THE STUDY

Nikola Filby and Danielle Briggs of WestEd, a Regional Educational Laboratory based in San Francisco, have carried out a systematic study of preservice teachers at these five campuses. They administered questionnaires to students asking what topics had been covered in coursework and how confident they felt in using particular skills in their first year of teaching.

By reviewing the data together, the authors of this chapter have developed several generalizations concerning the teaching of nonroutine strategies of cooperative learning at the preservice level. Each of these lessons learned is a separate section of the chapter. Systematic data serves as the basis for generalizations. Teacher educators supplement the data with descriptions of problems and their solutions from particular campuses.

Survey of PreService Candidates: Setting and Sample

Questionnaires were administered to a sample of 481 preservice teachers at five California State University campuses during spring of 1998. Surveys were given to preservice teachers taking courses that included complex instruction principles and techniques. For comparison, Filby and Briggs included the courses of professors who did not have experience in complex instruction. For three campuses (CSU at San Jose, San Francisco State University, and California Polytechnic, San Luis Obispo), students filled out the questionnaire in their classes. For the remaining two campuses (CSU at Fresno and CSU at Stanislaus), the questionnaires went directly to the home addresses of preservice teachers, including a random sample of those who were not taking courses on complex instruction.

The 100 preservice teachers who returned the questionnaire constitute the sample for this study. See table 9.1 for the distribution of returned surveys by campus. Even after reminder post cards were mailed to preservice teachers from Stanislaus and Fresno, the response rate for the entire study was 20.8 percent.

The low response rate means that absolute estimates from the questionnaire items for the respondents are unlikely to be a good estimate for the entire sample. Those who returned the questionnaires may have been the students who were more interested in cooperative learning. More reliable are the relationships between variables within the sample of respondents.

Questionnaire

Preservice teachers filled out the questionnaires just before the completion of their credential program for all campuses except California Polytechnic, San Luis Obispo (Cal Poly). Because of the timing of the program for the cohort identified at Cal Poly, the questionnaire was distributed in two sections with the items on student teaching and expectations for beginning teaching administered in the spring of 1999. As a result, the second phase of data for Cal Poly was not available for this analysis.

The questionnaires provided data on amount learned about cooperative learning in coursework, routine and nonroutine topics learned in coursework, the frequency with which their master teachers used cooperative learning, opportunities to do or practice cooperative learning, expectations to use cooperative learning, and how well-prepared they felt to use cooperative learning. In the items of the questionnaire, cooperative learning was referred to as "groupwork." The questionnaire was tailored for each campus in order to reflect variations in what was offered.

FIRST LESSON: COURSEWORK AND EXPECTED USE

The first lesson learned is counterintuitive: *How much you have learned in coursework about "groupwork" has nothing to do with your expectations to use these strategies as a first-year teacher.* The professor who covers cooperative learning in

Table 9.1. *Response Rate to Surveys by Campus*

Campus	Surveys Distributed	Surveys Returned	Response Rate (%)
Cal Poly	158	26	16.5
Fresno	99	18	18.2
SFSU	50	22	44.0
SJSU	150	25	16.7
Stanislaus	24	9	37.5
Total	481	100	20.8

considerable detail certainly feels that the more extensive and detailed is the coverage, the more the new teacher will look forward to using the strategy in the classroom. The data, however, tell a different and more complicated story. Out of 70 respondents who answered the question on how well prepared they felt, only 7 or 11.4% felt "very well prepared," while 60% felt fairly well prepared and 28.6% felt poorly or not prepared. Those who had coursework in complex instruction learned significantly more ($t = 2.42$; $p < .02$) than the students who did not (a mean score of 30.3 in the first group as compared to 23.8 in the second). Given that 42 is the highest score on this index, an average score of 30.3 for students who have studied about complex instruction in coursework means that they are reporting extensive learning.

A simple cross-tabulation of the index of amount learned and the percentage of students who expect to use groupwork "most days" (see table 9.2) reveals the contradiction. Notice that out of seven students who learned the least, four of them expect to use it most days. Moreover, of those students who are in the middle range on amount learned, the percentage of students who expect to use groupwork most days is higher than the percentage in the highest category of amount learned. Evidently, some people who don't know very much are confident about their future use of groupwork, and many students who have learned quite a bit are none too confident about frequent use of groupwork.

In table 9.3, we see that the frequency with which the students expect to use groupwork is uncorrelated both with amount learned in coursework and with how well prepared the student feels. Obviously, something else is affecting one's plans to use groupwork. Students' sense of being well prepared, however, is related to how much they feel they have learned in coursework ($r = .376$; $p < .01$).

SECOND LESSON: ROUTINE AND NON-ROUTINE COMPONENTS

Cooperative learning components requiring nonroutine classroom decision-making are less likely to be learned than basic concepts or more routine activities. Cohen classified

Table 9.2. *Number and Percent of Students Who Expect to Use Groupwork Most Days by Amount Learned about Groupwork in Courses*

Amount Learned	N	Frequency	%
0–14	7	4	—
14–28	26	11	42.31
29–42	38	14	36.84

Table 9.3. *Intercorrelation of Perceived Level of Preparation, Amount Learned in Coursework and Expectation to Use Groupwork*

	Coursework-Learn	Expect to Use	Well-Prepared
Coursework: Amount Learned	1.000		
How Often Expect to Use Groupwork	.028 (*n* = 71)	1.000	
How Well-Prepared?	.376* (*n* = 72)	.074 (*n* = 70)	1.000

*$p \leq .01$ (2-tailed test)

five of the fourteen components of groupwork as routine topics and five of them as nonroutine topics. Routine components of groupwork are more predictable and procedural behaviors, while nonroutine components require more interpretation and application of principles tailored to the context. Routine components of groupwork included: how to form/compose groups; how to manage groups; how to delegate authority to students; assigning roles; and, group process skills. Group process skills were in the relatively routine category because there are a number of skill builders, all planned out and scripted that beginning teachers can use for preparing students for group work. Presuming that she had acquired a reasonable understanding of what she was doing and why, the new teacher could carry out the five routine components mostly by following some basic rules. Nonroutine components of groupwork included: appropriate tasks for groupwork; drawing on multiple abilities; how to develop open-ended tasks; what to do about status problems; and when and how to intervene in groups. One might argue with this categorization, but on the whole, the latter set of components seems more nonroutine than the former.

Table 9.4 shows that students learned significantly more about the routine components than they did about nonroutine concepts and decisions ($t = -4.5$; $p = .000$). An examination of the percentage saying that they "learned a lot" for each component of cooperative learning is very revealing (table 9.5). Although,

Table 9.4. *Mean Scores for Routine and Nonroutine Topics Learned in Coursework*

	N	Mean	SD
Routine Index	100	2.17	.72
Nonroutine Index	100	1.97	.73

Paired sample t test for difference between means
$t = -4.472; p = 0$

Table 9.5. *Percent that "Learned a Lot" about Routine and Nonroutine Topics in Coursework (N = 100)*

Course Topics	Item	%
Routine	How to Compose Groups	44
	How to Manage Groups	37
	How to Delegate Authority	45
	Assigning Roles	57
	Group Process Skills	36
Nonroutine	Appropriate Tasks for Groupwork	43
	Draw on Multiple Abilities	53
	Develop Open-Ended Tasks	23
	What to Do about Status Problems	28
	When to Intervene in Groups	30

on average, students learned more about routine than nonroutine topics, the percentages saying that they had learned a lot were not uniformly high for routine and uniformly low for nonroutine topics. The nonroutine topics where students did not report learning so much were developing open-ended tasks, what to do about status problems, and when to intervene in groups. Students felt that they had learned the most about assigning roles (57%), drawing on multiple abilities (53%), how to delegate authority (45%), and how to compose groups (44%).

THIRD LESSON: TARGETED PRACTICE

The reason that classroom follow-up has always been so critical to good implementation is that teachers have an opportunity to practice and to receive feedback on specific strategies in their own classrooms. There are various ways teacher educators have tried to match those conditions for preservice teachers with what we call "targeted practice." The third lesson we have learned is as follows: *The more opportunities there are for targeted practice, the more the sticking power of instruction in cooperative learning.*

The placement of the student teacher with a master teacher who is accomplished in complex instruction has been one of our major efforts at targeted practice over the last three years. The questionnaire sample can provide some pertinent information about the results of having the opportunity to do groupwork as part of one's student teacher placement. Table 9.6 is a correlation matrix for items concerning the chance to see the master teacher use groupwork, the opportunity to do groupwork during one's student teacher placement, and the items on how well prepared one is and how often one expects to use groupwork. Those students whose master teacher used groupwork during their first placement were more likely to say that they expected to use groupwork frequently in their own first year of teaching ($r = .262$; $p < .05$). A direct indicator of targeted practice is the item on the opportunity to do groupwork during one's student teaching. This item was strongly related to expected use of groupwork ($r = .583$; $p < .01$) and to feeling well prepared ($r = .368$; $p < .01$).

These intercorrelations suggest why the amount learned in coursework did not predict expected use. *It is the chance to see and practice groupwork* that affects the students' willingness to try cooperative learning in their first year of teaching. Briggs and Filby followed a sample of thirty-one preservice teachers into their first year of teaching. Again, the strongest predictor of their actual use of groupwork was the chance to see and practice these strategies during their student teaching. Almost every teacher in the follow-up sample reported using some type of groupwork in the first year of teaching. However, the beginning teachers who observed, practiced, and learned more about groupwork during their student teaching were more likely to use task structures that resembled the approach of complex instruction. For example, these beginning teachers had their students work as a group on a project, come up with one answer as a group to a problem or set of questions, and work in groups on a unit with multiple activities.

Alternative Forms of Targeted Practice

The authors of the paper have been well aware of the importance of targeted practice for a long time. The difficulty has been, as discussed in the next lesson, the organizational problem of arranging for student-teacher placement with accomplished complex instruction teachers. As a result, two of the authors, McBride and Swanson, developed alternative forms of targeted practice, forms that do not require particular student-teacher placements.

Professor Sue McBride of Cal Poly, San Luis Obispo is a language arts specialist in the teacher education program who teaches elementary credential candidates. She has developed two special experiences outside of student teaching: the first provides superior modeling of good practice in complex instruction, and

Table 9.6. Intercorrelation among Opportunities to Do Groupwork in Student-Teacher Placement, Perceived Level of Preparation, and Expected Use of Groupwork

	Model ST-1	Model ST-2	Do Groupwork ST-1	Do Groupwork ST-2	Well-Prepared	Expect to Use
1st Master Teacher Used Groupwork (Model ST-1)	1.000					
2nd Master Teacher Used Groupwork (Model ST-2)	.167 (n = 23)	1.000				
Opportunity to Do Groupwork 1st Placement	.583** (n = 23)	.017 (n = 23)	1.000			
Opportunity to Do Groupwork 2nd Placement	.316 (n = 23)	.487* (n = 24)	.311 (n = 23)	1.000		
How Well Prep	.277† (n = 48)	.098 (n = 24)	.368** (n = 48)	.254 (n = 24)	1.000	
How Often Expect to Use	.262† (n = 46)	.11 (n = 23)	.293 (n = 46)	.325 (n = 23)	.074 (n = 70)	1.000

$**p < .01; \; *p < .05; \; †p < .10$

the second provides an actual opportunity for students to carry out a complex instruction lesson in teams with their classmates.

She describes these experiences as follows:

> The students are scheduled to observe complex instruction in action with a very accomplished teacher and her well-trained students. I have done it with small groups of four to twelve students observing, and I have done it with a whole class observing (20–24). Of course it is awkward because the classroom gets really crowded, but it is well worth the effort. The children are told that they are being observed in advance, and these are youngsters who have been using complex instruction on a regular basis. I cannot stress enough the competency of the teacher as a stellar teacher and the children as well trained in complex instruction. This has always been the case. I have great faith in the teachers whom I ask to do this. They are masters! They are able to run the CI rotation[2] and presentations and make comments to the Cal Poly students simultaneously.
>
> When possible, the observation is scheduled so that lunch, recess, or dismissal follows, thus allowing time for the teacher to chat with the Cal Poly students. The Cal Poly students are in a methods class prior to student teaching. They have had the following introductory experiences prior to the observation: (1) reading an article about complex instruction, (2) examining materials for teambuilding, (3) participating in teambuilding activities, (4) participating in group activities using complex instruction principles based on the content for the class, (5) discussion and presentation of material about complex instruction, (6) viewing an introductory video on complex instruction and a video [Cohen, 1994b] on status problems and their treatment, (7) information about what they will see and what to look for during the class visit.
>
> After the observation, we debrief back in the classroom on campus. The students can hardly believe what they have seen. They are amazed at the cooperation, the depth of explanations offered by the children, the skills of the teacher, and the great display of organization.
>
> A second type of experience is when the Cal Poly students create and implement complex instruction in a classroom for their fieldwork with a methods class prior to student teaching. They start with the same seven steps in the methods class described above. Then they create, as a class, ideas for tasks using curriculum content requested by the classroom teachers where we will do fieldwork. In groups, they create tasks that will be suitable for the unit that the whole class has

discussed. As a class, we also decide on teamwork activities and norms[3] to use in an introductory lesson.

My students have a preliminary visit to see the classroom, introduce themselvesto the children, chat with the teacher, and generally get a feel for how they might operate successfully in the classroom. Then my students return to several days of class to do planning, create materials, plan other lessons, and get a handle on the complexities of the situation. It's all very confusing!!! One of the days is a workshop to create materials, name tags, role cards, and do a walk-through of events.

Then there are four mornings of fieldwork, stretching over two weeks. The teacher has divided the class into groups that she believes will provide a good mix of personalities and will represent the make-up of the class. If children have special needs that the teachers believe we should be aware of to help children be successful learners, the teacher shares that information with us. The team of four Cal Poly students prepares a schedule that includes an introductory day with one rotation, two more days of one rotation each, and a culminating day to wrap things up and celebrate and review learning. This is the pattern we have used most often. Each team member takes responsibility for being the lead teacher one of the four days. The other members are support buddies, providing assistance as needed, and especially observing the lesson and providing feedback to the lead teacher in charge for the day. We typically divide the class of children into six groups, so a class of thirty has five in a group. We create three tasks and duplicate them to so that there will be the six activities. This works conveniently for our four days of fieldwork. Cal Poly students create simple roles if the teacher does not already use some. They are simple because we have only a short time to teach the roles and procedures in our four days.

One big thing I emphasize is that the children must do the task without our interference if at all possible. With so many of my students around, who know the task, who want to get to know the kids, and who are dying to act as a teacher, it's tough to get them to stop hovering. We work on it.

As the whole project is going on in five or more classrooms at one school site, I visit the teams operating in each classroom. Mostly I just watch and take notes. The notes consist of little messages I give to my students trying to provide positive and constructive feedback. I have been known to pull them aside and suggest that they stop *hovering*!! The best situation is when the classroom teacher had already trained the children in complex instruction, and I have come close to it on a

few occasions. I work with the teachers to get them to at least introduce the roles and some of the norms and post these. I've been pretty
successful with this. Many times there have been some teambuilding
and norm-building activities done too.

My students go crazy with all the organization. It is simply too
much for them to grasp as we begin the planning. I tell them to bear
with me, that it is impossible to comprehend it all right away. We
slowly tackle one piece at a time—keep in mind, they are also responsible for three other kinds of lessons besides those associated with the
complex instruction tasks. I feel it is important for them to get a sense
of a language-arts block of time and not just one kind of lesson. By the
time we finish—Wow, have they accomplished a lot!!! The first day is
the roughest, by far. After that, things fall into place for them. They
really "get it," so to speak, as far as the organization is concerned. They
come away from the first day greatly worried about how long the complex instruction portion takes, all the questions the kids have, the silli-
ness that some kids demonstrate. I try to assure them that the second
rotation will really smooth out. The children have a hard time with
the first rotation, as we know. I warn them about this, but they worry
anyway. They are usually thrilled with the creativity children bring
forth. They are usually amazed at how smoothly things flow on the
second day. When I have been able to run this kind of fieldwork program, I feel confident that the preservice teachers have a pretty solid
picture of how complex instruction is organized and played out in a
classroom. They have a good concept of an open-ended task, individual accountability, group wrap-up time, roles, and norms.

As just described, McBride has been able to design a field experience for all
her students that provides a high quality of targeted practice of a complex
approach to cooperative learning—an experience that occurs in the context of
coursework. She has been able to build into her courses practice with most of the
processes of curriculum planning through implementation with young students.

As we learned from the survey, understanding and using status treatments is
a nonroutine intervention that is very difficult for prospective teachers to grasp
in most forms of coursework. Dr. Patricia Swanson of San Jose State University
has developed special exercises involving targeted practice for this purpose. As
part of a capstone course, she created a set of three assignments for students completing their student teaching placements. She centered the course on the concept of status and status treatments. Because the students were simultaneously
completing their student-teaching, they could immediately apply and practice
the concepts and strategies discussed during coursework. She supervised about
one-third of the students in the class, and was familiar with many of their class-

rooms and their schools, all of which were in a school-university partnership program.

The status segment of the course utilized about six instructional hours, divided into three classes. In the first session she assigned background reading so that they would be prepared to explore what they meant when they talked about a student as "really smart" or "slow." The class also discussed motivation as not just "wanting to do well" but believing that one can do well in a given situation. Swanson wanted them to recognize that no child enters kindergarten not wanting to do well, but that in a few short years, many view their probability of doing well in a traditional school context as very low. They learn that they *cannot* do well. With this framework she hoped that the students would be less quick to judge students as "trouble makers" or "slow learners." Following this session, she asked students to analyze a lesson that they or their master teacher had taught in terms of the access to learning it provided to the range of students in the class. Who had access to learning? Who did not? She explained that this assignment was not about describing the perfect lesson, but rather about analyzing any lesson in terms of access to learning—that this is something they should think about every time they teach. They might not be able to provide perfect access, but they should be aware of who has it and who does not.

In the following two sessions, Swanson used an introduction to the concepts of status problems and their treatment that had shown good results with preservice teachers in her research (Swanson, 1997). The second session involved identifying status problems and the third session introduced two treatments for status problems: the multiple abilities treatment and assignment of competence to low-status students (Cohen, 1994a). In each session, she used video tapes of groups with low-status members and teachers using status treatments. She facilitated a discussion and provided opportunities to practice in the classroom. Swanson's research had demonstrated the value of modeling and practice opportunities along with the development of a conceptual understanding. Therefore, while she introduced the theory to develop basic conceptual understanding (underscored by a reading assignment), her discussions, modeling, and practice opportunities were concrete and practical.

At the close of this session on identifying status problems, she asked students to identify one or two students whom they perceived as "low-status" in their student-teaching classroom. She required them to write a one-page analysis describing these students and including specific evidence they used to decide that these students were low status. They had no trouble doing this—indeed they tended to focus on these students as they often presented behavioral or instructional challenges.

In the third session, she introduced the multiple abilities treatment and had the students practice identifying multiple abilities. She spent the bulk of the session as well as the next assignment on the treatment of assigning competence to low-status students. She asked them to observe students they had chosen as acting "low-status" during activities that required more than just reading and writing, and to attempt to assign competence to these students. If they were unable to observe the student doing something concrete and intellectual that would serve as the basis for assigning competence, she asked them to state this. They were then to write hypothetically about what they wished they had seen and how they would have assigned competence. They were required to write in quotation marks exactly what they said or would say. As Swanson put it, " I wanted them to not talk about students' performance abstractly, but rather to think practically about what they would say to a student and the group that would effectively improve that student's status."

In her research, Swanson had developed a written assessment of the effectiveness of her instruction, short of observing students using status treatments in the classroom. The test included open-ended questions on theoretical issues and responses to written and video vignettes. When she administered the test to her students, she reported that students did an outstanding job on each of the status assignments—as well or better than students in her previous research. They were specific in their evidence for identifying status, and in their feedback to students, and most were able to state concretely the ability that students exhibited. They demonstrated a sophisticated understanding of when they could assign competence, many correctly judging that the student's performance did not merit assignment of competence in that instance.

The students found the assignments tremendously useful. At this stage in their career (the end of their student teaching) they had mastered the practicalities of management and basic instruction and they were aware that traditional strategies were not working for all their students. They were concerned about those students whom they perceived as "low-status." There was considerable variation in terms of their perception of status treatments. Several commented that these status treatments were an excellent strategy for "engaging" low-status students and a valuable "management" strategy. Only a few saw the treatments for what they are—a strategy for enhancing equity in groups. Swanson's strategies illustrate how a course can provide practice of a demanding skill with a combination of simulations with vignettes and targeted practice with actual students.

FOURTH LESSON: ORGANIZATIONAL SUPPORT

The fourth lesson has to do with organizational support. Cooperative learning in a teacher education program can often be found in a particular professor's courses. In making and implementing the decision to teach cooperative learning, that professor may be working in isolation from the rest of the faculty. As soon as faculty members decide that they want to integrate the student-teaching experience with the coursework on cooperative learning, there is a much greater demand for organizational support. There has to be some way to link the placement process at the campus with the parallel process at the school in order to suggest that a particular student should be placed with a particular master teacher. This turns out to be a weak link. Not only is the relationship between the university and the school often a relatively weak one, but professors may not even be able to influence the process of student-teacher placement on their own campus unless they have administrative support at the university. The linkages between K–12 schools and the department or school of teacher education run the gamut from bits of bureaucratic cooperation to a tight relationship with a professional development school where teachers from that school have a presence on campus and are coinstructors of the preservice teachers. To make cooperative learning placements work, there have to be well-prepared teachers in the placement area at the right grade levels who can serve as models of cooperative learning. This often requires inservice before placement of preservice candidates.

The five campuses represent both ends and the middle of a continuum of organizational support and linkages with the public schools. These factors made some difference for the success of cooperative learning on a given campus. Thus the fourth lesson we learned was: *Campuses with more organizational support and closer linkages to schools will be more successful in preparing future teachers to use a demanding type of cooperative learning than campuses with less organizational support and weaker linkages to schools.*

We have two different ways to judge that success: one is the number of credential candidates who took coursework on complex instruction. The other is the number of student teachers who did their placement with a complex instruction master teacher in the schools. Although there were not a large number of such placements on any of the five campuses, their total number varied considerably across the campuses.

Table 9.7 provides data for 1998–99 for each campus on the number of professors knowledgeable and committed to complex instruction, estimates of the strength of administrative support from the university, and estimates of the strength of linkages with K–12 schools for each campus. The number of complex instruction placements and the number of credential candidates taking related coursework appears in the last two columns of the table. Administrative support was adjudged "weak" if the Department Chair and/or Dean were unaware of the work, or if aware, were uninvolved. Support was classified as "medium" in those cases where turnover in administrative positions had left faculty with some positive remainder from a previous, supportive administrator followed by one who was at least nominally supportive. "Strong" administrative support means that the administrator takes positive steps to assist with coordination and resources necessary for the innovation in teaching. The links with schools were described

Table 9.7. *Organizational Support, Links with Schools, Complex Instruction Coursework and Placements: Five CSU Campuses 1998–1999*

| Campus | Organizational Support for CI | | Links with Schools | Number of Credential Candidates | |
	No. of Profs.	Admin. Support		in CI Courses	in CI Placements
Stanislaus	2	Weak	Strong	100	6
Fresno	4	Medium	Strong	150	18
Cal Poly	4	Strong	Weak	335	0
S. F. State	2	Weak	Weak	170	0
San Jose	4	Medium	Medium	112	5

as "weak" if there were few complex instruction teachers in the area and if there was no working relationship between the university and complex instruction schools or districts. The links were "strong" if there were a professional development school or a school district featuring complex instruction with deep ties to the campus. The "medium" cell was used for campuses where there were numerous complex instruction teachers in the area and the universities or the professors had ties to some sites.

The first thing to note about this table is that the two campuses with weak linkages to the schools were unable to make complex instruction placements even though they prepared a large number of credential candidates through coursework. Cal Poly, a relatively small program, had the highest number of students taking complex instruction courses. This was a product of the major commitments of four senior faculty members and the Director of Teacher Education.

Professor Elaine Chin of this faculty describes how her colleague, Sue McBride, involved her in this mode of cooperative learning:

> More of the faculty at Cal Poly are probably aware of complex instruction (even minimally) than at any other CSU campus because of Sue McBride's work in educating us individually and in her organizing the faculty seminars held this last year. I was first introduced to complex instruction through a conversation with Sue and subsequent coaching she provided me about using groupwork differently in my own classroom. That initial introduction was what motivated Alice and me to attend the Stanford seminar three years ago. Since then, we have continued to read and think about complex instruction and to try to involve more of our colleagues in this project.

Except in the case of Cal Poly, the number of students taking relevant courses is not necessarily a direct consequence of administrative support. Professors in teacher education have considerable autonomy in deciding what to include in their courses. Even if they are assigned basic courses and even without support for complex instruction from the departmental administration, it is possible to include these materials in a wide variety of courses. The case of San Francisco State illustrates this point. Here the 170 students who were exposed to complex instruction were mostly exposed as the result of one committed and determined professor. However, without trained teachers at the secondary level in the city and with weak linkages to the schools, it was impossible to manage complex instruction placements.

The campus with the most placements was CSU Fresno where Professors Susanna Mata and Robin Chiero worked very closely with the principal and teachers of one school to develop a site where their student teachers could be placed. The principal of the school even came to Stanford for a week of the faculty seminar.

San Jose and Stanislaus showed an intermediate number of placements and we rated their linkages to the schools as having medium strength. In the case of San Jose, there were a number of university-school partnerships in the process of development and these show promise of more placements in the future. However, Swanson of that campus estimates that this will take deliberate planning and involvement of teachers at those schools, with the faculty committed to complex instruction at the campus. San Jose was also fortunate in having a large number of trained teachers in the area as a result of long-term professional development activities. Those students with a complex instruction placement from this campus were primarily the result of Professor Rosalinda Quintanar's close ties with the bilingual community, and her extensive experience with different schools and cooperating teachers in bilingual education programs. She supervises the candidates directly and is able to direct placement with teachers who are not only complex instruction teachers but teach in bilingual programs. Through her supervision, she can follow up her coursework, and provide observation and feedback for her student teachers.

Stanislaus also had the benefit of a number of complex instruction teachers in the area as well as the Ceres school district that had a close, long-term relationship with Stanford and with the California International Studies Project at Stanislaus (not located in the School of Education). But it is critical to note that these favorable conditions were not enough to produce anything like the numbers at Fresno, where the linkages were much more deliberate and tighter between particular schools and particular faculty members in the School of Education.

STRUCTURAL BARRIERS

Following the logic of our own argument and supporting data, it is very important for student teachers to have the opportunities to practice cooperative learning in a supervised classroom setting. One would imagine that with a reasonably amenable master teacher who did not use cooperative learning, the university faculty could either supervise the student's attempts to use complex instruction in the classroom or train the university supervisor to do so. Swanson of San Jose State says that neither of these solutions is very practical. For example, at San Jose State, the supervision of six student teachers equals a three-unit class for a faculty member. Supervision will often take twice as many hours as teaching a class. Consequently, faculty working under the heavy teaching load of the CSU system often choose to avoid supervision. Obviously Professors Swanson and Quintanar are exceptions to this rule in that they have undertaken the supervision of some of their own students.

Supervision tends to be poorly organized and under-funded in most teacher education programs. Supervisors are often part-time faculty and it is considered low-status faculty work. We have never been successful in working with these supervisors in conducting the classroom follow-up for student teachers. They do not have the organizational clout to persuade the classroom teachers to allow the conduct of a lesson in cooperative learning. Moreover, most of their work with student teachers focuses on classroom control and on the organization of reasonably coherent lessons. Working at the level of survival, there is little room to move on to more sophisticated strategies of cooperative learning.

Perez calls the difficulty of working closely with the schools a systemic one. She says:

> At CSU Fresno, as in most CSUs, there is a separation between the university (charged with teacher education) and our public schools. We live on two different planets due in large measure to organizational factors that preclude "crossing over," to the other side. There is also no mechanism by which classroom teachers can be involved in the training of student teachers in any but the most peripheral ways (as master/cooperating teachers only, which does not get much beyond the basic activities of lesson plans, demonstrating teaching, management, etc.). What I was looking for was a systematic, collaborative process by which university faculty and classroom teachers could plan the student teaching experience so that it would include the full range of what as known as "theory to practice."

Perez wanted to directly teach how to transfer what student teachers learned in the university classrooms to the field setting and she could not accomplish this without partnering with the classroom teacher. She went on to establish a remarkable collaborative relationship with one school. She even persuaded the district to put up a portable building on site where she and her fellow team of university instructors could teach all the classes for the twenty-nine student teachers in their cluster. The cooperating teachers could also carry out some instruction of the student teachers on site. This took the cooperation of administration on both "planets." There were many sessions with the classroom teachers in which they discussed with university personnel what the classroom experience for the student teachers would include and what role each would play. After a classroom demonstration of complex instruction, the teacher would return to the university portable classroom and debrief with the entire class.

Professor Mary Male of San Jose State also reports on the great benefits of university-school partnerships. In a partnership, faculty members from the university are more likely to work together to plan and deliver instruction and supervision, either through team teaching or collaborative planning meetings. Most partnerships feature joint selection of master teachers by a committee of university faculty and district personnel. San Jose State University established a precedent in partnership programs of taking the money for part-time supervision and allocating it instead as a supplement for the stipends for master teachers who then served as the university supervisor. This helped to produce more of a shared allegiance to the university and the district, rather than to the district alone.

CONCLUSION

If we want prospective teachers to be able to implement more demanding strategies of cooperative learning, the experience of these five campuses suggests that some changes from "business as usual" will have to take place. It is relatively easy to persuade faculty to include components of cooperative learning in coursework, and these courses can even be relatively well integrated without requiring major organizational change. What is very difficult to bring about is the provision of opportunities to see first-rate practice of these demanding strategies, and even more important, the chance for the student teacher to practice these strategies in the classroom. The survey data clearly shows that the students' willingness to implement cooperative learning in their own classroom is more closely connected to targeted practice than it is to coursework. Coursework is a necessary but not a sufficient condition for preparing a new teacher who will implement more demanding strategies of cooperative learning. Students, according to our survey, learned a great deal about cooperative learning from their coursework, covering a variety of important topics. This learning helped them to feel relatively well prepared, but it did not embolden them to state that they would try these strategies out when they were on their own in their first year of teaching.

We have reviewed extensively the structural barriers that occur between the teacher education programs at the university and the school. Because intimate connections are the exception rather than the rule, it is very difficult to arrange for student teachers to obtain the critical forms of classroom experience with master teachers who are highly skilled and sophisticated in their own practice of cooperative learning. The quantitative and qualitative data suggest that the most promising innovations are the professional development schools where a cluster of faculty in partnership with the cooperating teachers supervises a cohort of student teachers. Together, they shape a program of coursework and targeted practice in cooperative learning. Short of this major organizational change, the qualitative data suggest alternative forms of targeted practice that take place *in the context of coursework* but with opportunities to try out one's skills in classrooms.

Many studies of teacher education recommend closer linkages between higher education and the schools. Our study certainly concurs with this recommendation, but the devil is in the details. For a demanding and complex method of teaching such as some forms of cooperative learning, one must specify the conditions under which students can experience sufficient success to engage in a continuing program of trial and improvement. Then the pattern of organizational change must flow from the demands of the teaching technology necessary to meet these conditions. As the teacher educators from these campuses have elegantly illustrated: if you know exactly what you need to achieve, there is more than one way to solve these organizational problems.

NOTES

1. The study was supported by the Stuart Foundation of San Francisco, CA and by the Hewlett Foundation of Menlo Park, CA.

2. In complex instruction there are multiple groups, each carrying out a different task. The groups rotate from task to task. After each task, each group makes a presentation of their group product.

3. These norms are rules for behavior in cooperative settings.

REFERENCES

Brody, C. M., & Davidson, N. (Eds.) (1998). *Professional development for cooperative learning: Issues and approaches*. Albany: State University of New York Press.

Cohen, E. G. (1994a). *Designing groupwork: Strategies for heterogeneous classrooms* (2nd ed.). New York: Teachers College Press.

Cohen, E. G. (1994b). *Status treatments for the classroom* [video]. New York: Teachers College Press.

Cohen, E. G. (1997). Equity in heterogeneous classrooms: A challenge for teachers and sociologists. In E. G. Cohen & R. A. Lotan (Eds.), *Working for equity in heterogeneous classrooms: Sociological theory in practice* (pp. 3–14). New York: Teachers College Press

Ellis, N., & Lotan, R. A. (1997). Teachers as learners: Feedback, conceptual understanding, and implementation. In E. G. Cohen & R. A. Lotan (Eds.), *Working for equity in heterogeneous classrooms: Sociological theory in practice* (pp. 209–222). New York: Teachers College Press.

Lotan, R., Cohen, E., & Morphew, C. (1998). Beyond the workshop: Evidence from complex instruction. In C. M. Brody & N. Davidson (Eds.), *Professional development for cooperative learning: Issues and Approaches* (pp. 123–145). Albany: State University of New York Press.

Swanson, P. E. (1997). Linking sociological theory to practice: An intervention in preservice teaching. In E. G. Cohen & R. A. Lotan (Eds.), *Working for equity in heterogeneous classrooms: Sociological theory in practice* (pp. 240–259). New York: Teachers College Press.

CHAPTER 10

STEPPING INTO GROUPWORK

RACHEL A. LOTAN

> I hope I wouldn't interfere with the groups. I would try not to but I'm
> sure it would make my stomach hurt.
>
> —Paige Price, Student teacher,
> Stanford Teacher Education Program, Class of '99

Learning to teach in heterogeneous classrooms has become a critical component of many preservice teacher education programs. Preparing beginning
teachers to use strategies that promote learning at a high intellectual level in
classrooms where students have a wide range of previous academic achievement
and varying levels of proficiency in the language of instruction is one of the
greatest challenges facing these programs today. Teaching in such classrooms
requires complex instructional strategies that rely to great extent on small group
instruction.

When using groupwork, many teachers worry about how to manage and
organize the classroom to create an environment where students work cooperatively on intellectually challenging tasks. For groupwork to be equitable and productive, students need to make sure that all group members understand the
learning task, participate actively, and contribute equally to the success of their
group. Students need to learn how to request help and how to provide help to
members of their group. They need to learn how to engage in meaningful conversations about subject-matter content, and how to resolve substantive or interpersonal conflicts. Teachers need to know how to set up, promote, and sustain
such groupwork, how to hold groups and individuals accountable for being on
task, and when and how to intervene when problems arise.

In this chapter, I present a framework for teaching beginning teachers how
to manage and organize the classroom for small-group instruction. I draw from
my experiences with teaching a course currently entitled "Teaching in Heterogeneous Classrooms," in the Stanford Teacher Education Program (STEP) for

the past eight years. To illustrate my argument, I describe the curriculum and the pedagogy as well as selected student contributions and products in this course taught during the 1998/1999 academic year. Thirty-three beginning teachers participated in the fall quarter and twenty-four took the course during the winter quarter.

CURRICULUM AND PEDAGOGY UNDERLYING THE COURSE

In planning and designing this course, I took a particular curricular and pedagogical stance. My intent was to apply a solid theoretical framework and to use empirical evidence for the instructional strategies to which student teachers were being introduced. Furthermore, it was important to me to collect and to show curricula, student work samples, video vignettes, teacher-authored cases, hand-outs and assignments, in other words "existence proofs" that the strategies I presented to the STEP teachers were indeed effective in getting the expected results. For this purpose, I relied extensively on the work of the Program for Complex Instruction at Stanford University (Cohen and Lotan, 1997).

Conceptually, the course had three major goals. The first goal was to convey to the student teachers the notion that the classroom is a social system rather than a collection of thirty-some individuals directed, managed, led, and controlled by a teacher. This perspective allows teachers to incorporate an additional lens through which to view and analyze their students' behaviors and performances in the classroom.

In many teacher-education programs, courses that deal with classroom management have a basic psychological orientation. In these courses, understanding classroom interactions focuses mainly on single, and frequently unidirectional interactions between the teacher and individual students. In such cases, classroom management means knowing how to discipline and how to address, restrain, and repair students' disruptive behavior more effectively. Most of the classroom norms and routines prescribed in such courses deal with how to support the teacher in controlling the students while she is lecturing, how to ensure that students are attentive, on-task, and ready to complete in-class and homework assignments in a timely manner. Often these norms and routines are lengthy lists of a few "do's" and many "don'ts," sanctioned by mostly unpleasant consequences such a referrals or detention. In presenting to the teachers a framework of the classroom as a social system (see Cohen, 1986), I introduce sociological concepts such as power, authority, role, evaluation, and status—all useful to understand interaction processes and activity patterns of teachers and students in the classroom. In the forthcoming parts of this chapter, I describe how the teachers learned about delegation of authority, a central concept in organizing the classroom for small-group instruction.

The second goal of the course was to demonstrate to the teachers how, in addition to unique personal characteristics, dispositions, and attitudes, the structure of the situation or the context in which they find themselves influence students' and teachers' behavior and performances. Recognizing and understanding this relationship can be an empowering idea for many teachers. Rather than trying to control behavior by manipulating or attempting to change a student's personality (i.e., "fixing the kid"), teachers come to understand that they can define, shape, construct, or change the parameters of the situation. For example, by creating productive and safe learning environments and by designing inherently motivating, conceptually challenging, and intellectually rich learning tasks, teachers can establish optimal conditions for on-task, productive interactions between and among teachers and students.

The third goal of the course was to demonstrate how conceptions of intelligence, a psychological construct, translate into the practical design of learning tasks and how they affect teachers' expectations for and assessments of their students' contributions and achievements. In this course, intelligence was defined as "what one can do with what one knows" (DeAvila, 1985) and viewed as multidimensional and incremental (Sternberg, 1985; Gardner, 1983; Dweck & Henderson, 1989, Ben-Ari, 1997). This conception of intelligence allowed teachers to recognize that in their classrooms, in addition to being strong readers and writers and quick at calculating, students could be smart in many different ways. Building on this idea, the student teachers could choose any format or genre to demonstrate their understanding when completing the assignments of the course. (For more details, see a detailed description of one of the assignments below.)

Principles of Pedagogical Wisdom

To accomplish these goals, I followed four principles of conventional pedagogical wisdom. I am presenting one example for each of them.

Model and practice what you preach. As described above, the goal of the course was to develop teachers' conceptual understanding of an underlying knowledge base and to connect this conceptual knowledge base to practice. Course participants came to class with a range of previous expertise and experiences in the classroom. Conceptual learning goals and participants with diverse expertise are the conditions under which groupwork is recommended. Therefore, the STEP teachers participating in the course had numerous opportunities to work in small groups as groupwork was used in each and every session. Although the tasks ranged from simple (e.g., short buzz groups to quickly swap comments or reactions) to complex, (e.g., designing learning tasks for the high school students in the STEP teachers' classrooms), the student teachers constantly were able to voice their thoughts and opinions, and to exchange ideas with their colleagues. Furthermore, because the course emphasized the use of multiple intellectual abilities in group tasks, presentation of materials was accomplished through varied media: from lecture to role play, and from video analysis to multimedia assignments.

Provide real-life examples and give teachers opportunities to experience what they are asking their students to do. Skill-building exercises recommended for use in high school classrooms to train students how to work productively in small groups were introduced to the STEP teachers and they actually went through these exercises themselves. The important debriefings at the conclusion of each exercise fulfilled two purposes: first, to understand and to reflect about the group interactions that had just occurred; and second, to consider the exercises in light of having to conduct similar skill-builders for their high school students. An added benefit of experiencing these skill-building exercises was that the STEP teachers became better acquainted with one another and thus developed stronger personal and professional ties.

Be metacognitive and explicit to show how a knowledge base can be used to make instructional decisions. As the instructor, I made a particular effort to verbalize and voice my own thoughts and considerations in making pedagogical decisions. For example, I noticed that one of the groups was discussing an important issue that was basically unrelated to the task at hand. I debated whether to intervene and redirect the group. I decided against it because I assumed that the group had noticed that I was aware of the situation. I hoped that this might have been enough to signal to the members of the group to return to the task. During the debriefing, when it became clear that the group had not been able to complete their task because of lack of time, I described my dilemma about whether or not to intervene. My decision not to interrupt the group had clear consequences. We discussed and debated the advantages and the disadvantages of my pedagogical decision. This discussion of a particular classroom event illustrated to the student teachers that in teaching there rarely are unambiguously right or wrong answers and that effective teaching must rely on deliberate decision making, informed by general theoretical principles.

Reflect and provide ample opportunities for teachers to reflect on classroom experiences and pedagogical dilemmas. Classes usually started with STEP teachers sharing experiences from their classrooms as they related to the content of the course. I frequently shared my own reflections about previous lessons and often commented on what I would do if I could "rewind the tape." Furthermore, classroom activities (e.g., case discussions, analyses of video segments) as well as the assignments and the final project for the course included an important reflective component. The phrase "rewinding the tape" became almost a slogan for the course.

DELEGATION OF AUTHORITY: A CENTRAL CONCEPT

As a whole, the course covered five major areas: organizing the classroom for small group instruction, producing equal-status interaction in small groups, designing multiple-ability group tasks, developing language proficiency and academic discourse for English language learners, and assessing individual and group products. Because issues of power and authority are particularly challenging for many beginning teachers (as well as veterans), I will describe in detail how I introduced, taught, and assessed students' understanding of delegation of authority.

The Role of the Teacher

During groupwork, the organization of the classroom is vastly different from the structure of the classroom in whole-class or individualized instruction. With six or even nine groups, it becomes impractical, if not physically impossible, for teachers to oversee all groups personally. They cannot single-handedly see to it that groups run smoothly and that students understand what needs to be done and how to best complete the task. In other words, they cannot directly supervise and exercise authority over all groups simultaneously.

When the teachers delegate authority, they hand over specific responsibilities to the groups and to the individuals in the groups. The teacher accomplishes this by holding groups accountable for managing themselves and for making sure that all members are engaged in learning and working on completing the task. Delegating authority then becomes sharing with the students the power to make decisions about how to accomplish the task, how to work together productively, how to evaluate and enhance the quality of the group product, and how to recognize the contributions of individual members of the group. Delegating authority, however, does not mean relinquishing authority. Indeed, I often remind the student teachers that one cannot delegate authority if one does not have it in the first place.

To develop a concrete view of what successful groupwork might look and feel like, the course started with a simulation of a lesson. Because its activities could be completed during a single period, I chose a life-science unit on the visual system (Holthuis, Bianchini, Schultz, & Lotan, 1999). Playing the role of the teacher, I conducted a brief orientation. I posed to the students the central question of the activities, referred them to the cooperative norms posted on the walls of the classroom, and reminded them to play their assigned roles. Wanting to instill a sense of urgency, I informed them that in spite of the short time, I expected a quality product from the groups. Furthermore, since everyone had important contributions to make, they needed to make sure that all members of the group participated actively. Next, I proceeded to monitor the groups through observing and providing feedback. As the students were working, I intervened three times: to clarify the instructions to the task for one of the groups, to ask a question about a group's product, and to praise a student for a particularly creative solution to a problem.

In debriefing the lesson, the conversation proceeded on two levels: First, the student teachers reported on their experiences as members of the groups, and described their products and what they had learned about the visual system. Second, they projected their experiences onto their own high school classrooms. While they acknowledged the benefits of groupwork, they also voiced many genuine and legitimate concerns: Their classrooms were overcrowded and there was no physical space nor adequate furniture for small groups. Groupwork is too time consuming when one needs to cover many topics and keep pace with the rest of the teachers in the department. Many high school students are rowdy and do not know how to work together. The STEP teachers were greatly relieved when they found out that they were about to learn how to address and alleviate many of these problems.

Following the simulation that continued to serve as a reference point, I made connections to the theoretical argument underlying the simulation and the approach it represented through a short lecture and a discussion of the assigned readings from Cohen's *Designing Groupwork* (1994). Although the principles and the findings underlying complex instruction were emphasized throughout, the extensive empirical evidence about the academic, cognitive, social, and affective outcomes of small-group instruction as reported by researchers such as Slavin (1983), Johnson and Johnson (1990), and Sharan (1990) were presented to the participants in the course.

Cooperative Norms

When delegating authority, teachers redefine their traditional role. This redefinition does not come easily for many teachers, be they novices or veterans. Some struggle with the loss of being the focal point in the classroom—the sole provider of information and knowledge—who continually and persistently regulates students' behavior and learning. Others worry that without direct and constant supervision, the classroom might deteriorate into chaos, that is, students will not understand what needs to be done, they will make too many mistakes, and they won't complete their assignments. To avert such an alarming scenario, a system of cooperative group norms and student roles aids teachers in their delegation of authority. This system supports the changed role of the teacher and of the students during small-group instruction. Like the teachers, students need to learn how to adjust to delegation of authority. New ways of interacting with their peers require new norms of behavior.

The norms that teachers instill in students as they collaborate in small groups have to do with allowing students to serve as academic, linguistic, or other intellectual resources for one another. The right to request assistance and the duty to provide it is one of the first norms students need to learn. They also need to learn how to conduct constructive conversations in small groups by justifying their arguments and by explaining how, rather than by doing the work for someone else.

As mentioned above, in teaching these norms, we used a series of skill-building exercises (see Cohen, 1994). Applying the principles of social learning theory (Bandura, 1977), the STEP students were given opportunities to recognize the new behaviors, to practice them, and to receive feedback that reinforced internalization of norms. Taking time in every session of the first three weeks of the course, we were able to learn about and practice six different skill builders. All the student teachers immediately prepared their own sets of skill builders and many of them were able to use them with their high school students. Without exception, they were anxious to share the results of their experimentation with their classmates. They also reported that many cooperating teachers who were using small-group instruction welcomed this practical and immediate contribution of their student teachers. At the time of the midquarter course evaluations, the STEP teachers overwhelmingly rated the skill-building exercises as the most immediately useful (and "fun") part of the course.

Student Roles in Groups

As mentioned earlier, in addition to the use of cooperative norms, students assume specific procedural roles to support teachers as they delegate authority. By playing these roles, students manage the groups and themselves; they take over the responsibility for some of the practical, yet mundane, functions and duties that traditionally have been the teacher's purview. Thus, in each group the facilitator, the reporter, and the materials manager see to it that the group functions smoothly. Depending on the task and the teacher's priorities, additional roles may be assigned: time keeper, peace keeper, safety, or resource person.

These roles are different from "content" roles such as theorist, questioner, or explainer that reflect metacognitive functions necessary for groupwork; they are also different from "professional" roles such as artist, musician, poet, or director—roles that potentially lead to a strict division of labor. Although division of labor is often an efficient way to get the job done quickly, it also reduces interaction. In groupwork, when peer interaction is what we strive for, we need to achieve a healthy balance between division of labor and interdependence. Each student in the group must have a role to play, and roles rotate. In addition to participating fully in the content-specific, substantive task of the group, all students learn how to play all roles competently. In this way, students develop important social skills highly relevant for adult life.

Similar to using the new norms, assuming various roles usually does not come naturally to most students. In the course, we used short scenes to become acquainted with the roles and to practice teacher interventions when roles are misused or not used at all and groups break down. In small groups, the student teachers read short scenarios that focused on how groupwork can go awry when students do not play their assigned roles. For example, in one scenario only one student could read the instructions to the task and prevented others from touching the materials. In another scenario, group members kept arguing about who is to do what. In yet another scenario, a student kept interrupting the group and diverted the attention of his peers. In their small groups, the STEP teachers analyzed these vignettes and proposed teacher responses that make use of group roles. Then they role-played their short scripts, and the audience of their classmates evaluated the proposed teacher interventions.

Despite this preparation, becoming comfortable with the suggestion to assign roles to their high school students was a challenge for the STEP teachers and their reactions to the use of roles were mixed. As well-socialized adults, highly skilled in the interpersonal domain, they took harmoniously functioning groups for granted. Some of them perceived the roles as uncomfortable, artificial, and often limiting. Even at the end of the course, a number of them remained quite unconvinced of their usefulness. It was not until they implemented the final project in which they conducted a groupwork lesson in their classrooms that some of them were ready to acknowledge the benefits of well-implemented student roles. In addition to the skill-building exercises and the role plays, the student teachers also watched a short video that included vivid classroom scenes, teacher remarks, and a summary of the empirical evidence. The video shows that delegation of authority leads to increased student interaction that, in turn, produces greater learning gains.

Dilemmas of Delegation

As teachers learn how to delegate authority effectively, they ask themselves poignant questions: When and how do I intervene? Do I let kids fail when groups clearly don't work out? Am I abdicating my role as a teacher when I don't help my students? Cohen (1994) advises teachers not to hover over the groups and to refrain from rescuing the students when they can find their own solutions to the problem. Humorously, in class we formed a support group of "Hoverers Anonymous" and frequently confessed our transgressions when the pressures became too great and hovering and rescuing were unavoidable.

The STEP teachers enjoyed reading and discussing cases authored by experienced high school teachers about difficulties and dilemmas of delegating authority (Shulman, Lotan and Whitcomb, 1998). In two of these cases, (*One Group's Inertia* and *Do You Let Kids Fail*) the teacher-authors are taken aback by their students' reluctance and resistance to accept the authority delegated to them. Having decided that they will not rescue the groups, these authors wrestle with the pain of watching their students "fail." In another case, the teacher-author refuses to become the referee when two students are unable to resolve a conflict in their group. He requests that they produce a concrete plan of action to complete the task the next day. In a similar situation, another teacher-author resolves the conflict by separating the adversaries. These cases illustrate how delegation of authority is a constant negotiation between teachers and students, as well as the teachers' conflicting and at times contradictory views of their own pedagogical identity.

As they grow more comfortable with making students responsible for their own work, and as they hover less over groups and rescue more and more infrequently, teachers find that they are free for the kind of teaching that attracted them to the profession in the first place. Relieved from the burden of management and direct control, teachers, through feedback and questioning, encourage the students to move beyond the procedural aspects of the task and to interact with one another at a higher conceptual level, making sense of difficult intellectual problems.

The cases were the students' favorite reading assignments and they reported reading most of the sixteen cases in the book (Shulman, Lotan and Whitcomb, 1998) even though only six were formally assigned. These case discussions were a powerful tool for deepening the student teachers' understanding and for connecting theory to the practice. Case discussions always ended with the question: "If you were the teacher, what would you do?" The student teachers were asked to respond to this question via email to a listserve that included the whole class.

Some students agreed with the authors and would have refrained from rescuing the groups. Diane wrote matter-of-factly: "I would do what the teacher did, because if you go ahead and give the information, the students will never learn." Amelia elaborated, but, like many of her classmates, was less sure of herself: "Echoing the sentiments of many of my colleagues, I believe that I would let the students fail. In teaching, I often find myself trying to find the balance between two extremes: doing everything I can to 'help' students (which sometimes involves rescuing them) and using 'tough love' to help them take responsibility.

Given the circumstances, I hope I would not rescue the students." Carolyn recognized that the author's decision was well grounded, but wasn't sure whether she could have done the same:

> We really are doing students the biggest of favors by forcing them to accept responsibility for their own work. This is not an easy task, especially for those of us "softies" who would gladly let them off the hook so that they can feel safe and happy. But we have to make them accountable, and we have to do it consistently. Not only do the students who are slacking lose out when we allow them to slack, but other students pick up on the unspoken message. Firm standards are always a good thing. In other words, I would have let them flounder, at least for a minute or two.

Like some of her colleagues, Kristen completely agreed with the author at first, but found that in her own practice she would have been less confident:

> I would let the students fail. The assignment was one that the students were capable of handling. Giving them too much aid would undermine their capability or lower the expectations. If students know they are expected to need help from the teacher in every group project, they will need help in every group project. My answer (to let them fail) would have been different last week, as I rescued a nonfunctional group in my class. It takes time to learn.

In his response, Tim recognized how complicated delegating authority can get. After the first case discussion, he wrote the following comment:

> I am really enjoying the class for a variety of reasons, but the biggest reason is that it is REALLY challenging my views on how I handle groups in the classroom. I am a stereotypical "rescuer" (or at least I have been for these first few weeks of teaching) and I am really seeing the danger in this. I am looking forward to the rest of the class and getting ideas on how I can teach in a more efficient and helpful way.

A week later, in response to the second case discussion, he added:

> I suffer from "rescuism" so I probably would have stepped in early and given them some ideas on how to get started and checked back with them periodically. I would have sat down and said: "What is your end goal?" and then I would try to divide up the responsibilities between them. I tend to do this a lot in my sheltered class right now. I am strug-

---

Delegation of Authority: Me and My Classroom

To convey understanding of this concept, you may choose any format/genre/artistic expression that you like. For an excellent presentation, your work needs to incorporate information and ideas from the readings and from class discussions (including the case discussions):

- Provide a theoretical articulation of delegation of authority as well as a description of its practical implications for the classroom;

- Express your personal opinions/dilemmas/thoughts/feelings about delegating authority;

- Clarify the match between the form/style of your presentation and its content.

Figure 4. *Delegation of Authority.*

gling with this whole concept of not stepping in to help because I think that there are some instances when the kids don't know the instructions and they may not know exactly how to proceed.

Tim's second response emphasizes the necessity of taking into account a multitude of factors when making sound pedagogical decisions. Doug, a self-proclaimed "rescuer in recovery" acknowledged how useful reading and discussing the cases could be:

> After reading Susan's case I thought she did the right thing though it took courage. Without this example, I would most certainly have rescued them. Of course, there would have been consequences; they'd be working after school for the next several weeks and then presenting the information to the class just like everyone else. I also find that I have a problem with holding the entire group accountable for the failings of a few. I liked the case and hope to attain this level of delegation. It has definitely taken the quickness and ease out of a good old-fashioned swoop rescue, they are not as comfortable anymore. The first step.

Assessing Student Teachers' Understanding of Delegation of Authority

After completing this first part of the course that dealt with organizing the classroom for groupwork, the student teachers were asked to perform the "Delegation of Authority" assignment shown in Figure 4.

The astonishing variety of formats and the inspiring creativity of the responses to this assignment were extremely rewarding. Not only did the students show remarkable understanding of the theoretical definitions, the empirical findings, and the practical implications of delegation of authority, their choices of the various media reflected the fact that they were able to transfer their understanding to other situations and contexts. While a small proportion of students wrote "traditional" essays, most students chose alternative ways to convey their understanding. Students' work ranged from poems, odes, songs, short stories, and children's stories, short plays, letters (to the principal, to parents, and to students), and a special edition of the *Stanford Daily* newspaper, to posters, political cartoons, collages, dioramas, 3-D models, picture books, video clips, and a web-page. Students read, performed, and showcased their work in front of the class. Although I had not planned to do so when constructing the syllabus (mainly because I had not anticipated these responses), we agreed to devote a whole class period to enjoying the students' presentations. In their final evaluation of this course, a number of students commented that one of the most valuable experiences was the opportunity to select a personally engaging mode of expression to complete the assignments for the course. They realized that one could show "smarts" and understanding in many different ways. Sheldon's mobile is a good example of such a student product. Here is part of his commentary:

> I have chosen to use a mobile to represent my "Delegation of Authority: Me and My Classroom." I am using this metaphor for a number of reasons. The teacher is at the top and in reality has the ultimate authority over all the students. But this is not obvious to us at first glance. Each group does appear to be independent and have authority over themselves. We don't see a direct connection to the teacher's authority. It is only when we look closely at the groups that we see the thread and follow that to the teacher who is ultimately supporting them and guiding them. The trick the teacher must play is to have the ultimate authority but not make this obvious. In the end the students have control over what they do and the product they produce.
>
> Each group is made up of different colored M&M's to represent a culturally diverse classroom. Some M&M's are on longer strings and some are on short strings within their groups to represent the high- and low-status students. Some M&M's are hanging from their feet and some from their hands. This represents how some members of the group can be off task.
>
> When you first hang up the mobile you might notice that group two is off balance. Did you try to fix it? If so, you must confess in class: "I am a rescuer!" When you see the one group off-balance your initial

instinct is to fix it and get it back in balance. It is very difficult to ignore an off-balance group and let it fail. It takes a lot of restraint to stare at the failing group without intervening. But, as we have learned, we must let the group continue to work on their own. We must not step in and rescue. The bottom line is that running a class and all the components that go with it is a balancing act.

As much as I would like to, it is impossible to describe in detail all the products of the students' work. Without doubt, the quality of the students' work attested to their conceptual understanding of the content covered in this part of the course. However, more interesting than the straightforward "understanding" were students' reflections on what delegation of authority meant to them and how they viewed themselves mastering the concept in practice. For example, Laura, who had designed an elaborate map and tour guide, wrote:

In many ways, I see a conflict for myself as I consider just how much authority I am willing to give to my students in my classroom. . . . Using the classic Robert Frost metaphor of paths which represent decisions ("I chose the one less traveled"), I saw my decisions as a question of paths to choose. Do I delegate authority or not? And depending on my decision, the results of what happens in my class vary. These ideas led naturally to an extended metaphor on the roads that teachers decide to take as they choose their pedagogical methods. I saw the method of delegating authority as potentially leading to great things in my classroom: student interaction, student independence, and so forth. Unfortunately I also have fears: what if students fail and don't learn what I want them to? What if my class degenerates into chaos or my students are resistant to my methods? Alternatively, direct instruction might be a safer choice, but would my students be learning as effectively using this method? What benefits would they miss? This quandary reminded me of a recent trip I took along the Northern California coast, during which we drove the longest way, allowing us to see beautiful vistas, but at a cost of sickeningly winding roads and an increased driving time. Taking Rt. 101 would have been easier, but we would have missed out on so much of the beautiful scenery. With this recollection, my metaphor was complete. I decided to express the decision-making process involved in creating groupwork as a choice between various paths, offering different sights as well as pitfalls along the way.

Heather designed a mandala. She wrote:

I chose the form of a mandala. I wanted to show that there are positive and negative sides, and that those will always exist; they make up part of a whole. Like the yin and the yang of a mandala, the "light" and "dark" sides of delegating authority are part of the total sum. There is a "light" or positive side to delegating authority. These reasons are listed on the sun side of the mandala, on the sun's rays. They include higher student participation and higher learning gains for the students. There is also a "dark" or a negative side of delegating authority. These are listed on the moon. They include greater chance for teacher to lose control of the class, possible reinforcement of exclusion of low-status students and lower learning gains for the students, who for whatever reason, don't participate very much. I hope to avoid the "dark" side as much as possible. However, I remain aware that I can't control everything and that it only takes a minute when my back is turned to turn a group learning activity into a painful experience for a student.

Amanda had written a particularly sophisticated one-act play entitled "Help, I'm Hearing Voices" in which different voices were speaking in the teacher's head:

It seemed far too difficult to formulate one coherent piece that could encapsulate all of the conflicts and the contradictions that formed the core of my thinking about delegating authority. That was when I came up with the idea of a dialogue, or script: I could give voice to these various ideas and opinions, all within one unified piece! I also liked this idea because it would allow me to negotiate conflicts internally while personifying these arguments in written form. By creating a script, I could work out my feelings about delegation of authority and fulfill the requirements of the assignment.

The voices that I chose to personify all represented a different opinion or belief about delegating authority. The Idealist wanted to delegate authority and believed everything would work out fine. The Realist (also known as Mr. Practicality) also wanted to delegate authority if it would work in his classroom context. The Pessimist didn't want to delegate authority because he felt it wouldn't work. The Impartial Observer didn't have an opinion but was interested in seeing how choices about delegating authority affected the classroom. The Rescuer (also known as "Softy") liked the idea of delegating authority in principle but wanted to reserve the right to intervene if things went wrong, and the Analyzer believed in delegating authority and was the expert on readings and theories.

CONCLUSION

The work of the STEP student teachers reflected their understanding of the concept of delegation of authority. As the course progressed, we covered other important elements of productive groupwork (such as the features of a "groupworthy" task, assessing group and individual products). We reviewed different approaches to cooperative learning, from structures (Kagan, 1992) to academic controversy (Johnson & Johnson, 1994), and group investigation (Sharan & Sharan, 1994). Using an analytic framework, the students were able to evaluate the benefits and the costs of these various approaches and thus became educated consumers of various classroom strategies designed for heterogeneous classrooms. Although the student teachers seemed to have developed a solid knowledge base for this instructional approach, finding out to what extent they actually used, or will be using groupwork in their own teaching, will remain the nagging question for a future study.

REFERENCES

Bandura, A. (1977). *Social learning theory.* Englewood Cliffs, NJ: Prentice-Hall.

Ben-Ari, R. (1997). Complex instruction and cognitive development. In E. G. Cohen & R. A. Lotan (Eds.), *Working for equity in heterogeneous classrooms: Sociological theory in practice* (pp. 193–206). New York: Teachers College Press.

Cohen, E. G. (1986). On sociology of the classroom. In M. Lockheed & J. Hannaway, (Eds.) *The contributions of the social sciences to education policy and practice 1965–1985.* Berkeley, CA: McCutchan.

Cohen, E. G. (1994). *Designing groupwork: Strategies for heterogeneous classrooms* (2nd ed.). New York: Teachers College Press.

Cohen, E. G., & Lotan, R. A. (Eds.) (1997). *Working for equity in heterogeneous classrooms: Sociological theory in practice.* New York: Teachers College Press.

De Avila, E. A. (1985). Motivation, intelligence, and access: A theoretical framework for the education of minority language students. In *Issues in English language development: Information exchange.* Rosslyn, VA: Inter-America Research Associates. [Co-sponsored by the National Clearinghouse for Bilingual Education and the Georgetown University Bilingual Education Service Center.]

Dweck, C. S., & Henderson, V. L. (1989, April). *Theories of intelligence: Background and measures.* Paper presented at the biennial meeting of the Society for Research in Child Development, Kansas City, MO. Available through ERIC Document Reproduction Service.

Gardner, H. (1983). *Frames of mind: The theory of multiple intelligences*. New York: Basic Books.

Holthius, N., Bianchini, J., Schultz, S, & Lotan, R. (1999). *Nervous system: An interdisciplinary life science curriculum for the middle grades*. Chicago: Everyday Learning.

Johnson, D. W., & Johnson, R. T. (1990). Cooperative learning and achievement. In S. Sharan (Ed.), *Cooperative learning: Theory and research* (pp. 23–37). New York: Praeger.

Johnson, D. W., & Johnson, R. T. (1994). Structuring academic controversy. In S. Sharan (Ed.), *Handbook of cooperative learning methods* (pp. 66–81). Westport, CT: Greenwood Press.

Kagan, S. (1992). *Cooperative Learning*. San Clemente, CA: Kagan Cooperative Learning Co.

Sharan, S. (Ed.) (1990). *Cooperative learning: Theory and research*. New York: Praeger.

Sharan, Y., & Sharan, S. (1994). Group Investigation in the cooperative classroom. In S. Sharan (Ed.), *Handbook of cooperative learning methods* (pp. 97–114). Westport, CT: Greenwood Press.

Shulman, J., Lotan, R. A., & Whitcomb, J. A. (1998). *Groupwork in diverse classrooms: A Casebook for educators*. New York: Teachers College Press.

Slavin, R. E. (1985). *Cooperative Learning*. New York: Longman.

Sternberg, R. J. (1985). *Beyond IQ: A triarchic theory of human intelligence*. Cambridge, England: Cambridge University Press.

PART II

COMMENTARIES

CHAPTER 11

THE INSTRUCTIONAL DESIGN OF COOPERATIVE LEARNING IN TEACHER EDUCATION

CELESTE M. BRODY

When the editors hold conversations with teacher educators about how to improve the preparation of teachers in cooperative learning, we are often asked, "What are the best ways to prepare novice teachers so that they can use cooperative learning well in their classrooms? Are there teacher education programs that can advise us about what works and what novice teachers can reasonably be expected to master as they enter teaching?" Whether the teacher education programs are offered in small private colleges or large public universities that educate thousands of new teachers each year, the narratives in this volume point out the foundational beliefs that guide the decisions teacher educators make regarding the structure of programs, the curriculum for cooperative learning, and desirable as well as possible outcomes.

The editors asked the contributors how they knew whether they were achieving their goals with respect to student mastery of cooperative groupwork. The contributors report on data they gathered and analyzed: student journals and portfolios; observations of how well student teachers were implementing cooperative learning in classrooms; and assessments of their programs through school personnel who also work with their students. Many concluded that they need additional data about the longitudinal effects of their preparation of novices for cooperative learning—an ongoing challenge common to teacher educators who are practitioners more than researchers.

Celeste M. Brody

CRITICAL ASPECTS OF A
COOPERATIVE LEARNING PEDAGOGY

With respect to cooperative learning, are there points of agreement on what novice teachers should understand and be able to put into practice during student teaching or at the end of program? The teacher educators in this volume do differ in the complex understandings and abilities they want their novice teachers to achieve with regard to cooperative group work. Novice teachers, however, must at least understand why and how to develop groups and group tasks, and distinguish the kinds of group processes for different kinds of outcomes. They should understand that cooperative learning requires a sharp change in the organization of the classroom and thus a change in the ideas and practices surrounding classroom management. They need to grasp the elements of task design, how to delegate their authority to a group; how to hold students accountable to one another and for the outcomes of the task; and how to structure a debriefing of groupwork. Novices need practice in coaching students for communication and groupwork skills. They should know how to monitor and evaluate student interactions to determine if productive exchanges are occurring, how to intervene to further learning or avert problems, as well as how to apply insights to improve group learning in subsequent attempts. There are questions about teacher beliefs in regard to social justice and the larger purposes of groupwork—whether the novice teacher can place actions into a larger framework regarding equity and educational ends.

Can a beginning teacher manage the complexities of cooperative learning within the larger complexities of teaching? The contributors believe novices can achieve minimum competence but it is decidedly difficult to achieve mastery. And, to achieve a minimum standard of competence in the aspects described above there are questions that teacher educators must ask themselves about the design of their programs. I have selected five areas that the contributors might generally agree are important considerations for instructional design in preparing novice teachers for the effective use of cooperative learning. There is no formula for executing peer learning, particularly cooperative groupwork, thus teacher educators must resolve for themselves some perennial questions if they are to succeed at this endeavor.

1. Program Goals and Philosophy

- How do the program goals and philosophy direct the teaching of cooperative learning and instill the values of cooperation?
- Do faculty share the goals and regularly evaluate their outcomes?

Contributors who have worked consciously to reform their programs spent considerable time in developing and revisiting a coherent philosophy and program rationale. The size of the teacher education programs is an obstacle to the kind of dialogue that is required of a group of faculty to achieve agreement about the values and beliefs that will bind their collective work and facilitate whether they can evaluate the implications of these over time. In response to the problem of unmanageable size, West Chester University faculty (chapter 8), for example, have created "boutique" experiences that serve not only students but faculty as well.

Several programs place cooperative learning into a broader view of a teacher's role, a view that telegraphs important values and ideas to the novice teachers. These programs intentionally—through both program structure and curriculum—seek to develop teachers who are: "visionaries," "change agents," "decision makers," and "leaders" who can construct (in the contributors' words) "learning communities," "learner-centered classrooms," "democratic schools," and "equitable alternatives to competitive classroom practices." In the Anderson College program, for example, cooperative learning reinforces the idea that "teachers are competent *builders* of knowledge, and committed builders of community, and caring builders of values." The cooperative learning processes that the programs design then become central to students being able to enact these goals in their field settings. Anderson College (chapter 4) emphasizes modeling of cooperative learning by faculty, as well as teaching about cooperative learning as a curricular topic. By evaluating whether "we do as we say," faculty reflect on how well they are achieving their goals and philosophy in terms of what their students are capable of doing. Lewis & Clark College faculty (chapter 2) identify key ideas as to "teacher as decision maker" that spiral through the curriculum to provide context for learning to apply cooperative learning processes. The State University of New York at New Paltz program (chapter 3) is one of the most explicit in its philosophical orientation of promoting social justice by teaching a cooperative learning course framed around "Socially Conscious Learning."

2. Learning to Teach by Experiencing Cooperative Learning

- How will novice teachers experience cooperative learning in the program?
- Do these experiences tie to competencies in the teacher's role?

Experiencing cooperative learning is at the core of being able to understand it and eventually transfer and apply its principles to classrooms. If teacher candidates are to value professional relationships, understand how to work as a member of a school team, develop communities of learners, create democratic schools, or improve conditions for achieving social equity, they start by experiencing the realization of each of these goals in their teacher education programs. They might, for example, experience what a "learning community" is through how the teacher education program itself is structured. Learning communities may be created through small cohorts as in the West Chester University program, OISE/Toronto, and the Lewis & Clark College programs or they may develop through long-standing base groups as in Anderson College and the Kassel University (chapter 7) approach. Such structures provide not only the foundation for understanding and experiencing cooperative learning processes—the basis for transfer and application—but they also require students to be accountable in new ways to one another. The novice teachers create a "feedback loop" involving dialogue, multiple forms of assessment, and reflection. For example, on a topic such as how to integrate special needs students into small groups, students might prepare for an assignment individually, bring their work to a small group for discussion and critique, and then create a new synthesis of these ideas through a group presentation to the whole class. Finally, the students would be expected to write independently in their journals to analyze their own learning and draw additional lessons for future teaching. Because they are working within cohorts or base groups that relate to one another over the course of a year or more, students are expected to connect the theories of how effective small-group processes work for their own learning as a professional. They also have an arena in which to learn how to develop healthy whole-class learning communities that are vibrant social and intellectual environments for studying and exploring questions of significance to the participants.

Programs rely on different forms of experiential learning to promote active connections between theory and practice. Stanford University-STEP (chapter 10) and West Chester University, Swanson of State Jose State University, and McBride of Cal Poly, San Luis Obispo (in Cohen, et al., chapter 9), for example, use prepared or student-generated video clips, case studies, and structured observations extensively. Lyman and Davidson (University of Maryland, chapter 8) describe how microteaching creates teaching moments, and Finkbeiner of Kassel University applies a unique model (LMR-Plus) in recursive and incrementally challenging real teaching assignments throughout the entire program. It is important to experience cooperative learning frequently throughout the teacher preparation in order for prospective teachers to (1) appreciate its value, (2) confront their own learning histories and resistances to these approaches, (3) experience the difference that cooperative learning processes make in their own learning, and (4) provide a context for studying the principles guiding the application of cooperative learning.

3. The Primacy of Reflection in Teacher Learning

- What reflective practices will be central to the program?
- How will the faculty model reflection during their teaching processes?

Contributors point out the efficiency of using metacognitive approaches to teach about complex instructional processes through the cycle of: modeling, talking out-loud as they teach, and then reflection on what happened. Brody and Nagel (Lewis & Clark College), Rolheiser and Anderson (OISE/Toronto), and Lotan (Stanford University) prefer this form of "self-reflexion" because it allows them to verbalize and voice [their] own thoughts in making pedagogical decisions and it models the idea that teacher decision making is not about right or wrong answers but of making choices between competing courses of action in the moment.

Consistent with the emphasis in teacher-education reform there is a common understanding among contributors that practicing systematic reflection produces the greatest transfer of learning to new settings (Henderson, 1996; Schon, 1987) and is a critical variable in developing teachers who are "decision makers" (Lewis & Clark College), "socially conscious teachers" (SUNY at New Paltz), or "competent curriculum builders" (Anderson College). Going further, Lyman and Davidson (University of Maryland) have done extensive and important work on providing novices with an analytic vocabulary for reflection to enhance their practices of cooperative learning. Reflection, whether it is through the creation of a culminating professional portfolio (OISE, Toronto), or frequent written exercises that require students to analyze what they know and how they know it is a skill that makes a difference in terms of knowing how and when to use cooperative learning.

4. Learning to Teach as a Developmental Process

- When and what will students learn about cooperative learning?

The level of control teacher educators have over the timing and duration of the teacher preparation may be important in novices' abilities to implement cooperative learning effectively. The context for learning to teach with cooperative learning includes discrete, planned, and conscious curricular and pedagogical experiences that reflect a developmental view of the learning and the learner. Contributors generally agree that novice teachers are more likely to understand what they are doing and why if they start by learning how to organize simple approaches to group learning, such as dyads. The novice should "start small," with simpler tasks that are supported by coaching students in one or two skills, such as listening or paraphrasing, to make sure that everyone participates and students understand what it means to cooperate. Through informal processes such as pairs that meet briefly for specific, narrow objectives, the prospective teacher can observe students' interactions, and then master some fundamentals of classroom management (e.g., using cues for helping students to begin and end) before moving on to more sophisticated processes such as a base group structure, or even conducting small-group discussions. Anderson College and Niagara University (chapter 6) provide this developmental structure through a progression of experiences with the major "models" of cooperative learning. Their curriculum moves from simple approaches to more complex approaches, drawing from Kagan (1994), then the Johnsons' conceptual approach (1990), then STAD as developed by Robert Slavin (1986), and finally elements of complex instruction (Cohen, 1994).

The Stanford University complex instruction programs are research-based and the most challenging because of the need to understand and use status treatments while managing five or six groups each doing a different task. Contributors at institutions where the faculty have had explicit training in the complex instruction approach (see Cohen, et al., chapter 9) report that their students can, indeed, accomplish this approach in the time they have with the novice teachers. Other teacher educators, on the other hand (Anderson College and Niagara University), who try to integrate complex instruction into their cooperative learning curriculum report that it is a stretch for students to master or even become superficially acquainted with in the time they have with their students. This may suggest a reliance on psychological paradigms for instruction that do not account in any depth for questions about status and the classroom as a social system.

5. Recursive Learning through Key Courses

- Where is the cooperative learning curriculum—in the general and/or content-specific methods courses?
- How does classroom management integrate the teaching about cooperative learning?
- Where do novices address the issues of teaching for social justice, supporting diversity and fostering educational equity?

It takes multiple experiences of different intensity, duration, and sophistication with this pedagogy to transform even willing teacher candidates into those who can hold their own in an increasingly complex, challenging, and even reactionary school climate. Two program areas that are particularly critical to the ability to apply cooperative learning are classroom management and methods courses—both general and specific to content areas. The third area, teaching for social justice, is a concept that also needs to be supported with recursive experiences and plenty of time for novices to consider the practical implications of their actions for educational goals.

Classroom Management

The timing of classroom management in teacher-education programs is an ongoing debate: too early in the preparation, and the novice teacher has no context for transfer and thus understanding the relationship between theory and practice. Too late in the program, and the novice teacher does not have enough theory for making effective decisions in, for example, student teaching. In terms of a complex pedagogy such as cooperative learning, if the basics of a management system are not understood and in place in the classroom, the novice teacher will most likely fail at implementing these lessons. The connection between aspects of cooperative learning and classroom management are critically important to novices' learning and the level of use they will achieve.

The Stanford University-STEP, the CSU Programs, Lewis & Clark College, and West Chester University are examples that develop the idea that the classroom is a social system and make it central to classroom management. This means that the novice teacher understands that learning happens best in environments where people develop shared understandings and norms for communication. The novice learns to develop strategies to promote group and class cohesiveness, hold groups accountable, and delegate authority for learning to groups. At the same time, the novice coaches students in the skills necessary for effective participation specific to the task at hand. This approach is in sharp contrast to traditional classroom-management approaches that have a basic psychological orientation. Lotan aptly defines the limits of traditional classroom management in her chapter: "where classroom interactions focus mainly on single, and frequently unidirectional interactions between the teacher and individual students and management means knowing how to address, restrain and repair students' disruptive behavior more effectively."

The idea that a teacher considers the classroom as a group of students that works together on each other's behalf and confers social rewards on one another is not new. Class-building and creating a sense of community as the cornerstone of effective classroom management, however, is relatively recent in the guides to cooperative learning.

General Methods and Content Methods Courses

Cooperative learning is typically taught as a discrete pedagogy in either or both types of courses: general methods and methods in the content areas. Programs such as those at the University of Maryland, Niagara University, West Chester University, OISE/Toronto, and Lewis & Clark College have included cooperative learning in both forms of methods courses. The advantage is that novice teachers can grasp general principles for cooperative learning in one course, and then be expected to consider the relationship of groupwork to the requirements of different content areas. This produces a spiral effect that provides recursive and multiple approaches to learning pedagogy. General methods may encourage the novice teacher to integrate learning theory, classroom management, and their own beliefs about the teacher's role and teaching. Understandings about cooperative learning can be framed around a series of decisions teachers make regarding selecting an appropriate instructional strategy for different learning goals.

Going further, methods in the content areas allow novice teachers to delve more deeply into the nature of the task for groupwork and the relationship of different forms of dialogue to disciplinary structures. For example, mathematics teachers may need to learn to coach for specific skills relative to getting and giving help in a conference-type setting and the use of small-groupwork for problem solving where there is only one right solution to a specific problem (Farivar & Webb, 1998). In contrast, when the learning task is more open-ended, novices will need to know how to prepare students for a different type of conversation. Language arts methods may structure questions about the importance of talk in language learning, the criteria for holding discussions, and the problem of negotiating relevant learning experiences with children that relate to literacy development (Meloth & Deering, 1994; Stahl, 1995). Science teachers can be introduced to real-world problem solving (Nagel, 1996) in relation to group investigation methods (Sharan & Sharan, 1992). Art teachers focus on the support of independent performances through peer conferencing for different aspects of a production process. Physical education teachers may concentrate on ways to promote full and equitable participation in competitive and non-competitive sports and activities for a range of student abilities and interest (Baloche & Blasko, 1992; Kohn, 1992).

The ability to construct rich tasks worthy of groupwork requires that novices have a deep understanding of content and the processes of inquiry and knowledge construction related to that discipline (or disciplines, in the case of interdisciplinary curriculum or elementary school) as well as pedagogical challenges that teachers consistently face in these areas. On the other hand, there is a danger that teaching about cooperative learning through content methods courses only leads to narrow understandings about teacher decision making and may reinforce traditional notions of what are acceptable ways of teaching a particular discipline.

Finally, teacher educators who want to include values related to social justice in their program should analyze whether these values should be represented across the program, including traditional "methods" courses. Or, if these questions are relegated to traditional "foundations" courses, how can these courses bring the relationship between theory and practice to life through the "methods" courses (Schniedewind & Davidson, 1998)?

THE IMPORTANCE OF DEFINING COOPERATIVE LEARNING OUTCOMES IN PROGRAMS

A college curriculum is a necessary but not sufficient condition for learning. The lack of good models of cooperative learning in schools, particularly in secondary schools, puts pressure on the teacher preparation program to provide frequent opportunities for the prospective teacher to practice groupwork in the laboratory setting of the college. Nothing substitutes for real classroom models of cooperative learning with mentors who have the skill and acumen to support the novice in thinking through the practical problems of application in classrooms where everything happens at once. But as contributors attest, there are many factors that make this difficult or impossible. (See the Cohen and Brubacher commentaries for further discussion on this.)

Having performance standards as outcomes for enacting cooperative learning in teacher education programs is a step toward articulating for the novice teacher, school personnel, and other faculty what is expected, what the criteria are, and approximately when over the course of the program the student teacher should demonstrate them. Continuing these outcomes into continuing licensure programs (Lewis & Clark College, for example), master's degrees (SUNY at New Paltz, for instance) and inservice programs that colleges offer in conjunction with public schools (e.g., University of Maryland and OISE/Toronto) can do a great deal to promote a consensus about what is possible, what it looks like in practice, and how colleges and universities can work together to educate prospective teachers. Faculty need to invest in defining the formative and summative competencies and outcomes in relation to cooperative learning. Then, they need to decide where and when to integrate cooperative learning into the instructional design. They may find as did several contributors (OISE/Toronto, for example) that these discussions lead to the redesign of the entire program, or as with the West Chester University faculty, to the creation of smaller units where teachers and students can work closely with particular schools. The ability to do this depends on faculty commitment, a good deal of leadership, and a desire to create something new by faculty members themselves. Engaging these challenges is, indeed, a daunting, but exceptionally satisfying task.

REFERENCES

Baloche, L., & Blasko, J. (1992). Learning together—A new twist. *The Journal of Physical Education, Recreation and Dance, 63* (3), 26–28.

Cohen, E. G. (1994). *Designing groupwork: Strategies for the heterogeneous classroom* (2nd ed.). New York: Teachers College Press.

Farvivar, S. & Webb, N. (1998). Preparing teachers and students for cooperative work: Building communication and helping skills. In C. Brody & N. Davidson (Eds.), *Professional development for cooperative learning: Issues and approaches.* Albany: State University of New York Press.

Henderson, J. G. (1996). *Reflective teaching* (2nd ed). Englewood Cliffs, NJ: Merrill Press.

Johnson, D. W., Johnson, R. T. & Holubec, E. J. (1990). *Circles of learning: Cooperation in the classroom* (3rd ed.). Edina: MN: Interaction Book Co.

Kagan, S. (1994). *Cooperative learning: Resources for teachers.* San Juan Capistrano, CA: Resources for Teachers.

Kohn, A. (1992). *No contest: The case against competition.* Boston: Houghton Mifflin.

Meloth, M. S. & Deering, P. D. (1994). Task talk and task awareness under different cooperative learning conditions. *American Educational Research Journal, 31,* 138–165.

Nagel, N. (1996). *Learning through real-world problem solving: The power of integrative teaching.* Thousand Oaks, CA: Corwin Press.

Schniedewind, N. & Davidson, E. (1998). *Open minds to equality: Learning activities to affirm diversity and promote equity.* Needham, MA: Allyn and Bacon.

Schon, D. (1987). *Educating the reflective practitioner.* San Francisco: Jossey-Bass.

Sharan, S., & Sharan, Y. (1992). *Expanding cooperative learning through group investigation.* New York: Teachers College Press.

Slavin, R. E. (1986). *Using student team learning* (3rd ed). Baltimore, MD: The Johns Hopkins University Press.

Stahl, R. (Ed.) (1995). *Cooperative learning in language arts: A handbook for teachers.* Menlo Park, CA: Addison-Wesley.

CHAPTER 12

POCKETS OF EXCELLENCE

Implications for Organizational Change

ELIZABETH G. COHEN

The authors of the chapters in this volume honestly described their struggles against difficulties in achieving their vision of a new generation of teachers playing new and different roles. In one sense, their trials and tribulations are case studies of the organizational difficulties with current arrangements in teacher education operating in a turbulent environment. Cooperative learning is a fine illustration of more general problems faced by teacher education: What happens when the objectives for credential candidates include the mastery of challenging methods of instruction? These new objectives have arisen in response to the need for more effective techniques for an increasingly diverse school population and in response to the drive to be more successful in reaching all students. Other innovations in instruction, such as teaching for understanding, reciprocal teaching, or improvement of intergroup relations fall into the same category of strategies requiring considerable understanding and staff development.

Some teacher education programs in these chapters have reorganized around a new vision of teaching, such as constructivist teaching, professional collaboration, or the goal of social justice, while others have differently organized clusters within larger programs that may be more conventional. Such programs or clusters are "pockets of excellence" where faculty and master teachers work closely and consistently with credential candidates and with each other. For example, Slostad, Baloche, and Darigan (chapter 8) describe a "boutique" experience amidst the "shopping mall" constructed for a thousand students working for an elementary credential at Westchester University. In a 15-credit block for a semester, approximately eighteen students and three faculty members develop literacy skills using cooperative learning as an important framework. Students gain intensive field experience as well as specific training in strategies of cooperative learning. The fact that this powerful experience is found in one small cluster of coursework and faculty in a large program argues for larger structural reform. Why shouldn't all the preservice teachers have such a strong experience?

ORGANIZATIONAL DIFFICULTIES

The chapters document a set of organizational difficulties with multiple references to some central problems. As one of my sociological colleagues is fond of saying, "I think the data are telling us something."

Placement of Student Teachers

The placement of student teachers or interns is at the heart of any teacher education program. Placement is especially critical for preservice teachers who are studying cooperative learning because the chance to *see and practice* groupwork affects the students' willingness to try cooperative learning in their first year of teaching (Cohen et al., chapter 9). Authors reporting on experience in student teaching find that when modeling and practice opportunities during student teaching are infrequent, there is much less chance that graduates will be able to use techniques of cooperative learning well.

Despite heroic efforts to guarantee the nature of this experience, there are persistent difficulties. For example, Slostad, Baloche, and Darigan report that even with the careful placement of students in the field, some students were in classrooms where the use of cooperative learning was less than ideal. Not only do some of the student teachers find themselves with cooperating teachers who have negative attitudes toward cooperative learning (Foote et al., chapter 6) and who think that there is no way to hold individuals accountable and are thus opposed to its use in their classroom, but some candidates are in schools where the principals do not approve because they expect a quiet classroom (Harris & Hanley, chapter 4).

Professors may not be able to influence the process of student teacher placement. Sometimes there is centralized control of this function at the university such that groups of professors who are teaching cooperative learning cannot request placement with teachers who use these techniques (Cohen, et al., chapter 9). At Niagara University (Foote, et al., chapter 6), each district has its own policy on selecting cooperating teachers and because the teacher education program needs to place all of its students, they must take all available placements.

Relationships between the universities and schools are often relatively weak and counterproductive. As Theresa Perez put it "We live on two different planets due in large measure to organizational factors that preclude 'crossing over,' to the other side" (Cohen, et al., chapter 9). The principal linkage between the university and student-teacher placement is the supervisor who is often not the professor of the course on cooperative learning. Supervision of student teaching is a poorly organized and usually underfunded function.

Consistency of Teaching among Teacher Educators

A second organizational difficulty lies in the weakly integrated faculty within the program of teacher education. Many of the authors argue that if credential candidates consistently experience more cooperative learning in their classes, they will be much more likely to try these strategies when they are on their own. However, the authors suggest that this can only be achieved in small faculties or in small clusters of faculty and students within larger programs. In the integrated semester of Westchester (Slostad, Baloche, and Darigan) there is a collective collegial experience that allows the three faculty members to collaborate and problem solve with respected colleagues, thus producing consistent teaching. Even in a small college like Lewis & Clark College (faculty of ten to twelve full-time teachers who work closely together), Brody and Nagel speak of faculty turnover and use of adjunct faculty as undermining the consistent use of cooperative learning at the college. At Anderson College, the head of teacher education at the time, Joellen Harris, (Harris & Hanley, chapter 4), was able to run a class on cooperative learning for seven of her colleagues. At Niagara University, Foote et al. report that although all full-time faculty members in the education department use cooperative learning to some degree, some full-time faculty and adjunct faculty are not very confident about being able to instruct preservice teachers in these strategies. As a result of observing this inconsistency, a number of authors speak of the need for continuing staff development for faculty in teacher education programs—something for which there is very little organizational precedent.

The need for collegial interaction and support along with continuing staff development is closely related to the weakness of instructional leadership in the administration of teacher education programs. The chapters reveal heroic attempts by faculty members to integrate programs around a unified philosophy of teacher education. This is best exemplified at Lewis & Clark (Brody and Nagel, chapter 2).

A unifying philosophy may not be enough to produce a consistent and well-integrated program. As Brody and Nagel conclude, an underlying agreement on philosophy is not a substitute for close coordination of ways to instruct candidates in methods of cooperative learning. The case of OISE at the University of Toronto comes closest to the ideal of instructional leadership where Rolheiser and Anderson report Dean Michael Fullan's strong leadership in reshaping the teacher education program. Another example is that of Susan Roper as head of teacher education at California Polytechnic State University at San Luis Obispo (Cohen et al.). Roper sponsored, attended, and participated in faculty workshops in complex instruction, workshops that she sponsored for her faculty.

Higher education pays lip service to collegial norms, but most teacher education programs are no more collegial than the rest of the university. Small groups of professors can be successful as a team in teaching cooperative learning, but leading the entire faculty into more teamwork and coordination is like the proverbial task of trying to herd cats.

The Problem of Timing

In training teachers, we try to cram everything into the preservice phase followed by the first year of teaching in which there is no further contact with university experts. This presents a practical difficulty in that the student teacher may be overwhelmed with issues of classroom management and is not ready to practice innovations that assume a well-managed classroom.

Looking at the experience of veteran teachers developing their skills in cooperative learning, one can see that it often takes more than one year to produce a confident user of these methods. As with all more complex innovations, one's understanding becomes deeper over time, with practice and feedback. Very often, despite a rich program, graduates fail to use cooperative learning in their first year of teaching. For example, after four years of work with cooperative learning, Anderson college reports from a follow-up study that only two out of sixteen first-year teachers made frequent use of cooperative learning in their first year of teaching (Harris & Hanley).

Turbulence of the Organizational Environment

The pressure for accountability and standards is reducing the ability of teacher education programs and that of faculty in schools to implement more sophisticated methods of teaching. According to Brody and Nagel, "The gaps between our recommendations about best practice and actual school practice have increased in the last five years—the effects of the state's emphasis on standardized testing as measures for benchmarks have been devastating to the progressive practices including the use of cooperative learning in the school." The pressure for test scores pushes teachers into a constant mode of test preparation that often translates into traditional teacher-dominated classes and a neglect of cooperative learning (Harris & Hanley). If preservice programs focused on innovations are to survive in this environment, Rolheiser and Anderson have found that they must constantly adapt to subject-based learning expectations by grade level and annual standardized testing. Dictation of educational policies and practices by politicians and corporate executives impede Schneidewind's attempts to introduce concepts of social conscience along with cooperative learning.

The general tendency for schools and districts to mandate specific instructional strategies works against student teachers receiving support from their cooperating teachers for trying out their skills. The classroom teacher may regard these new skills, learned at the university, as incompatible with the mandates under which she labors. In the future, the universities and colleges of education may become the repositories of more demanding methods of instruction that are not in general use at the present time.

IMPLICATIONS FOR REFORM

The success of a number of the programs suggests new ways of accomplishing objectives in a reform of teacher education. Their successes tell us how things might be better, just as their difficulties tell us something of the underlying organizational problems.

Integration of Teacher Education with the Schools

The effectiveness of various partnerships speaks to the potential of a new form of teacher education that universities run jointly with selected schools. The strongest form appears when the classroom teachers become partners in the instruction and supervision of student teachers. At the University of Toronto (Rollheiser and Anderson, chapter 1), the faculty negotiated programmatic partnerships with school districts and clusters of schools, called the Learning Consortium. The partners chose cooperative learning as a focus for teacher learning. Host teachers and university instructors observe the candidates teach and provide on-the-spot feedback. Rolheiser and Anderson collected systematic evidence of coaching by the host teachers.

Working with a single school, Perez involved the teachers with the instruction of preservice candidates in a portable building at the school site. University faculty teaching in a cluster within the teacher education program at CSU Fresno and the cooperating teachers took joint responsibility for instruction of the student teachers (Cohen et al.).

Alternative to a full-fledged partnership, other methods of reorganizing and controlling student teaching showed some success. At the Howard County Teacher Education/Professional Development Center (Lyman and Davidson, chapter 8), student teachers attended seminars in connection with their placement in schools in five surrounding districts. The students received direct encouragement from the center coordinator to implement cooperative learning. This program was helped by the fact that cooperative learning is relatively widely implemented in schools in this area due to many years of active work of Neil Davidson and the Maryland Association for Cooperation in Education (MACIE).

In the integrated semester described by Slostad, Baloche, and Darigan, the practicum professor determines all student placements at three schools where he has worked consistently for five years. He knows all the teachers and they trust him. In the Master's-level program at Lewis & Clark, there is a year-long placement with a mentor teacher. Interns are matched with mentors in a careful process of initial visits, interviews, and discussion. Mentors are expected to allow students to experiment with different forms of peer learning and to attend an ongoing seminar at the college.

All these reorganizations require a willingness on the part of cooperating teachers to become truly expert in innovative techniques taught at the university. The University of Toronto faculty who were involved in the Learning Consortium (Roheiser and Anderson) staged a series of summer institutes in cooperative learning for practicing teachers, interested university faculty, and prospective student teachers. And yet with all this elaborate work, these authors state the need for more coaching to further develop the expertise of host teachers.

Integration within the Teacher Education Faculty

The faculty of teacher education programs and its administration need to be more tightly coordinated and instructionally integrated without undesirable forms of standardization that we now see in the public schools. Given the traditional professorial model of total autonomy, this is a tall order in higher education.

The experience of Niagara University is instructive (Foote et al.). Full-time faculty members take on the responsibility of being a course facilitator for several courses to provide consistency and high standards and to provide support for instructors who teach these courses. They have also found team-teaching helpful in faculty coordination and staff development.

Particularly in very large programs, there is a temptation to use standardization as a way to solve the problem of coordination of faculty and objectives.

Rolheiser and Anderson speak of the shift to a program cohort structure as conducive to more coordination and coherence of student experience *within* one of the cohorts or clusters. However, the success of their particular cohort is not consistent across all program options in their institution. As they describe the problem, "The challenge is how innovative approaches in teacher education are shared with colleagues and diffused over time within a large preservice program." We need to study the use of cohorts within large programs to determine the type of leadership that will be necessary to meet this challenge.

Changing the Timing

There seems to be real merit in staging teacher training such that the full credentialing occurs after preservice instruction and after some years of classroom experience. Teachers who are experienced and have full control of their classrooms are in an excellent position to learn new techniques that they can try out and then receive feedback from their university instructors. The experience reported by Schneidewind attests to the efficacy of this model. All of the practicing teachers in her follow-up study were using cooperative learning in their classrooms. Oregon has put in a Continuing Licensure requirement that means that faculty will have an opportunity to work with program graduates and inservice teachers over the course of six years (Brody and Nagel).

CONCLUSION

University-school partnerships, professional development schools, collaboration of teacher education faculty, and staging of teacher preparation are not new ideas. What is new is the proposal to combine these features so that organizational arrangements are specifically linked to development of new roles and instructional strategies for the next generation of teachers. Starting with the technical demands of what we want teachers to be able to do, we need to move to arrangements that will support and enable teacher educators to meet those demands.

CHAPTER 13

COOPERATIVE LEARNING AND TEACHING FOR SOCIAL JUSTICE

MARA SAPON-SHEVIN

The chapters in this volume evidence a wide range of approaches to teaching cooperative learning (and teaching cooperatively) within teacher education programs. These programs differ in many ways: the centrality of cooperative learning to the overall program, the types of cooperative learning students are taught and expected to practice, and the relationships between classroom and field experiences. There are also noticeable differences in the extent to which concerns about equity and social justice are addressed explicitly or embedded within the teacher education program generally and the teaching of cooperative learning specifically.

This commentary section raises issues and concerns about the ways in which broader societal concerns about justice, fairness, equality, voice, and power are linked to the teaching of cooperative learning. While there is little doubt (and these chapters confirm) that cooperative learning is an effective teaching strategy, how does the cooperative learning modeled in these chapters link this promising pedagogy to broader societal and cultural conditions and concerns? As teacher education continues to evolve and come under close scrutiny, it is imperative that teacher educators be clear about the value base that informs their pedagogical and curricular choices and their commitment to understanding the broad-ranging results of particular choices.

The following represents points of struggle and possibility in the teaching of cooperative learning. Each of these questions allows us to examine more closely the intended and unintended consequences of how we prepare teachers.

How do concerns about broader issues of social justice
connect with teaching cooperative learning?

Issues that might be labeled as social justice are embedded in these program models in many ways—through the curriculum, the pedagogy, and the program philosophy. Many of the programs described here discuss the importance of preparing teachers for heterogeneous classrooms, a reality linked to issues of fairness, equity, and representation. Rolheiser and Anderson (OISE/UT, chapter 1) state that they expect their teachers to be "active agents of educational improvement and societal change," and one of the key images of their program relates directly to issues of diversity. Cohen et al. and Lotan (chapters 9 and 10) address the importance of giving teachers strategies that enable them to work successfully with diverse learners, particularly in terms of issues of power, authority, role, evaluation, and status. Teachers are specifically taught to be alert to marginalized and excluded students and to actively intervene to promote more equitable participation and outcomes. Harris and Hanley use a variety of approaches, including Cohen's model that demands attention to low-status students and multiple abilities. Slostad et. al attend to the relationship between classroom management and teaching and ways in which issues of control are managed. They explore the importance of having students become "humane authoritarians" while continuing to make them "move towards more interactional and democratic practices." The Lewis & Clark program (chapter 2) also has students wrestle with the relationship between classroom management and cooperative learning and uses cohorts as a purposeful way of exploring justice, equality, and equal access. Finkbeiner at Kassel University (chapter 7) attends to issues of marginalization and exclusion by attempting to make all classroom participants "experts" and disrupting prevailing hierarchies of skill. Lyman and Davidson (University of Maryland, chapter 5) include discussions of social justice concerns (tracking and mainstreaming) as content through which they teach cooperative learning strategies. Lastly, Schniedewind's program (SUNY at New Paltz, chapter 3) completely embeds issues of cooperative learning within a broader context of developing a "socially conscious" vision of a cooperative, inclusive society.

How can the process of teaching cooperative learning be used to
look at the social justice issues that arise in our own classrooms?

At the same time that these programs teach students about issues of power, voice, authority, and democratic decision making in the elementary and secondary classrooms in which they will teach, these same issues arise in college classrooms. While programs such as those described by Cohen et al. (chapter 9) and Lotan (STEP, chapter 10) talk to future teachers about multiple abilities and the implications of acknowledging the many different ways of being "smart," how do these imperatives transfer to the preservice teacher education program? How do teacher educators themselves struggle with issues of status, stigma, and representation in their own programs? What are the challenges of negotiating the conflicts and inequities that arise in the teacher education program at the same time that there is curriculum to be "covered"? Do we "preach" better than we "practice"? Is that inevitable given the differences between university-level teaching and public school education, or should we be more troubled by those discrepancies? How much time can a teacher educator take in class to deal with complex interpersonal conflicts and relationships when they are also charged with teaching students how to teach? And yet, how can they not attend to the very issues they want their students to address in the field? Lewis & Clark's use of cohorts, and the relatively small size of some of the other programs make it quite likely that interpersonal concerns will surface during the program (Sapon-Shevin and Chandler, 2001). Teacher educators' skills in attending to these issues are as important as models as the particular cooperative learning program they espouse. Lotan's students struggle with issues of hovering, rescuing, and the delegation of authority both within their own classroom and during their field placements, providing instructive parallels of the hard decisions teachers make.

*Are there contradictions between recognizing cooperative
learning as critical pedagogy and requiring its use?*

Some of the programs included here are ones in which only a small segment of the teacher education students are actively engaged in cooperative learning instruction. In Slostad et al.'s program (West Chester University, chapter 8), the individual teacher education programs are referred to as "boutiques" and contrasted with more institutionalized programs. The OISE/UT program (chapter 1) is also one in which only some students are given extensive preparation in cooperative learning. This raises complex structural and ethical concerns. If teacher educators really believe that cooperative learning is an essential strategy for producing equitable, just classrooms, then what about the future classrooms of those who do not receive this preparation? At a practical level, how do higher education institutions change, and can pedagogical and curricular changes be mandated across faculty and programs?

On the other hand, even if we firmly believe that cooperative learning should be a critical component of every future teacher's education, is *requiring* critical pedagogy an oxymoron? What is the relationship between empowering teachers and teacher educators to make their own decisions about teaching and curriculum and yet privileging specific kinds of strategies? In my Teaching Strategies course, for example, I must make decisions about which strategies to teach. Some students complain that they get "too much cooperative learning." How do I, as a teacher educator, evaluate the ethical and pedagogical limits of my own strong bias for teaching strategies that are constructivist and grounded in a specific vision of the way the world could be? It is difficult to declare certain teaching strategies "more effective" without asking, "effective for what?" Given a climate in which the purposes of schools are hotly debated and contentious, decisions about methods cannot be made in a political or economic vacuum.

> *Are we (or can we be) as committed to preparing diverse teachers*
> *as we are to the diverse students they will teach?*

Cooperative learning is often advocated as a successful teaching strategy for working with diverse student groups. Many of the programs described here share a commitment to preparing teachers for diverse (and often urban) schools and purposefully teach cooperative learning strategies to increase the likelihood of student success. What is our commitment to teacher education students who are from nontraditional or underrepresented backgrounds or who lack some of the typical skills and preparation deemed necessary for success within the teacher education program? This question raises both pedagogical and ethical dilemmas. Many of the programs described here prepare teachers who come from largely white, middle-class backgrounds. Several of the authors lament the limited diversity of students (and faculty) within their own programs. What about students who perform poorly in the teacher education program? How do we sort out the differences between "nonstandard" and "below standard" in the teachers we prepare? How do we interrogate our own biases so that we do not further decrease the heterogeneity of the teaching force while still maintaining the "quality" we aspire to? When future teachers do not master the basic skills of cooperative learning, what kinds of accommodations are we expected or able to make and what is our level of commitment to ensuring the success of a diverse teacher education group? Lotan explores the fact that equal treatment is not necessarily "fair" treatment, and that we must base our differential treatment of students on actual student needs rather than on stereotypes or prejudicial low expectations. But, within a teacher education program, how do we manage this, and what are the limits of time and resources that make this commitment to equality of outcome challenging? How do we make sure that our own prejudices and values do not obscure us to the potential within our own "nonstandard" students?

> *What will happen to the important relationships necessary to teach and implement*
> *cooperative learning in a growing climate of standardization and testing?*

Many current trends in education are completely antithetical to the underlying values and practice of cooperative learning. Both the growing use of high-stakes testing and a focus on standardized tests as the measure of educational achievement work against teachers' ability and willingness to engage in creative, collaborative pedagogical and curricular projects. Brody and Nagel's experience demonstrates that the focus on standardized testing "distracts from best practice" and leaves teachers with "no time to experiment and learn." Harris and Hanley describe administrators who perceive cooperative learning as being in conflict with "real teaching" which occurs when the room is quiet. If teachers are judged on the ways in which their teaching strategies resemble testing strategies, they will not feel supported to engage in cooperative learning. When teachers feel under the gun, fearing for their jobs and their reputations, then their willingness to broaden their pedagogical repertoire is sharply diminished. When student achievement will be measured by multiple-choice questions on standardized tests and those tests are directly linked to rigid, lock-stepped curricula, the chances that teachers will develop exciting, participatory, cooperative learning projects and activities will be decreased as well. In Massachusetts, a teachers' group protested the state testing program by constructing a graveyard of rich educational opportunities they could no longer provide their students because of the limitations and demands of the mandated testing. Cooperative learning activities and a focus on collaborative projects will no doubt be among the casualties of these educational "reforms."

Also likely to suffer from an increased emphasis on high-stakes testing are some of the relationships that are fostered within cooperative teacher education and elementary and secondary classrooms. Many of the programs described here are clearly strong because of the relationships that exist among the people involved. Student and faculty cohorts that build community and decrease loneliness and isolation, close relationships between cooperating teachers and student teachers and between teachers and students—all of these suffer when what is evaluated (and thus valued) is test scores above all else. Maintaining a commitment to the principles and practices of cooperative learning will be increasingly challenging and important as various school constituencies struggle to define the true purpose of education and the ways in which success will be judged.

How can we balance our commitment to developing strong university-school partnerships with our commitment to working with schools that allow our students to learn to become good teachers?

It was clear that the success of many of the programs described here depends on having student field placements that allow beginning teachers to practice cooperative learning, receive thoughtful feedback, and be mentored by experienced, competent cooperating teachers in schools that value and promote cooperative learning. What ethical issues arise as we try to bridge the university-field connection? In some programs, future teachers are placed only in settings in which cooperative learning is already well entrenched and respected. This provides the powerful advantage of allowing practicing teachers to explore their new skills in a nurturing, supportive atmosphere. Even in those schools, however, the departure of a key staff member can challenge the school's commitment to cooperative learning.

But what about the schools (described by many of these chapters) where cooperative learning does not happen, or those with a pedagogy and curriculum that are antithetical to the use of cooperative learning strategies? We must struggle with our responsibilities to our future teachers and the need to provide them with good learning opportunities and the reality that many of the students in schools that do not embrace cooperative learning will therefore never be able to benefit from this pedagogy. While some of these schools may be schools with resources and a different but equally successful orientation, it is also likely that these schools will be poor, inadequately supported or staffed, and with few resources. Are we, then, perpetuating hierarchies of privilege and discrimination by working closely with schools that are already doing well and avoiding those in struggle? Are there ways in which colleges of education can form relationships with poor and struggling schools so that students in those schools can also experience cooperative learning and other cutting-edge teaching strategies as part of their school experience?

Establishing working partnerships with schools involves negotiating discrepancies in the missions, schedules, and work responsibilities that discriminate public schools from colleges and universities. But it is only through these collaborations that we can hope that our future teachers will be able to practice what we have taught them and that our teaching can remain responsive to the very real challenges facing the public schools.

> *What preparation and support will teachers need if they are to move their use and understanding of cooperative learning outside their classroom walls to look at broader societal concerns such as racism, capitalism, violence and poverty?*

It is sad, but undeniable, that vast discrepancies exist between what we teach future teachers at the university and what they see when they enter many schools. While sharing a positive vision of what schools and society *can* be like is critical, we must also equip future teachers with the political and advocacy skills they will need to negotiate the gap between the schools they see and the schools they want to create. Brody and Nagel describe the ways in which secondary school teachers resist cooperative learning and the ways that resistance is linked to broader societal norms of competition, marginalization, and meritocracy. How can we help students transfer their understanding to bigger venues? Almost seventy years ago, George S. Counts asked, "Can the School Build a New Social Order?"(1932). He inquired about the possibility of schools serving as beacons, models, and catalysts for the kinds of systemic, structural changes that a more inclusive, democratic society demands. Seventy years later, we are still asking this same question. Schniedewind explicitly challenges the teachers in her program to think beyond cooperation as a teaching strategy and to explore ways in which cooperative thinking and a growing social consciousness about cooperation can inform institutions and problems outside of the school walls. What are the implications of cooperation for how we think about non-school forms of selection, sorting, competition, hierarchies, and exclusion? How can we help our students think about issues of health care, racism, violence, and poverty from a cooperative, inclusive perspective?

In an article entitled, "Cooperative Learning: Liberatory Praxis or Hamburger Helper?" (Sapon-Shevin, 1991), I raised concerns about the ways in which cooperative learning had become, in some instances, and could become more generally, a relatively value-free pedagogy, de-coupled from broader concerns about social justice. This is a danger to which we must remain alert. We have the potential to help our future teachers not only learn powerful educational strategies but also see how those are and can be connected to building more democratic, multicultural, inclusive communities. Let us seize every opportunity to help teachers link their "school work" to broader social agendas that improve the lives of all people.

REFERENCES

Counts, G. S. (1932). *Dare the school build a new social order?* Paper presented at the Progressive Education Association in Baltimore, MD., February, 1932.

Sapon-Shevin, M. (1991). Cooperative learning: Liberatory praxis or hamburger helper? *Educational Foundations, 5,* 5–17.

Sapon-Shevin, M. & Chandler-Olcott, K. (2001). Student cohorts: Communities of critique or dysfunctional families. *Journal of Teacher Education.* 52(5), 350–364.

CHAPTER 14

THE ROLE OF THE CLASSROOM TEACHER IN TEACHER EDUCATION

MARK BRUBACHER

The classroom teacher is a critical link between the coursework and practical field experience of the preservice teacher. As many authors in this volume have explained, unless the preservice teacher has the opportunity to work with a classroom teacher who is a model and who provides guided experience in cooperative learning, it is very difficult for the novice to adopt this strategy for instruction in her/his own classroom. The difficulty of finding such mentor teachers within the typical organizational arrangements of universities and public school districts is one that a number of authors have described. Although mentor teachers are highly valued by the authors, with the exception of Mary Murray [one of the co-authors of chapter 6, on Niagara University], we do not hear directly from the classroom teacher in this volume.

The contributors to this book report on the continuing difficulty of locating well-prepared mentors who can model, coach, and supervise the student teacher's learning effectively. In the area of cooperative learning it is especially challenging at the secondary level to find teachers who share the same educational philosophy and practice as the college faculty. At the secondary level, potential mentor teachers in cooperative learning may be isolated within the practice of their own schools. However, finding mentoring teachers is also a problem for the elementary level. For example, although Anserson College faculty (chapter 4) prefer to place teacher candidates in sites that use cooperative learning, they often meet the implementation problem of a true difference in teaching philosophies between the teacher candidate and the cooperating teacher in the public school classroom.

In this commentary, I would like to examine the possibility of a new and more equal partnership of university educators and classroom teachers in the process of teacher education. There are several chapters where such new and different arrangements are suggested. I would like to bring these ideas together in these pages along with some suggestions for how such a reform could work to the advantage of all three parties: the university-based teacher educator, the preservice teacher, and the classroom teacher.

MOVING TOWARDS A COEQUAL RELATIONSHIP

There is a growing realization that institutions of teacher education must work more closely with school boards and schools. Rolheiser and Anderson (chapter 1) at IOSE/UT have created a program where classroom teachers and university faculty become partners in the instruction and supervision of student teachers. Cohen et al. (chapter 9) is encouraged by one example at CSU Fresno of a "tight relationship with a professional development school where teachers from that school have a presence on campus and are co-instructors of the pre-service teachers." The Lewis & Clark College program (chapter 2) provides a year-long seminar for their mentors to support their learning and to invite their expertise in the design and execution of the internship. West Chester University faculty (chapter 8) in the boutique approach work closely with teachers from selected school districts who understand the philosophy of the particular program and become cooperating colleagues in the teacher preparation.

It is not at all unusual for the university to hire a classroom teacher to teach a methods course in a particular content area. This step, in itself, does not constitute an equal partnership, nor does it lead automatically to a solution to the problems of field placement in preparing teachers in cooperative learning. In the case of Lewis & Clark College and Niagara University (chapter 6), we have examples of close collaborations between the teacher who is working at the university and a team of faculty members—a collaboration with cooperative learning as a central goal. At Lewis & Clark, the faculty actively recruit practitioners—teachers recently retired, on leave of absence or teaching simultaneously in the two organizations—as clinical experts who supervise the field experiences and teach courses. At Niagara University, Mary Murray is a current public school teacher and also an adjunct professor teaching the social studies methods course with a central emphasis on cooperative learning. By selecting "master" adjuncts, the faculty feel they are sending a signal to the schools that they view these individuals as outstanding teachers and want their practices to be held up as models. This should help to reduce the isolation of the secondary school teacher who is expert in cooperative learning.

When classroom teachers have an important role in preservice instruction *at their school site*, there is an additional step toward a partnership that will result in integrated supervision of the preservice teacher who is attempting cooperative learning. For example, the Ryerson University Now (RIN) program in Ontario, Canada has developed the practice of paying high school teachers to give an accredited university course at the high school location. An example of this type of arrangement was reported by Carol Cameron who was an adjunct professor at York University, also in Ontario Canada.[1] She was located in a school and had her own classroom, but had release time to work with colleagues as an inservice instructor and with the group of student teachers. When Carol taught, cooperative learning was at the center of her instruction on assessment and evaluation. Furthermore, she provided a model of this practice in her classroom. In other long-term arrangements, universities pay for relieving practicing/host teachers from one or more of their regular classes. This frees them up to become coequal teaching associates in which they plan and deliver programs as equal partners with the university faculty.

A New Partnership Paradigm

Ideally, classroom teachers should be actively involved in the training of new teachers from the coursework stage to the fieldwork stage. One way for this to happen is a better integration of practicing teachers with the university faculty. One organizational structure that reflects this approach is what Cohen et al. (chapter 9) describe as professional development schools: "The quantitative and qualitative data suggest that the most promising innovations are the professional development schools where a cluster of faculty in partnership with cooperating teachers supervise a cohort of student teachers. Together they shape a program of coursework and targeted practice in cooperative learning."

In addition to the professional development schools described in this chapter in connection with CSU Fresno, Swanson of San Jose State describes her experiencing three professional development schools in San Jose Unified School District:

> I could create the conditions we know are necessary to teach complex instruction. Coursework and student teaching were simultaneous (two days of coursework and three in the field) so students could try any idea in their student teaching. I worked with their cooperating teachers in monthly seminars so I could explain their assignments. I took the time to teach cooperating teachers about status and how to treat it. I could emphasize that they had to give their students the latitude to

try multiple ability tasks in order to treat status. While there was defi-
nitely tension between the schools' prescriptive back-to-basics curriculum and the kinds of teaching I wanted my students to try, we had
good rapport and ongoing communication to make it work.[2]

Swanson reported that just as she developed a cadre of cooperating teachers with
the help of observation and feedback in their classrooms so that they could play
a fully equal role, the foundation grant supporting the professional development
schools ended. Although efforts were made to seek new funding, no school university partnerships were funded with the foundation's new initiatives. This
event illustrates the fragility of organizational arrangements that try to bridge
the two different worlds of the university and the public schools. They do not
represent a fundamental organizational change, but a temporary partnership
dependent upon external funding.

Similarly, Perez in the chapter on the California State University campuses
(Cohen et al., chapter 9) reports success with a school whose teachers are co-
instructors of the preservice teachers at CSU Fresno. In most cases, however,
Perez states that "intimate connections are the exception rather than the rule."
Swanson goes on to explain about alternative models of partnership:

> Whether a cooperating teacher offers several sessions of groupwork for
> a university class, or the university professor goes to the schools and
> teaches the cooperating teachers about complex instruction, you bring
> together the two essential partners. If we want student teachers to
> practice what they learn in coursework, it will only happen with com-
> munication between the course instructor and those who structure,
> monitor, and teach in the student teaching setting.[3]

In the state of California, the reduction in class size in early elementary
grades brought about an acute shortage of teachers. Preservice teachers just
beginning their programs were offered the opportunity to teach with emergency
credentials. As a result, alternative certification programs sprang up in which
there was deeper cooperation between school districts and the California State
University system then ever before. At San Jose State, there is a partial intern
program in which the interns teach in the class of a faculty associate and take
over the class one day a week while the associate mentors other beginning
teachers. They take coursework simultaneously at the university. In the second
year they are full-time teachers with ongoing support, some coursework, and
mentoring from both the district and the university. The communication
between university faculty and schools is ongoing and tailored to bringing
together ideas presented in coursework with their application in the classroom.

Here is an unexpected opportunity to provide a unified experience of coursework and practice in cooperative learning.

The schools and the universities are still two very different organizations with many barriers in between. Moreover, cooperative learning is still outside the mainstream, especially in secondary schools. However, I hope that these examples illustrate what can be done by seizing opportunities such as professional development schools, new alternative certification programs, and other breaks in the traditional barriers between university-based teacher educators and classroom teachers.

CONCLUSION

Classroom teachers and first-year teachers who are experimenting with cooperative learning both need and deserve some ongoing support. Some of the arrangements we have described provide that extra ongoing support within the schools. Insofar as practicing teachers receive support for their work in cooperative learning, they will be more willing and able to provide support for student teachers. When university personnel reach out to work with their own graduates as well as with cooperating teachers, they will find that placement of student teachers with strong models of cooperative learning becomes less problematic.

Promoting approaches that foster a coequal relationship between classroom teachers and university faculty could go a long way in solving the problem of finding enough mentors who are dedicated to helping new teachers with cooperative learning. If structures are set up enabling teachers to become fully professional copartners, the gap between the teacher training institution and the schools could virtually disappear. As teachers are empowered through their own growth, and through the design and implementation of programs, they will see themselves as professionals in contexts similar to law internships and teaching hospitals. Teacher educators need to explore more vigorously innovative teacher training approaches that directly involve experienced, expert classroom teachers.

NOTES

1. Transcription of proceedings of a cooperative learning conference sponsored by the International Association for the Study of Cooperative Education (IASCE) and the Great Lakes Association for Cooperation in Education (GLACIE), held in Toronto, Canada, May 27–29, 1999.

2. Personal Communication, Patricia Swanson.

3. Personal Communication, Patricia Swanson.

CONCLUSION

MARA SAPON-SHEVIN AND ELIZABETH G. COHEN

This book marks the first time that information has been collected on how cooperative learning is conceptualized and implemented within teacher education programs. The cases selected for inclusion are not a random sample. Indeed, each program represents significant, longstanding commitment by faculty to the importance of this instructional strategy. A study of these cases has yielded important new knowledge. We are now significantly smarter than we were at the inception of the project about what can be accomplished and how teacher educators have brought about a measure of success. But the programs and research described in this book have also illuminated many challenges for teacher educators and helped us to identify areas of necessary future exploration and research.

TWIXT THE CUP AND THE LIP, THERE'S MANY A SLIP

Taken as a whole, we are acutely aware that there are major differences between claims that our students are instructed in "cooperative learning" and a detailed understanding of what exactly future teachers learn and practice. Like many "best practices" in education, "cooperative learning" has become something of a code word for a set of practices that involve students working together, but there are multiple interpretations of the nature of that instruction as well as the goals for its implementation. Extensive future documentation will be required in order to fully understand the nature and quality of what teachers are learning and to evaluate the quality of their implementation of cooperative learning in the field.

PROCESS/CONTENT RELATIONSHIPS

One area of concern is the relationship between cooperative learning as a *process* and an understanding of the content or *curriculum* that cooperative learning is used to teach. The models and approaches described here include those in which a fairly standard curriculum is taught cooperatively, a few in which a multilevel curriculum (one that addresses a wide range of student skill levels within the same activity) has been elaborately designed specifically for cooperative learning groups, and those in which the content itself relates directly to issues of collaboration, conflict resolution, and cooperation. We have yet to fully understand whether presenting teachers with already-prepared curricula to be delivered cooperatively is a helpful step in mastering the complexities of cooperative learning or whether removing teachers from decision making about curriculum represents a step towards overall deskilling. When teachers implement a complex cooperative learning curriculum designed by others, this may help them to understand the complexity of curriculum design, but it might not lead (without extensive support) to them designing their own complex lessons. It is not clear whether all cooperative learning must be constructivist (drawing on students' own knowledge and experiences) in order to be successful.

What is clear is that teachers must become skilled in constructing student tasks that are *interdependent*—for example, those that require students to actively work together in order to be successful. Simply putting students in groups and urging them to work cooperatively on what is essentially an individualized task does not occasion the most powerful results or help teachers to become thoughtful about the content they teach. There is much work to be done in helping teachers to become thoughtful about the curriculum they design and implement. Further research needs to examine the nature of the curriculum that is taught cooperatively. In addition to this descriptive research, we need to understand how we can best help teachers to become skilled curriculum designers who use cooperative strategies in their classrooms.

THE TEACHER'S ROLE

A greater understanding of the teacher's role vis à vis cooperative learning is also critical. It is evident that cooperative learning changes the teacher's interactions with students. Teachers with a tendency to micromanage may be seriously challenged when implementing a teaching strategy in which they are not privy to every small detail of discussion or interaction. Lotan refers to the need for cooperative learning teachers to join "Rescuers Anonymous," resisting the strong pull to rescue cooperative learning groups that are floundering or even temporarily stalled. Teachers need to monitor, but also trust the process, recognizing that part of learning to work in a group may involve exactly the kind of problem solving and conflict resolution occasioned by lack of clarity or lack of immediate success. What are the differences between problems within groups that will get worked out if the group is given adequate skills and time, and those that do require teacher intervention? And how do we teach teachers to tell the difference, neither micromanaging the process nor abandoning groups that struggle? Although we are not proposing that only teachers with particular personality traits can become good teachers of cooperative learning, we do need to help teachers to reflect on the ways in which their own ideas about the teacher's role may facilitate or impede the work of small groups.

THE CHALLENGE OF HIGH-STAKES TESTING

Perhaps the biggest challenge to the consistent adoption of cooperative learning teaching strategies is the new focus (some might say obsession) with high-stakes testing and meeting state and national standards. Many teachers are feeling extremely stressed by the demands of the new high-stakes tests and with the accompanying change in their own responsibilities from teaching to test preparation.

We firmly believe that there is no fundamental conflict between cooperative learning strategies and the demand for high standards in schools. In fact, teaching students higher-order thinking and processing skills is highly compatible with the increasing demands they must meet within school and beyond. There is, however, a dangerous erosion of the ability of teachers to be thoughtful decision makers about their own students, teaching, and curriculum when they are faced with outside pressures that often conflict with their own understanding of their students and their needs. The loss of teacher autonomy that often accompanies the new focus on testing clearly challenges teachers' abilities and opportunities to design their own instruction. Many of the student-learning gains achieved through cooperative learning may be lost when teachers must teach to tests they themselves did not design. Similarly, when teachers are evaluated based on their students' performance on standardized tests, they will be less willing to engage in creative curriculum design and pedagogy. Turning teachers into deskilled employees who must use standardized teaching materials and are held accountable to external criteria is a troubling phenomenon with serious potential to erode the already fragile process of teacher empowerment.

DIVERSITY AND STATUS ISSUES

Many of the teacher education programs described here are clear in their commitment to the education of diverse students. They try to prepare teachers who will be eager and skilled in the education of a wide range of students, including those of different races, dis/abilities, language backgrounds, religions, and socioeconomic statuses. We are concerned that cooperative learning continues to take seriously the principle of *heterogeneity* as one of its key organizing beliefs. A teacher recently told one of us that the gifted students in her class do cooperative learning while the other students do worksheets. This kind of curriculum differentiation is very problematic, based as it is on misconceptions and stereotypes about who can profit from what kind of instruction. It is also evidence of teachers' lack of skill in designing cooperative learning tasks that are meaningful and accessible to all students. Those who have written about cooperative learning in diverse classrooms (Thousand et al., 2002) emphasize the need to design cooperative learning so that students at a variety of skill levels can participate and be challenged within a common task or project. Creating multilevel cooperative learning activities is a design issue, particularly for those teachers most comfortable with and accustomed to a curriculum highly differentiated by ability grouping. Increasing pressure on teachers and schools to produce results may also make less-experienced teachers abandon the challenges of designing multilevel cooperative learning tasks, seriously threatening our commitment to diversity and fair and equitable schools. Serious attention to status issues is also critical to cooperative learning that truly moves each child forward individually as well as the group. Simply designing a cooperative learning task that allows students at many levels to participate is not sufficient unless there is constant monitoring and assessment of who is participating and how, and the nature of interactions among students. The growing emphasis on product, sometimes to the exclusion of other goals, including group interaction, may erode careful attention to *how* the group reached consensus, created the "shared" poster, or participated in the cooperative learning process.

PROCESSING ISSUES

While many of the programs described here stressed the importance of teaching future teachers and students to "process" the cooperative learning experience, there are considerable differences in *what* is being processed or debriefed. Debriefing both the process and the content of curriculum learning is critical to issues already raised above. The nature and quality of student participation, particularly with reference to diversity and status issues, must be a critical part of the debriefing process. Debriefing the content of cooperative learning will obviously be directly related to the nature and quality of the curriculum content.

Asking whether everyone in the groups got the same answer on the worksheet is very different from having students analyze the differences in the three texts they examined on Civil Rights and asking them to discuss questions of point of view, bias, and stereotypes. Sophisticated debriefing skills go far beyond making sure that each group got the "same right answer" and will require teaching specific ways of asking questions, checking for understanding, challenging discrepancies, and reconciling differences.

EVALUATION AND FUTURE RESEARCH

Almost all of the above issues have a direct evaluation component. How well is our cooperative learning working? What is being achieved? For whom is it working? What are the intended and unintended outcomes of this kind of orientation or instruction? Each of these questions can form the basis for future evaluative (and not simply descriptive) research.

The chapters in this book suggest many different ways to evaluate one's program. Some authors analyzed student reflections from journals. Others interviewed or gave questionnaires to graduating students, asking them how well prepared they perceived themselves to be and how beneficial their coursework had been. Still others used reports from teaching supervisors and from the candidates themselves on the extent to which student teachers had the opportunity to practice cooperative learning during their supervised classroom experience. The samples were typically small, and the analysis was often not systematic. Clearly, the motivation to ascertain the effect of one's program is very strong, but lack of financial and personnel resources may make elaborate and systematic evaluation difficult.

As formative evaluation, questionnaires given to students can be very useful in revising coursework and the program itself. For such research to have practical effects, it is essential for faculty to decide in advance which issues regarding the program are problematic and whether or not survey responses could possibly affect future decisions or occasion program changes. If one collects only anecdotes about how important students find their cooperative learning coursework and how favorably they feel about the strategy, one is unlikely to collect data that will really change faculty behavior. In contrast, students might be asked to report on inconsistencies in the ways cooperative learning is taught in their various courses and the challenges they experienced in implementing these strategies during their field placements. Students can also report on the problems they experienced in lack of support for cooperative learning from their cooperating teacher in the schools. They could also report on which aspects of cooperative learning they learned well and which ones they feel they need more help with. Collecting this kind of detailed feedback can move questionnaires beyond instruments seen as "merely attitudinal" to ones that can be useful for program redesign.

Summative evaluation deals with the effectiveness of the program as a whole: whether or not preservice teachers graduating from a particular program go on to use cooperative learning in their first year of teaching—and use it well. This, unfortunately, is the question most difficult to answer.

It is no accident that there was very little such systematic evaluation reported by the authors in this volume. Finding out whether and to what extent new teachers apply what they have learned in their preservice coursework and student teaching requires tracking the newly credentialed teachers into their first year of teaching. If this is possible, and if they are willing to find the time in one of the most challenging years of their lives, we may be able to collect data on frequency and manner of implementation.

Although certainly an improvement over "no data," this data collection is also problematic. Given that so many of these teachers have experienced an intense program of indoctrination on the value of cooperative learning, they may be tempted to exaggerate reports of their use of these strategies. Moreover, those who do not find the time to fill out their questionnaires are especially likely to be those teachers so overwhelmed with problems of classroom management that they are not using cooperative learning.

The strongest and best method of evaluation would be the observation of teachers' classrooms in operation. If, for example, a teacher reports that she makes the most use of cooperative learning in social studies, one could arrange to visit a series of social studies' classes. To ascertain the quality of those cooperative lessons, one could examine the lesson plans, the instructions to the students, the observed percentage of students who actively talk and work together, and the character of wrap-up and debriefing. It would also be possible to evaluate the quality of the products produced by the group (Cohen et al., 2002). Different teacher education programs stress different features of cooperative learning. For example, one program might stress the importance of reflection on group processes, while another might emphasize the use of tasks that are open-ended and require higher-order thinking. The evaluation should include the special features of cooperative learning approaches that have been central to the preparation program.

It is not easy to evaluate how much use of cooperative learning is "enough," and how sophisticated one could expect the practice of a first-year teacher to be. Since it is very difficult to determine the answers to these questions in advance, a better option might be to include a comparison group of other first-year teachers teaching in the same settings but who have not been through the same teacher preparation program being evaluated. At minimum, this design will yield information as to whether the emphasis in the program is reflected in the classroom practice of graduates more than those who completed a different program with a different emphasis. This is made even more complex, however, by the compounding differences of very different instructional contexts for first-year teachers. Very valuable information could be obtained by combining observation with questionnaires/interviews. For example, it might be that those graduates who are not practicing cooperative learning did not have a student teaching experience that allowed them to practice their new strategies and did not provide an adequate model in the cooperating teacher. By contrasting the coursework and student-teaching experiences of those who are making extensive use of cooperative learning and those who are not, program evaluators can learn much that is valuable. We might also want to extend our assessment of teacher competencies and outcomes beyond preservice education and continue to provide support and monitoring for teachers in the field. New teacher mentoring programs might help us to monitor whether and how graduates are using the skills of cooperative learning.

Such an analysis, however, will require a sufficiently large sample of graduates so that variability in observed practice can be correlated with variability in experiences within the program. Such an elaborate design may seem beyond the methodological expertise of those who have the major responsibility of running the program. A group of teacher educators from different institutions might be able to provide the necessary assistance, perhaps sharing evaluation instruments and observation tools that cross program designs and priorities. Cooperation with resident methodologists and statisticians within the larger school of education might also be beneficial. Doctoral and masters students might want to collect this kind of data as part of required research projects.

It is also critical to help teachers themselves identify their own research questions about cooperative learning. Outsiders are rarely positioned as well as insiders who can engage in action research about curriculum, pedagogy, and class climate that stem directly from teachers' personal experiences.

We remain committed to the value of cooperative learning as an organizing principle and a set of values as well as a teaching strategy. We believe that future research in this area is essential to understanding what we now do and how we can do it better. Building school communities that embrace cooperative learning requires a thoughtful analysis and evaluation of current practices, and multiple opportunities for continued implementation and redesign.

REFERENCES

Cohen, E. G., Lotan, R. A., Abram, P. L., Scarloss, B. A., & Schultz, S. E. (2002). Can groups learn? *Teachers College Record, 104,* 1045–1068.

Thousand, J. S., Villa, R. A., & Nevin, A. I. (2002). *Creativity & collaborative learning: The practical guide to empowering students, teachers, and families* (2nd ed.). Baltimore: Paul Brookes Publishing Co.

CONTRIBUTORS

STEPHEN E. ANDERSON is Associate Professor in the Department of Theory and Policy Studies in Education at the Ontario Institute for Studies in Education of the University of Toronto. His research focuses on teacher capacity to improve student learning, school choice policies, and school improvement.

LYNDA BALOCHE is Professor of Education at West Chester University where she teaches courses in creativity and cooperative group processes. She is the author of *The Cooperative Classroom: Empowering Learning* and enjoys working with teachers and schools that are moving towards cooperative community.

CELESTE M. BRODY is Instructional Dean at Central Oregon Community College, formerly on the faculty at Lewis & Clark College where she specialized in instructional theory and adult development. Her publications include *Professional Education For Cooperative Learning: Issues And Approaches* with Neil Davidson.

DANNIELLE BRIGGS was a research associate at WestEd at the time of the study with Stanford University, and is currently Education Researcher at SRI International where she focuses on the evaluation of multisite, community-based initiatives that support improved outcomes for youth.

MARK BRUBACHER was Head of English at York Memorial Collegiate and Student Centered Learning Consultant with the Toronto District School Board. With Ryder Payne and Kemp Rickett he is author of *Perspectives on Small Group Learning: Theory and Practice.*

ELAINE CHIN IS Professor of Education at Cal Poly State University, San Luis Obispo where she specializes in secondary teacher education and conducts research on alternative certification programs. She authored with Kozma, Russell and Marx, "The roles of representations and tools in the chemistry laboratory and their implications for chemistry instruction" in *The Journal of the Learning Sciences*.

ELIZABETH G. COHEN is Professor Emerita of the Stanford University School of Education and Department of Sociology. For twenty years, she directed the Program for Complex Instruction at Stanford. Her publications include *Designing Groupwork: Strategies for Heterogeneous Classrooms* and a coedited book with Rachel Lotan, *Working for Equity in Heterogeneous Classrooms: Sociological Theory in Practice*.

DAN DARIGAN is Professor of Children's Literature and Literacy at West Chester University. He is the author of *Children's Literature: Engaging Teachers and Children in Good Books*.

NEIL DAVIDSON is Professor Emeritus of Curriculum and Instruction at the University of Maryland, specializing in teacher education, faculty and staff development, and mathematics education. He is cofounder of the university's Academy of Excellence in Teaching and Learning.

ROBIN ERWIN is an Associate Professor of Teacher Education at Niagara University. His work focuses on literacy education, especially preparing teachers who will cultivate deep comprehension and critical thinking among their students.

NIKOLA FILBY is Associate Director, West Ed in San Francisco where she oversees the regional laboratory program that links research to practice in a four-state region. She conducts research and evaluation projects on school change.

CLAUDIA FINKBEINER is Professor of English, American, and Romance Languages at the University of Kassel, Germany. Her research and teaching concentrates on cooperative learning, literacy, intercultural education, learning strategies in reading, content-based language learning, and computer-assisted language learning.

CHANDRA FOOTE is Associate Professor of Teacher Education at Niagara University, specializing in educational research and human learning and development. She has written *Constructivist Strategies: Meeting Standards and Engaging Adolescent Minds* with Paul Vermette and Catherine Battaglia.

BOB HANLEY is Vice President and Dean of Student Services and Associate Professor of English and Education at Anderson College, South Carolina, and specializes in language, education, and diversity.

JOELLEN HARRIS is the Codirector of Teacher Quality at the South Carolina State Department of Education. She was formerly the division head for Education and the Director of the Teacher Education Program at Anderson College.

RACHEL A. LOTAN is Associate Professor and Director of the Teacher Education Program at Stanford University. Her interests are teaching and learning in academically and linguistically heterogeneous classrooms and teacher education.

FRANK LYMAN is formerly the Professional Development Center Coordinator at the University of Maryland where he worked with over one thousand student teachers and developed several techniques and tools for teaching and reflection.

MARY MALE is Professor in Special Education at San Jose State University. She has published *Technology for Inclusion: Meeting the Special Needs of all Students*.

SUSANA C. MATA is Associate Professor of Education at the Kremen School of Education and Human Development at California State University, Fresno.

SUSAN MCBRIDE teaches at Cal Poly State University in San Luis Obispo, CA. where students use her *Handbook for Teaching Reading and Language Arts*.

MARY MURRAY is currently an adjunct professor at Niagara University and a high school social studies teacher who is recognized for her success in designing classrooms for student active participation.

NANCY G. NAGEL is Professor of Education at Lewis & Clark College in Portland, Oregon. where she is Chair of the Department of Teacher Education. She is the author of *Learning Through Real-World Problem Solving: The Power of Integrative Teaching*.

ROSALINDA QUINTANAR-SARELLANA is Associate Professor at San José State University where she teaches language acquisition, multicultural education and student teaching. She has published on equity, language acquisition, and linguistic minority students.

CAROL ROLHEISER is Associate Dean of Academic Development at the Ontario Institute for Studies in Education of the University of Toronto where she focuses on instructional and assessment innovation, teacher education reform, and managing educational change. Her publications include *Beyond Monet: The Artful Science of Instructional Integration*, with Barrie Bennett.

MARA SAPON-SHEVIN is Professor of Inclusive Education in the Teaching and Leadership Division of the School of Education at Syracuse University where she prepares teachers for inclusive, heterogeneous classrooms. She is the author of *Because We Can Change the World: A Practical Guide to Building Cooperative Inclusive Classroom Communities*.

NANCY SCHNIEDEWIND, is Professor of Educational Studies and Coordinator of the Master's Program in Humanistic/Multicultural Education at the State

University of New York at New Paltz. With Ellen Davidson, she is author of *Open Minds to Equality: A Sourcebook of Activities to Affirm Diversity and Promote Equity*.

YAEL SHARAN has many years of international experience training teachers and principals for cooperative learning. She is the author, together with Shlomo Sharan, of *Expanding Cooperative Learning Through Group Investigation*.

THOMAS SHEERAN is Professor of Education at Niagara University. The author of over fifty articles and book chapters, his academic interests include active learning strategies, assessment, and measurement.

FRANCES SLOSTAD is a faculty member at West Chester University where she teaches both undergraduate and graduate courses and supervises early field-experience students and student teachers. Her research and publications focus on effective practices for inclusion.

PATRICIA SWANSON is Assistant Professor at San Jose State University where her research focuses on equity issues and developing strategies to assist beginning teachers in addressing classroom status problems.

JENNIFER WILSON-BRIDGMAN is Assistant Professor of Teacher Education at Niagara University specializing in literacy education, reading instruction, the study of teaching in higher education.

PAUL VERMETTE is Professor of Teacher Education at Niagara University and author of the book, *Making Cooperative Learning Work: Student Teams in K-12 Classrooms*. He currently teaches secondary methods and cultural foundations courses.

INDEX

Printed in the United States
36693LVS00002B/38